Ockham's Nominalism

Ockham's Nominalism

A Philosophical Introduction

CLAUDE PANACCIO

UNIVERSITY PRESS

OXFORD
UNIVERSITY PRESS

Oxford University Press is a department of the University of Oxford. It furthers
the University's objective of excellence in research, scholarship, and education
by publishing worldwide. Oxford is a registered trade mark of Oxford University
Press in the UK and certain other countries.

Published in the United States of America by Oxford University Press
198 Madison Avenue, New York, NY 10016, United States of America.

© Oxford University Press 2023

All rights reserved. No part of this publication may be reproduced, stored in
a retrieval system, or transmitted, in any form or by any means, without the
prior permission in writing of Oxford University Press, or as expressly permitted
by law, by license, or under terms agreed with the appropriate reproduction
rights organization. Inquiries concerning reproduction outside the scope of the
above should be sent to the Rights Department, Oxford University Press, at the
address above.

You must not circulate this work in any other form
and you must impose this same condition on any acquirer.

Library of Congress Cataloging-in-Publication Data
Names: Panaccio, Claude, 1946– author.
Title: Ockham's nominalism : a philosophical introduction / Claude Panaccio.
Description: New York : Oxford University Press, 2023. |
Includes bibliographical references and index.
Identifiers: LCCN 2022027373 (print) | LCCN 2022027374 (ebook) |
ISBN 9780190078980 (hardback) | ISBN 9780190079000 (epub)
Subjects: LCSH: William, of Ockham, approximately 1285-approximately 1349. |
Nominalism. | Philosophy, Medieval.
Classification: LCC B765.O34 P363 2023 (print) | LCC B765.O34 (ebook) |
DDC 189—dc23/eng/20220805
LC record available at https://lccn.loc.gov/2022027373
LC ebook record available at https://lccn.loc.gov/2022027374

DOI: 10.1093/oso/9780190078980.001.0001

Printed by Integrated Books International, United States of America

Contents

Acknowledgments   vii
Ockham's Writings: Abbreviations   ix

Introduction   1

1. Nominalism   8
   A proposed definition   9
   Six Ockhamist theses   17
   Outline of a nominalist program   27

2. Against Realism   31
   Universals   31
      The argument from numerical unity   32
      The argument from separability   33
      The argument from mereology   36
      The argument from the indiscernibility of identicals   37
   Relations   41
      The argument from infinite regress   42
      The Razor argument   47
   Quantities   53
      Extension   54
      Numbers   57

3. Ontology   63
   Individuals   63
      Substances and qualities   63
      The composition of material substances   70
      Intensive qualities   76
      Artifacts   79
   An ordered world   81
      Motion, space, and time   81
      Inherence and information   84
      Essential similarity   86
      Causation   90
   Possible beings   96

4. Semantics	101
Natural kind terms	101
Signification	102
Supposition	105
Truth-conditions	109
Relational terms	119
Connotation	120
Relations as signs	122
Relational statements	125
Quantitative terms	128
Propositions connoted	129
Pseudo-names	132
Collective terms	136
5. Epistemology	142
Cognitive acts	142
Intuition	144
Abstraction	149
Connotative concepts	153
Judgement	156
Mental language	159
Grammar	160
Natural signs	164
Syncategorematic terms	168
Knowledge	172
Evident cognition	174
Demonstration	177
Induction	180
Sciences	184
Conclusion	188
Bibliography	195
Ockham's works	195
On Ockham and medieval philosophy	196
Other works cited	201
Name Index	207
Subject Index	211

Ackowledgments

I was greatly helped by a number of persons in the preparation of this book. First and foremost, I want to thank Jenny Pelletier, who kindly accepted to look at it with the critical eye of a native speaker of English. Her many judicious suggestions had a significant effect on both the form and the substance of the work.

I also wish to express my gratitude to Susan Brower-Toland, Calvin Normore, Robert Pasnau, and an anonymous reader for OUP, who all generously made me benefit from their precise comments, questions, and objections on partial or complete preliminary versions. Almost all of their remarks led me to rewrite some passages here and there, sometimes importantly.

Martin Pickavé was the spark for this book since he first recommended me to OUP for an introduction to Ockham, and Peter Ohlin acted from then on as my guide and my contact with the publisher with great efficiency and kindness. I am very grateful to the two of them.

Although I have been officially retired since 2016, the University of Quebec at Montreal and its department of philosophy have kindly offered to keep me around by generously granting me the status of emeritus professor along with certain academic facilities. I want to acknowledge the significant support that this has brought to my work.

My greatest debt in the end is to my wife, Claude-Élizabeth, for her daily and affectionate care, especially in the pandemic period, during which most of this book was written.

Ockham's Writings: Abbreviations

All references to Ockham's writings will be to the St. Bonaventure critical edition of the Latin text of his philosophical and theological works:

Opera philosophica. Ed. Gedeon Gal, et al. St. Bonaventure, NY: The Franciscan Institute, 7 vols., 1974–1988 (henceforth: *OPh*).
Opera theologica. Ed. Gedeon Gal, et al. St. Bonaventure, NY: The Franciscan Institute, 10 vols., 1967–1986 (henceforth: *OTh*).
When an English translation is available, the reference will also be given.

For individual works, the following abbreviations will be used:

Brev. summ. libr. Phys.	*Brevis summa libri Physicorum* [*A Short Summa on the Books of* The Physics]
Exp. in libr. Perih.	*Expositio in librum Perihermenias Aristotelis* [*Commentary on Aristotle's* On Interpretation]
Exp. in libr. Phys.	*Expositio in libros Physicorum Aristotelis* [*Commentary on Aristotle's* Physics]
Exp. in libr. Porph.	*Expositio in librum Porphyrii de praedicabilibus* [*Commentary on Porphyry's* On Predicables]
Exp. in libr. Praedic.	*Expositio in librum praedicamentorum Aristotelis* [*Commentary on Aristotle's* On Categories]
Exp. sup. libr. Elench.	*Expositio super libros Elenchorum* [*Commentary on Aristotle's* On Sophistical Refutations]
Ord.	*Ordinatio* [Commentary on Book I of Peter Lombard's *Sentences*] (NB: This huge work is divided into 48 parts called "Distinctions," each one being subdivided in turn in a number of "Questions")
Quaest. in libr. Phys.	*Quaestiones in libros Physicorum Aristotelis* [*Questions on Aristotle's* Physics]
Quaest. var.	*Quaestiones variae* [*Various Questions*]
Quodl.	*Quodlibeta septem* [*Quodlibetal Questions*]
Rep.	*Reportatio* [Questions on Book II, III and IV of Peter Lombard's *Sentences*]

SL	*Summa logicae* [*Summa of Logic*]
Summ. phil. nat.	*Summula philosophiae naturalis* [*Summa of Natural Philosophy*]
Tract. de corp.	*Christi Tractatus de corpore Christi* [*Treatise on the Body of Christ*]
Tract. de praedest.	*Tractatus de praedestinatione et de praescientia Dei respectu futurorum contingentium* [*Treatise on Predestination, God's Foreknowledge and Future Contingents*]
Tract. de quant.	*Tractatus de quantitate* [*Treatise on Quantity*]

Introduction

This book is about William of Ockham's views on universals, relations, and quantities. The underlying conviction is that his ideas on these matters are still of interest for today's philosophical discussions and that taken together they constitute a rich network of positions and arguments that deserve to be taken into consideration in metaphysics, epistemology, and philosophy of language. Ockham indeed is a towering figure. He is arguably the most important Western thinker between Aquinas in the thirteenth century and Descartes in the seventeenth. Although most of his non-political works were written in the span of about a decade, between 1315 and 1325 or so, his thought quickly spread across Europe and was both highly controversial and exceptionally influential for more than two centuries. Significant traces of it are found in Descartes and Leibniz, for example. Yet, his fame progressively faded in the early modern period. By the early twentieth century, whatever was kept alive from the medieval Latin scholastic period was confined to Catholic milieus, where Thomism was triumphant, and Ockham was no longer seriously studied. Nowadays, although his way of philosophizing bears important affinities with contemporary analytic approaches, most of his works remain untranslated into any modern language; for those that are translated, such as the *Summa of Logic* and the *Quodlibetal Questions*, their technicality is an obstacle that dissuades casual readers who are primarily interested in philosophy, as they heavily combine the vocabularies of Aristotelianism and medieval logic with scholastic modes of exposition that now seem rather odd. This is why an introduction is needed.

The focus will be on three central Ockhamist theses that can be brought together under the label of "nominalism." Here they are in preliminary formulations:

(1) Everything in the world is singular; generality is a semantic feature, not an ontological one: universals are nothing but signs.
(2) Relations are not a special kind of beings; relational signs are special indeed, but this is a matter of the distinctive ways in which they refer to non-relational things.
(3) Quantities, such as numbers and geometrical dimensions, are not a special kind of beings either; quantitative signs are special, but this is also a matter of the distinctive ways in which they refer to things in the world.

These theses are logically independent of each other. One could be a nominalist with respect to universals while accepting singular relations or singular quantities in one's ontology. Conversely, one might want to countenance universals, but only non-relational ones, or non-quantitative ones. But we can prima facie detect a common inspiration for all three ideas: Ockham wanted to keep the ontology as simple as possible. As we shall see, he did maintain a real distinction between singular substances and singular qualities, but he firmly rejected any additional multiplication of entities. The conjunction of theses (1), (2), and (3) is basically what I call Ockham's "nominalism"—although he himself never used the term.

Ockham did not mean these theses to invalidate our usual ways of speaking: general predication in his view is a perfectly legitimate tool for describing the world; and relational as well as quantitative statements can be mind-independently true. The challenge, then, is to hold all of this together in a systematic, coherent, and plausible theory without falling into extreme skepticism and relativism. This is precisely what Ockham strives to accomplish. My aim is to explain how he does it, and thus to outline a fascinating nominalist system that is liable, I hope, to enrich the current philosophical conversation.

That this book is an *introduction* means in particular that it will avoid detailed discussions of interpretation. The exact nature of Ockham's positions on various subjects has given rise to many a scholarly controversy—which I have at times contributed to—but I will be content here to present my own understanding of his ideas with references to the main Ockham passages where they are developed and a few occasional quotations. On each particular topic, I will mention along the way a limited number of salient studies that the reader can turn to for further analysis and bibliographical references, and I will often take the liberty of referring to previous writings of mine in which I have more fully argued in support of some of my interpretations.

That this introduction is intended as a *philosophical* one means that it aims to bring out the significance of Ockham's thought for philosophical debates that are still on-going about universals, relations, and mathematics. It is in this spirit that the non-Ockhamist term "nominalism" occurs in the title of this book: it points both to the cluster of recent discussions which I think Ockham can fruitfully contribute to and to the school of thought he belongs to. A historian of philosophy always reformulates the doctrines he or she is talking about to some extent. Such reformulations are heavily constrained by a strong requirement of historical accuracy: we do not care much for a pseudo-Ockham! Historical accuracy, however, leaves room for wide variety in the modes of presentation according to what the historian is interested in in the works of the past, to the intended audience, and to the project the historian is engaged in. We always make selections in the original material, and we have significant leeway as to the vocabulary and categories that we use for describing the ideas we want to draw attention to.[1] Although I will not be comparing in any detail Ockham's positions with those of recent philosophers, I want to stress the aspects of his thought that I take to be relevant today and to present them accordingly. And I will occasionally develop certain ideas that are not explicit in Ockham but that he is committed to or that are strongly suggested by what he says. In such cases, I will make it clear that this is what is going on.[2]

I will mostly leave aside, on the other hand, the theological aspects of Ockham's thought. This is not innocuous, admittedly. Ockham was a Franciscan and one of the great theologians of his time. He was deeply and sincerely concerned with theological issues such as the Divine Trinity and the Eucharist, and many of his works are of a theological

---

[1] I develop this point in Panaccio 2019a.
[2] For references to contemporary philosophy, I will often be content to cite encyclopedia entries, where the reader will find good general presentations of relevant issues and debates and more bibliographical references.

nature. Even in philosophy proper his positions often had religious motivations, and he regularly made use of theological arguments, having to do most saliently with God's omnipotence.[3] His ideas about universals, relations and quantities, however, are interesting independent of this theological context and can be detached from it to a large extent. Indeed, Ockham himself thought of philosophy as capable of standing by itself, independent of one's religious convictions, and he considered that Aristotle—as he interprets him—mostly had it right despite not being a Christian. The theological arguments and examples Ockham used in logic, physics, and epistemology were usually treated by him as persuasive means given his intended audience, rather than as indispensable parts of these philosophical disciplines. I am not suggesting that he did not take them seriously. He did. And I will mention some of them along the way. But much of his nominalism is of philosophical value without them.

Here is how I will proceed. Chapter 1 introduces the general notion of "nominalism" that I will be using and shows how it applies to Ockham's positions on universals, relations, and quantities. Chapter 2 discusses some of Ockham's main arguments against the corresponding forms of realism. Chapter 3 offers a sketch of Ockham's positive ontology, with only singular substances and singular qualities in it. Chapter 4 expounds the semantic theory that Ockham devises to support his nominalist claims about general terms, relational terms, and quantitative terms. Chapter 5, finally, shows how he accounts for human knowledge with a theory of mental acts and an elaborate conception of thought as mental language (*oratio mentalis*).

Before we get to the heart of the matter, a few words must be said about Ockham's life, works, and intellectual environment. This will help to better understand what he was up to. As far as we know, he was born around 1287 in the village of Ockham, some twenty-five miles southwest of London, and he was entrusted to the Franciscan Order in his childhood. His school curriculum as an adolescent included a lot of Aristotelian philosophy, especially logic, in which he was to eventually become a prominent expert. He was ordained subdeacon in 1306 and

---

[3] For detailed presentations of Ockham's theology, see in particular Adams 1987: 901–1347, and Maurer 1999: 157–292.

began his theological studies in Oxford shortly thereafter. This was a time of rivalry between the Franciscans and the Dominicans for intellectual leadership in Christian theology. The Dominicans already had a well-established hero, Thomas Aquinas, who died in 1274. On the Franciscan side, the best candidate during Ockham's youth was the British philosopher and theologian John Duns Scotus. When Ockham was studying theology, Scotus had just died (in 1308), and Ockham eagerly scrutinized his writings. As it happened, though, Ockham found himself in disagreement with much of what Scotus thought.

Before receiving their doctoral degree, advanced medieval students in theology were required to teach a one- or two-year course that consisted in commenting on the standard textbook of theology at the time, Peter Lombard's *Sentences*, a treatise in four books dating from the twelfth century. This was their occasion to develop their own thoughts by discussing a wide variety of questions directly or indirectly raised by this textbook. Ockham did this in Oxford between 1317 and 1319, and his first major work, accordingly, is a huge commentary on the *Sentences*. The part that deals with Book One is by far the most important. It occupies four volumes in the modern critical edition, with a total of more than 2,300 pages. Because it was carefully revised by the author himself for distribution, it is referred to as the *Ordinatio*. The other three books circulated only as student transcriptions of the original lectures (approved by Ockham, however), and they are collectively known as the *Reportatio*. Throughout this commentary, Ockham systematically developed keen criticisms of both Aquinas and Scotus, among others, and put forward his own views on a great number of issues, philosophical as well as theological. On the matters of universals, relations, and quantities, in particular, he sharply broke with the dominant realist consensus and defended strong nominalist positions.

This got him into trouble. His doctrines were suspected of having unorthodox theological consequences, and before he could receive his doctoral degree (which he never obtained in the end), he was transferred by the Franciscans to their London college, where he taught logic and natural philosophy from 1320 to 1324. In connection with this teaching he wrote detailed commentaries on Porphyry's famous treatise on universals, the *Isagoge* (the Greek word for "introduction"); on Aristotle's logical treatises *On Categories*, *On Interpretation*, and

Sophistical Refutations, and on Aristotle's *Physics*; as well as two systematic treatises in natural philosophy, the *Short Summa on Physics* and the *Summa of Natural Philosophy*; plus a lengthy series of *Questions on Aristotle's Physics*. Even though he did not teach theology during this period, he did not drop it altogether. For one thing, he wrote two short works to defend himself against the suspicion that his views on quantity had unacceptable consequences for the Christian doctrine of the Eucharist: *On Quantity* and *On the Body of Christ*. And he participated in biannual public events, during which he answered a wide variety of questions about his innovative positions in both philosophy and theology, thus progressively bringing about one of his most important works, the *Quodlibetal Questions* (literally: Questions on any subject whatsoever).

Hostility did not calm down, however. In 1324, Ockham was summoned to the papal court in Avignon under suspicion of heresy. A special committee was appointed by Pope John XXII to investigate a list of fifty-one theses allegedly endorsed by Ockham. The work of the committee lasted a few years, during which time Ockham stayed at the Franciscan convent in Avignon. It is probably in this period that he wrote—or at least completed—his magisterial compendium, the *Summa of Logic*.[4] The committee eventually concluded that some heretical doctrines had indeed been defended by Ockham, but the official papal condemnation never came, as Ockham ran into even more serious trouble in the meanwhile by getting involved in a raging controversy between John XXII and the Franciscan Order over Apostolic poverty. The dispute reached such heights that at one point in 1328, the General of the Franciscan order, Michael of Cesena, was placed under house arrest along with Ockham and three other Franciscans. The five friars came to fear for their lives and daringly escaped from

---

[4] According to Ockham's modern editors, the *Summa* was written in London in the summer of 1323, but their arguments are not conclusive. It is a lengthy treatise (some 850 pages in the Saint-Bonaventure edition) and a very carefully crafted one, which could hardly have been produced in such a short time, especially given the impressive amount of other works Ockham is thought to have authored during his London period. The Avignon enforced stay, on the other hand, would have been an ideal occasion for him to systematically develop his logical views.

Avignon on the night of May 26, 1328. They were excommunicated shortly thereafter.

The small group found refuge in Pisa with the army of Emperor Louis of Bavaria, who had his own political disagreements with John XXII, and from there they were taken to Munich, where Ockham spent the rest of his life extensively writing on political issues until his death on April 10, 1347. Because of the works he then produced, Ockham stands out as one of the founders of modern political theory.[5] This aspect of his thought, however, will be left aside in the present book. My focus here is on doctrines that he developed before his Munich period and to which he never returned.[6]

---

[5] For an overview of Ockham's political thought, see McGrade 1974.
[6] For general introductory presentations of Ockham's life and thought, see Spade 1999, Keele 2010, Spade and Panaccio 2019.

1
Nominalism

The term "nominalists" (*nominales* in Latin) was introduced in philosophy in the second half of the twelfth century to designate the followers of Peter Abelard (1079–1142). The appellation had to do with their solution to the famous problem of universals: species such as *man* or *tulip* and genera such as *animal* or *flower* were held by them to be mere names (*nomina*). Their opponents, by contrast—of which there was quite a variety—were called "realists" (*reales*) because they took species and genera to be real things out there in the world (*res*).[1] By Ockham's time, a century and a half later, the term had been all but forgotten, and he never used it himself. It only reappeared in the early fifteenth century, sometimes under the slightly revised form "*nominalistae*," as the need was felt again for a taxonomy of the schools of thought that were competing with one another across Latin Europe. And again, although several theses were ascribed to the nominalists both in philosophy and in theology, the label was mostly evocative of their distinctive position that universals are signs rather than external things.[2] Nowadays, the term is common in philosophy, but it has gained a wider variety of uses. It is necessary therefore to explain in some detail what will be meant here by "nominalism" and how the label applies to Ockham.

---

[1] This is what I take to be the main conclusions of an interesting discussion among specialists that took place in Madison, Wisconsin, in the early 1990s about the origin and scope of the word "*nominales*" in the twelfth century. See the papers assembled in Courtenay 1992.

[2] See Kaluza 1988; Biard 2010, 2017. Kaluza, in particular, identifies three main schools of thought that were recognized as such in the fifteenth century: the *peripatetici* (followers of Albert the Great and Aquinas), the *formalizantes* (followers of John Duns Scotus), and the *nominales*, and he insists that "even though the subjects of disagreement between the schools were numerous, one of them was certainly predominant over all the others and was at the origin of the threefold division of the schools: the topic of universals" (Kaluza 1988: 22; my transl.).

A proposed definition

Nominalism is often defined as the thesis that every real thing is particular, or singular. In his groundbreaking 1978 book on universals, the Australian philosopher David Armstrong, for example, writes that "the fundamental contention of Nominalism is that *all things that exist are only particulars*."[3] This is a useful characterization and I have frequently used it myself in previous writings. It makes it clear that we are dealing with an ontological doctrine, a position that has to do with what kinds of things there are, and more precisely with what the most general kinds of things are. Thus understood, nominalism comes out as a position about the so-called problem of universals, just as it was taken to be in the twelfth and fifteenth centuries: Do universals exist out there in the world? If you say "yes," you are a realist; if you say "no," you are a nominalist.

Then again, there are those who prefer to say that nominalism is the refusal to countenance abstract entities in the ontology. And some purported abstract entities, they point out, might not be universals: numbers, for example, or the null set, the one and only set that, according to standard mathematical theory, has no member at all. Think of the opening declaration of Nelson Goodman and W. V. O. Quine's joint paper "Steps toward a constructive nominalism," published in 1947: "We do not believe in abstract entities. [. . .] We renounce them altogether."[4] Others, such as Keith Campbell, define nominalism as the denial of properties.[5] In this sense the so-called trope-theorists, including Campbell himself, are not to be called "nominalists," since they accept the reality of what they call tropes, which they take to be properties, albeit singular properties such as this particular patch of redness.

Now consider those who want to exclude relations from the ontology. Can't they be counted as nominalists, too, in a certain sense? One is tempted to say at this point that such philosophers are nominalists *with respect to relations*. My first suggestion is that this

---

[3] Armstrong 1978, vol. I: 12 (with Armstrong's italics).
[4] Goodman and Quine 1947: 105.
[5] Campbell 1990: 1.

relativizing strategy should be extended to the other characterizations I previously mentioned. We would thus have: nominalism with respect to universals, nominalism with respect to abstract entities, nominalism with respect to properties, as well as nominalism with respect to relations, each one of them being independently opposed to a corresponding form of realism.

Should we choose one of these or even a fifth one as *the* right way, or the privileged way, of applying these old labels? Any such choice, I am afraid, is bound to be unduly restrictive. This is best seen in the case of properties. If "nominalism" is taken to be the refusal to countenance properties, then even William of Ockham will be denied the label, since he admitted singular qualities in his ontology in addition to singular substances. And similar inconveniences will follow if we pick the denial of universals or the denial of abstract entities or the denial of relations as the single primary mark of nominalism. A more fruitful approach, I submit, is to take "nominalism" and the corresponding opposite term "realism" as *relational terms*. A doctrine will be said to be nominalist or realist *with respect to something*, rather than merely nominalist or realist, period. This makes room for important distinctions between various forms of nominalism and realism while stressing the prima facie connection between these positions: they all have to do with accepting or not accepting certain sorts of entities in the ontology.

This is only a first step, though. As Quine has famously remarked, a philosopher who wants to deny the reality of a certain sort of entities cannot simply say that there are certain things that do not exist.[6] What the philosopher has to do is to introduce a description of the purported entities and then deny that such a description applies to anything. Nominalism with respect to universals, say, must provide a reasonably informative description of what a universal is supposed to be. Nominalism with respect to abstract entities must provide a reasonably informative description of what an abstract entity is supposed to be, and so on. But new difficulties arise at this point.

---

[6] See Quine 1963: 1.

Take universals. In the medieval period, a universal was defined as what can be predicated of many. Yet several medieval authors who do not normally count as nominalists, such as Aquinas and Duns Scotus, were quite ready to grant that universals *in this sense* do not exist in the extramental world. Predication, they reasoned, occurs only in propositions, and propositions occur only in language or in thought; universals, therefore, occur only in language or in thought. Both Aquinas and Scotus, on the other hand, admitted mind-independent common natures within the external things themselves.[7] Are we to say that Aquinas and Scotus were realists with respect to common natures, but nominalists with respect to universals? This would be misleading. Things seem to turn out this way only because of the technical sense of the term "universal" (*universale*) in the Middle Ages, but surely the philosophically interesting feature of Aquinas's and Scotus's solutions to the problem of universals is that they countenanced mind-independent common natures even if they did not *call* them "universals."

If we want to devise a useful taxonomy of nominalist approaches across the history of philosophy, we should use our own vocabulary and investigate how well it retrospectively applies to certain doctrines of the past. This is not an easy task, either. In the *Nominalism* entry of the *Stanford Encyclopedia of Philosophy*, Gonzalo Rodriguez-Pereyra, for example, stipulates that something is a universal if and only if it can be instantiated.[8] "Instantiation," however, is itself a term of art, albeit in recent analytic philosophy rather than in medieval philosophy, and it is not immediately clear what it means and how it can be transposed to medieval philosophy. Professional historians of philosophy often insist that the theoretical vocabularies of distant periods in the history of the discipline are incommensurable with one another in a great number of cases.

What are we to do? On the one hand, we have arrived at the conclusion that the term "nominalism" should be a relational one. We want to speak of nominalism with respect to something or other. On

---

[7] See, e.g., Aquinas, *On Being and Essence* 3. For an introduction to Scotus on universals and common natures, see Noone 2003.

[8] See Rodriguez-Pereyra 2016.

the other hand, we would like, if possible, to provide descriptions of these "somethings" independent of the technical vocabularies of the doctrines we are thus classifying and in such a way that we could detect from the outside, as it were, what these doctrines have to say *about them*. But we must be careful not to presuppose in doing so that the things the nominalists want to reject do exist after all.

The key to this conundrum is to be found, unexpectedly, in a short text from the fifteenth century, known today as *Defense of Nominalism*, in which a group of Parisian philosophers apologetically reacted to a decree issued in 1473 by the King of France, Louis XI, prohibiting the teaching of nominalism at the University of Paris, a doctrine that the King himself traced back to Ockham.[9] At the very beginning of this text, the authors propose a definition of what they take nominalism to be:

> Those doctors are called nominalists [*nominalistae*] who do not multiply things that are principally signified by terms according to the multiplication of terms. Realists, on the other hand, are those who contend that things are multiplied with the multiplication of terms. [. . .] Also, nominalists are called those who apply diligence and study to know all the properties of terms from which depend the truth and falsity of speech, and without which there can be no perfect judgment of the truth and falsity of propositions.[10]

This characterization of nominalism has two parts to it. First, it says, in substance, that the nominalists do not take it that a distinct category of things in the world corresponds to every distinct category of terms in language.[11] And second, the nominalists typically apply great care to the study of semantics. As laconic as it is, the first clause is the one that will especially inspire us. The second clause hardly sorts out a distinctive feature of nominalists. Even in Ockham's time, there were realist

---

[9] An English translation of this text can be found in Thorndike 1944: 355–360.
[10] Ibid., 355–356.
[11] Note indeed that, strictly speaking, what the medieval as well as the contemporary nominalists refuse to multiply is not the singular things, but the *categories* of things. Ockham, for instance, considered that there are as many singular rednesses in the world as there are singular red objects, but he rejected any fundamental distinction between universal things and singular things.

philosophers who did apply diligence and care to the study of semantics. Walter Burley is a salient case in point.[12] And of course this is still true of many of today's realists. This second clause is not to be ignored, as we will see, but it is of interest to us only in virtue of its connection with the first one: insofar as nominalists refuse to multiply things according to the multiplicity of terms, they have to provide some appropriate semantic account for those categories of terms that do not correspond in their view to special categories of things. Nominalists, then, will typically care for semantics even if they are not the only ones to do so. Their distinctive characteristic, however, has to do with the refusal to construe the ontology by projecting the structure of language into it.

This is still too rough, though. Few philosophers ever wanted to multiply things according to the multiplicity of terms. Even among realists with respect to universals, most of them would deny that there is a distinct universal for every linguistic predicate. David Armstrong, for one, subscribes like many others to what he calls a "sparse" theory of universals, which does not, as he puts it himself, make an "uncritical use of predicates" to pick out which universals there are.[13] The idea that the distinctive feature of nominalism is that it does not posit a category of things for each category of terms requires some refinement if it is to be of any help. A first step is to take "nominalism" as a relational term as proposed earlier and to speak of "nominalism with respect to something" rather than of nominalism *tout court*. But here comes a second proposal, inspired by the fifteenth-century Parisian doctors: what nominalism should be relativized to are *linguistic* categories. We will cash out the idea that nominalists do not multiply entities according to the multiplicity of terms by defining a nominalist position with respect to a certain group of linguistic units as *that position according to which there are no special entities corresponding to such linguistic units*. This is the definition I will be working with from now on.

It significantly differs from what we had been considering so far. Instead of speaking of nominalism with respect to universals, or with

---

[12] Burley was a bit older than Ockham and he significantly influenced him, especially in semantic theory. On this important author, see Conti 2016.
[13] Armstrong 2010: 18. This use of "sparse" in ontology comes from Lewis 1986: 59–60.

respect to relations, or with respect to numbers, as I was informally doing, what will now be required to complete the phrases of the form "nominalism with respect to __" is a reference to certain linguistic items. We will speak of nominalism with respect to general terms (or a subgroup of them), or nominalism with respect to relational terms, or nominalism with respect to quantitative terms, and so on.

There are several advantages to this approach. First, "nominalism" now comes out as a genuinely relational term. It relates certain philosophers with certain linguistic units, regardless of whether those linguistic units have external referents or not. Should we keep saying that a philosopher is a nominalist with respect to numbers, for example, we would have to understand the term "number" as a shorthand for a description. And even if we agreed on a particular description of what a number would be if it existed—which might not be an easy task—we should be prepared to admit that this description might apply to nothing in the world, just as the nominalist claims. If so, saying that a philosopher is a nominalist with respect to numbers would not relate the philosopher in question with anything at all and it would not, consequently, be very informative. It would not tell us what the philosopher's claim is about. By contrast, saying that this philosopher is a nominalist with respect to numerical terms does relate the philosopher with certain real things—namely numerical terms— and tells us what his claim is about: it is about numerical terms.

A second advantage is that what this relational characterization of nominalism relates the philosopher to—namely, linguistic items—is in all cases something that we are familiar with independent of any philosophical theory, whether our own or those of the philosophers we are talking about. The categorization of linguistic items might require a minimum of theoretical framework, admittedly, but very little of it is needed for sorting out the varieties of nominalism we might be interested in. Whether on the basis of their syntax or of their most conspicuous semantic features, we usually have no trouble identifying general terms or relational terms or numerical terms in our language or in the language of the philosophers of the past.[14] Describing a given

---

[14] To be sure, identifying the category of abstract terms might be a bit more difficult. Ockham at any rate uses for this a purely morphological feature; see below, pp. 23–26.

doctrine as denying (or asserting, for that matter) that a special category of real things corresponds to general terms, or to relational terms, or to numerical terms is prima facie more manageable than saying that it denies (or asserts) the reality of universals or relations or numbers.

Furthermore, the philosophers we are dealing with were also quite familiar with linguistic units of the said categories. There were general terms, relational terms, and numerical terms in Greek, Latin, and Arabic, just as there are in English, French, Italian, and German. I am not claiming that such terms are to be found in *all* past, present, and possible future human languages. But they certainly are present in the languages of the philosophers we want to classify as nominalists or realists in the relevant respect. And these philosophers are (or were) usually aware that their theses—the theses at least that we want to stamp as nominalist or realist—had to do with such terms somehow. It was clear to Abelard, Scotus, and Ockham, as much as to Locke, Hume, and Russell, or to Nelson Goodman, David Armstrong, and Gonzalo Rodriguez-Pereyra, that their positions on "universals" crucially required an account of how general terms work. And it was clear to Ockham and to Leibniz as much as to Russell and Moore or to E. J. Lowe and Peter Simons that their theory of "relations" crucially required an account of how relational terms work. They might not have thought that providing such accounts was the primary goal of their respective doctrines, but they all more or less self-consciously knew or felt that it was a requirement they had to fulfil. Defining the different varieties of nominalism and realism by reference to linguistic categories thus allows us to pinpoint a common object for all of these theories from different periods in the history of philosophy and a common requirement with respect to which their degree of success can be evaluated.

This is not to reduce the question of universals, or relations, or numbers merely to a matter of philosophy of language. A satisfactory account of general, or relational, or numerical terms must involve metaphysics and epistemology as well as semantics. And we should not presume that semantics is necessarily predominant. The structure of the various theories we are interested in can vary indefinitely. But insofar as they can be labeled as nominalist or realist, they must deal with language at some point. Identifying the particular categories of linguistic units these theories are concerned with provides an efficient way of classifying them and of comparing them with one another.

There is indeed a case for the much stronger claim that the distinctive phenomena a philosophical doctrine should account for are mostly of a logico-linguistic character, that is, that they are in general linguistic phenomena liable to affect the validity of inferences, arguments, or justifications.[15] Ethics, for example, centrally deals with a special kind of evaluative statement, such as "A ought to do P" or "P is the right thing to do." Philosophy of mind deals with typical linguistic structures, such as "A believes that p" or "A desires that p," where the p-clauses have special logical properties. Even metaphysics can illuminatingly be seen as an attempt to say how the world has to be for certain types of linguistic statements to be legitimate, statements involving general terms, for instance, or relational terms, and so on. If this is correct, the relational definitions I am proposing do not merely hit upon some derivative feature of nominalism and realism that would happen to be useful for classificatory purposes, they draw attention to a central aspect of these doctrines, a privileged dimension along which they can best be evaluated as good or bad philosophical theories. According to this view, the philosophical value of a certain variety of nominalism depends on how well it accounts for a given sort of linguistic item by providing an ontology, a semantics, and an epistemology. Although this is not the right place to defend this view in any detail, it is the perspective that guides my approach to Ockham's doctrines in the present book.

It is by no means necessary, however, to endorse this general conception of philosophy in order to appreciate the usefulness of adopting the proposed relational characterizations of nominalism and realism as working definitions. They provide a unified way of identifying varieties of nominalism and realism while relating each of them to recognizable objects—linguistic units, namely—that we are familiar with independent of our philosophical preferences and that we know the

---

[15] The point is developed in Panaccio 2019a.

philosophers we want to study were interested in as well. A doctrine, then, will be said to be nominalist with respect to a certain category of linguistic items insofar as it incorporates in some way or other the claim that no special sort of entities corresponds in reality to this category of linguistic items. In this sense, a nominalist position with respect to general terms, for example, claims that nothing special is referred to by general terms in addition to what is referred to by singular terms; a nominalist position with respect to relational terms claims that nothing special is referred to by relational terms in addition to what is referred to by non-relational terms; and so on. This still leaves a choice between two possible nominalist approaches with respect to any given linguistic category: either to say that nothing in the world corresponds to it; or to say that it does require the real existence of some entities, but only of those that are independently required by the other terms of the language. The latter approach is what we will mostly be interested in here.

Six Ockhamist theses

I introduced this book as being about Ockham's theories of universals, relations, and quantities. As we now realize, this was not clear enough. We can hardly consider universals, relations, and quantities as commonly recognizable objects and ask what Ockham has to say about them. In accordance with the strategy proposed in the previous section, we must reconstruct the Ockhamist doctrines we are interested in by relativizing them to linguistic categories. This yields three central nominalist theses that can be attributed to Ockham:

N1 - Nominalism with respect to general terms: there is no special sort of entities that corresponds to general terms.

N2 - Nominalism with respect to relational terms: there is no special sort of entities that corresponds to relational terms.

N3 - Nominalism with respect to quantitative terms: there is no special sort of entities that corresponds to quantitative terms.

In all three cases, Ockham's position instantiates the second of the nominalist approaches distinguished at the end of the previous section: general terms, relational terms, and quantitative terms all refer to real things for him, but these are not extra objects in addition to the things that are referred to by non-general, non-relational, and non-quantitative terms. He thus needs a basic category of referential linguistic items that are altogether singular, non-relational, and non-quantitative. Ockham also defended nominalist positions with respect to syncategorematic terms such as prepositions and conjunctions, with respect to abstract terms, and with respect to sentences in general. I will come back to these shortly, but let us focus first on N1–N3.

A singular term for Ockham is a sign that is supposed to designate a single thing.[16] He distinguishes three kinds of singular terms: (1) demonstrative pronouns such as "this" or "that"; (2) proper names such as "Socrates" or "Plato"; and (3) complex expressions formed with a demonstrative and a general term such as "this man," "this red thing," etc. Although Ockham is not explicit about it, the category of demonstrative pronouns is the most basic one for him: everything that can be designated by a proper name or by a complex phrase of the form "this F" can be designated by a demonstrative pronoun alone.[17] What thesis N1 comes down to, therefore, is that only those things that can be designated by a demonstrative pronoun should be accepted in the ontology in order to give a correct account of general terms. The paradigmatic instances of such things are ordinary perceivable objects such as a human being, a tree, a fire, or a house, but Ockham is ready to include mental states and immaterial individuals such as God and the angels. God and angels, admittedly, cannot be pointed at here below, but he believed that they could be in the afterlife, at least mentally. In terms of Ockham's theory of cognition, a thing that can be designated by a demonstrative pronoun is any object that can be directly apprehended in such a way that the knower can thereby be certain that this very thing presently exists. Such an apprehension is what Ockham

---

[16] *SL* I, 19, *OPh* I: 65–67 (transl. Loux 1974: 90–92).
[17] See Panaccio 1980, 2004: 13–15.

calls an "intuitive cognition."[18] Thesis N1, then, is the claim that a correct account of general terms does not require the ontological admission of anything other than singular objects capable in principle of being directly and independently intuited by some mind or other.

Ockham was very much aware that the problem he was discussing in relation with what he called "universals" (*universalia*) crucially had to do with linguistic items. He endorsed the common definition of a universal as what is capable in principle of being predicable of many.[19] But anything that is predicable, he thought, has to be a sign, since it has to be able to occur in a predicative sentence and represent something other than itself in that sentence. The term "horse," for example, is predicable of many in the sense that it can be the predicate term of many true sentences with different subject terms. In particular, it can be the predicate of many true sentences the subject terms of which are demonstrative pronouns designating different singular objects, such as "this is a horse," "that is a horse," etc. The predicate in such sentences cannot merely represent itself: "this is a horse" does not normally mean that this thing here is the term "horse" itself; the predicate "horse" has to function as a sign for something else. Ockham admits of two kinds of such general signs: linguistic ones and mental ones. Only the former, however, are immediately given to our common experience. Mental signs have to be postulated, Ockham thought, for a correct understanding of our intellectual capacities and accomplishments, but what he treats in practice as the primary objects that a theory of universals has to deal with are the general terms of our public languages.[20] His contention, then, is that the things these linguistic items represent can all be intuitively apprehended and singularly designated by demonstrative pronouns.

Yet further specifying what these things are is not a merely logical or linguistic matter for him. The medieval problem of universals was

---

[18] Ockham's theory of intuitive cognition is laid out in *Ord.*, Prologue, q. 1 (transl. Boehner 1990: 18–25) and *Quodl.* V, 5 (transl. Freddoso 1991: 413–417). A detailed presentation is to be found in Adams 1987: 495–530. More on this in chapter 5.

[19] *SL* I, 14, *OPh* I: 47–49 (transl. Loux 1974: 77–79).

[20] See, e.g., *Ord.*, dist. 2, q. 4, especially *OTh* II: 134–137 (transl. Spade 1994: 136–138). In order to determine the structure of our mental language, Ockham turns to the linguistic categories that are semantically indispensable in spoken languages; see *SL* I, 3 (transl. Loux 1974: 52–54) and *Quodl.* V, 8–9 (transl. Freddoso 1991: 424–432).

commonly discussed in connection with three questions that the Greek philosopher Porphyry had raised in his *Isagoge*, also known as the treatise *On the Predicables*, which had become one of the basic textbooks of logic in Boethius's Latin translation. In this work, Porphyry provided a classification of the different sorts of predicates one has to deal with in logic, the two most salient of which are genera such as "animal," and species such as "horse."[21] Before addressing the logical issues directly, though, Porphyry listed three "profound" questions: Do genera and species exist in themselves or only in the mind? Are they corporeal or incorporeal? And do they exist apart or in sense objects? This was tantamount to asking whether anything corresponds to general terms out there in the world and, if so, what their ontological status is. Porphyry, however, refrained from discussing these questions himself, because they require, he said, a more detailed examination than what is possible in an introductory booklet. Ockham in commenting on this passage is explicit that Porphyry's questions do not pertain to logic but to metaphysics.[22] And he takes this very seriously. Metaphysics for him is a bona fide discipline concerned with the basic structure of reality.[23] In Ockham, then, the problem of universals is to determine whether there is a special kind of beings in the world that corresponds to our general terms in addition to the singular objects that can be pointed at. His answer is no, which is precisely why he counts as a nominalist in our sense. But in his view this ultimately is a metaphysical issue, not a merely logical one.

The situation is similar with thesis N2. "Relation" (*relatio*) was known to medieval philosophers as one of the four major categories identified by Aristotle in his treatise *On Categories*, the others being substance, quality, and quantity.[24] But what these categories are supposed to be categories of was the object of an age-old controversy in

---

[21] The other three Porphyrian predicables are *differentiae* (such as "rational"), *propria* (such as "capable of laughing"), and accidental predicates (such as "white" or "seated").

[22] *Exp. in libr Porph.*, Prologue, 2, *OPh* II: 10.

[23] On Ockham's conception of metaphysics, see Pelletier 2013.

[24] Aristotle's list of categories has ten items in it, but the other six (action, affection, position, time, place, and *habitus*) are dealt with by him very briefly and they continued to be considered of a lesser interest throughout the Middle Ages. For excellent presentations of the medieval debates over relations, see Henninger 1989 and Brower 2018.

the Aristotelian tradition: are they categories of things, of words, or of something else? Ockham's position is straightforward: the main goal of Aristotle's *On Categories* "is to discuss certain words that signify things."[25] The items included in each category are not the external things themselves, but terms that refer to external things somehow. What belong in the category of relation, in particular, are but relational terms.

A relational term is defined by Ockham as a nominal term that cannot be truly predicated of anything unless it is possible in principle to add another nominal phrase to it.[26] "Mother," for example, is a relational term because although it can correctly be said of somebody that she is a mother without further specification, this cannot be true unless it is possible to add a nominal phrase indicating whose mother she is. Ockham's nominalist position is that such relational terms refer in general to external things, but that their referents are not different from those of non-relational terms. The difference is in the mode of signification, not in the nature of the external referents.[27] We will discuss the semantics of these terms in chapter 4, but the point now is that for Ockham the truth of an affirmative sentence with a relational term in it such as "Eve is a mother" or "Eve is the mother of Abel" requires the existence of the mother and the child, and maybe of some singular qualities inhering in them, but no extra "little thing" is needed in between the *relata*.[28] Ockham thought that Christian theology requires the admission of some relational entities in order to account for Divine Trinity and Incarnation in particular,[29] but I will leave this aside here. Ockham is explicit that philosophy proper can and should do without such entities.[30] In his view, whatever exists in the natural world is an "absolute" thing, that is, a singular substance or a singular quality, such as can be referred to by standard non-relational terms.

---

[25] *Exp. in libr. Praedic.*, Prologue, *OPh* II: 135–136.
[26] See *SL* I, 52, *OPh* I: 172 (transl. Loux 1974: 171).
[27] See in particular: *Ord.*, dist. 30, q. 1–3, *Quodl.* VI, 16–20 (transl. Freddoso 1991: 539–559), and *SL* I, 52 (transl. Loux 1974: 171–174).
[28] Ockham frequently uses the phrase "*parva res*" (little thing) in *Quodl.* VI to characterize the special objects that realists postulate as referents for relational terms.
[29] *Ord.*, dist. 30, q. 4, *OTh* IV: 366–374.
[30] *Ord.*, dist. 30, q. 2–3, *OTh* IV: 320–365.

"Quantity" was also one of Aristotle's four main categories. Considered as such, it includes only significative terms for Ockham.[31] Thesis N3 is the claim that these terms refer to substances and qualities, but in some special way. In one sense indeed, the term "quantity" (*quantitas*) is applied by Ockham to the external things themselves. Quantities in this sense do exist in the outside world for him, but they are nothing but singular substances or qualities: Socrates or a given patch of redness can truly be said to be a quantity (or a *quantum*), and so do the twelve Apostles taken as a group. A quantity in general is defined as something that has parts which are external to one another, "parts outside of parts," as Ockham puts it.[32] Following Aristotle, he distinguishes two main kinds of quantities: continuous and discrete. A continuous quantity is a single extended entity with spatiotemporally contiguous parts, while a discrete quantity is a collection of countable singular entities. Two sorts of terms, then, are to be included in the corresponding Aristotelian category: geometrical terms, on the one hand, such as "point," "line," "surface," and "volume" or "body," that can be used to provide information as to how the contiguous parts of something are spatiotemporally arranged with respect to each other; and numerical terms, on the other hand, such as "one," "two," "three," that can be used to count the members of a collection. Thesis N3 says that all such terms can occur in true descriptions of the very same things that non-geometrical and non-numerical terms refer to without additional ontological commitment. All material substances truly are bodies, for instance, insofar as they are three-dimensional. And any collection of singular entities, whether substances or qualities, can truly be numbered. As in the other cases, the basic ontology is a matter for metaphysics to determine, but how it is that quantitative terms can be true of anything without the ontology being enriched pertains to semantics.

---

[31] Ockham's main developments on quantity are: *Exp. in libr. Praedic.* 10-11, *Quodl.* IV, 23-33 (transl. Freddoso and Kelley 1991: 336-383), *Tract. de quant.* as a whole (transl. Birch 1930—but not quite reliable), and *SL* I, 44-48 (transl. Loux 1974: 142-158). See on this Adams 1987: 169-213.
[32] *Quodl.* IV, 23, *OTh* IX: 407 (transl. Freddoso and Kelley 1991: 336).

N1–N3 will be discussed in some detail in the remaining chapters of this book. But three other nominalist claims in Ockham must be briefly mentioned. The first is:

N4 - Nominalism with respect to syncategorematic terms: there is no special sort of entities that correspond to syncategorematic terms.

The distinction between categorematic and syncategorematic terms is a basic one in Ockham. The former are all of those terms that refer somehow (or purport to refer) to something in the world, such as "man," "animal," "red," "redness," and so on. *Syncategoremata*, on the other hand, are the connectors, quantifiers, negations, and prepositions of a given language, such as "if," "no," "every," "some," "with," "of," "except," "insofar," etc. "None of these," Ockham says, "has a definite and determinate signification, nor does any of them signify anything distinct from what is signified by categorematic terms."[33] The point is that syncategorematic terms do not refer to anything at all. Ockham's approach to these terms is an instance of the first nominalist strategy we identified at the end of the previous section: nothing corresponds to them in the world. This is not to say that they are meaningless (in our sense of the word). They do have crucial semantic functions insofar as they affect the truth-conditions of the sentences in which they occur. What they do not have is a designative function. The sentences "All horses are white" and "Some horses are white" have different truth-conditions because their quantifiers differ, but neither of the two requires the existence of anything but what the categorematic terms "horse" and "white" directly or connotatively refer to.

Another one of Ockham's theses that can be counted as nominalist according to our criterion is:

N5 - Nominalism with respect to abstract terms: there is no special sort of entities that correspond to abstract terms.

---

[33] *SL* I, 4, *OPh* I: 15 (transl. Loux 1974: 55).

In Ockham's way of speaking, the distinction between abstract and concrete applies only to terms: external things are neither concrete nor abstract. The distinction, moreover, is first and foremost a morphological matter for him. Abstract and concrete terms, he says, "have the same stem but different endings," and the abstract ones usually (but not always) have more syllables than their concrete counterparts.[34] Typical examples of, respectively, concrete and abstract terms are "just" and "justice," "red" and "redness," "philosopher" and "philosophy," "animal" and "animality," etc. Semantically, this is not a homogeneous distinction. Ockham lists four cases. Sometimes, one of the two terms refers in some way to something that the other in no way refers to. "Red," for example, refers to red substances while connoting their rednesses, but "redness" refers only to the individual qualities of redness and in no way to their underlying substances. Sometimes, the abstract and the concrete terms are strictly synonymous with each other. This is so, Ockham thinks, with "animal" and "animality," at least in one sense of these words. Since being an animal does not involve any extra property in addition to the substance of the animal itself, Brunellus the donkey can—in a contrived way of speaking, admittedly—be said to be an animality as well as an animal. A third possibility—and an especially intriguing one—is that both terms refer either directly or connotatively to the same things in the world, but one of them implicitly incorporates some syncategorematic or adverbial determination. "Horseness," for example, might be taken as an abbreviation for something like "a horse necessarily" or "a horse insofar as it is a horse." It then refers to nothing but singular horses, but it is not substitutable in all contexts for its concrete counterpart "horse." Saying that "horseness is some sort of animality" thus comes down to saying that horses necessarily are animals. In such cases, the explicit reformulation with only concrete terms and syncategorematic or adverbial terms would typically require a rephrasing of some other part of the sentence as well, as in the example above where the predicate "is some sort of animality"

---

[34] *SL* I, 5, *OPh* I: 16 (transl. Loux 1974: 56). Ockham's views on abstract terms are expressed in *SL* I, 5–9, *OPh* I: 16–35 (transl. Loux 1974: 56–69) and *Quodl.* V, 9, *OTh* IX: 513–518 (transl. Freddoso 1991: 429–432).

is replaced by "are animals."[35] The fourth case, finally, is when the concrete term refers to certain individuals while the abstract one refers to several of these taken together. An example of this in English would be "associate" and "association," if the latter is taken to collectively refer to a group of associates.

In none of these cases, according to Ockham, does the abstract term normally import anything that is not somehow referred to by the corresponding concrete one. In some instances of the first case, admittedly, the abstract term is semantically simpler than its concrete counterpart. "Redness," for example, is a simple natural kind term—an "absolute" term, in Ockham's terminology—as it refers only to singular qualities of redness without connoting anything else; "red," on the other hand, is semantically more complex as it denotes the red substances and connotes their singular rednesses. This is generalizable to all cases in which the abstract term stands for certain qualities while the concrete one stands for the substances having these qualities. Yet even then, the abstract word does not designate anything that is not in some way referred to by the concrete one, be it connotatively.[36] As we will see in detail in chapter 3, Ockham's ontology does countenance indeed two sorts of basic entities: singular substances and singular qualities, but since a concrete qualitative term such as "red" denotes substances and connotes qualities while the abstract counterpart "redness" refers only to qualities, it turns out that everything that is referred to by the abstract term is also referred to somehow by the concrete term.

In the second and third ways of distinguishing concrete and abstract terms, the referential equivalence between them is straightforward. It holds in virtue of the definitions of what semantic relations hold between the two terms in such cases: plain synonymy in case number two and mere syncategorematic or adverbial difference in case number three (which, as we saw, involves no additional entities according to N4). The referential equivalence between the concrete and the abstract terms might seem less obvious in the fourth case, in which one of them refers to a collection while the other refers to separate individuals.

---

[35] More on this in the section on pseudo-names in chapter 4 below, pp. 132–136.
[36] Ockham's idea of connotation will be further explained in chapter 4.

Modern philosophers indeed often consider a collection of individuals to be a distinct entity with respect to its members.[37] But Ockham does not. For him, a group is nothing, ontologically, but its members. Yet, he believes, we can speak of them collectively, if we wish, rather than distributively.[38]

A last Ockhamist claim I want to mention is:

N6 - Nominalism with respect to sentences: there is no special sort of entities that corresponds to whole sentences.

There is no such thing in Ockham's ontology as an event or a state of affairs. An affirmative or negative assertive sentence—a "proposition" (*propositio*) in Ockham's vocabulary—is a grammatically well-formed combination of categorematic and syncategorematic terms that has a truth-value. It has truth-conditions, consequently, and Ockham is very explicit about them, discussing at length "what is necessary and sufficient for the truth of propositions."[39] But sentences (or propositions) have no significates of their own. Ockham's semantics is atomistic and it is based on what we today call the principle of composition: the truth-conditions of a sentence are a function of the signification of its categorematic terms as determined by whatever *syncategoremata* the sentence includes. As in the case of N4, his approach to sentences illustrates the first of our two nominalist strategies. While Ockham says that universal, relational, or quantitative terms signify certain things in the world, he never says so for sentences. Whether or not a sentence as a whole designates some special entity became the object of an interesting debate later on in the fourteenth century, and some authors indeed were realists about that,[40] but Ockham himself does not yet treat the point as controversial. He simply avoids saying that a sentence signifies anything, except in a very loose sense of "to signify."[41]

---

[37] See, for example, Goodman 1956.
[38] On collective terms in Ockham, see below, pp. 136–138.
[39] *SL* II, 1, *OPh* I: 241 (transl. Freddoso and Schuurman 1980: 79). Ockham's theory of truth-conditions is set out in *SL* II, 2–20 (transl. Freddoso and Schuurman 1980: 86–154).
[40] See, e.g., Nuchelmans 1973, Cesalli 2016.
[41] On the various senses of "to signify," see *SL* I, 33 (transl. Loux 1974: 113–114).

The ontological commitment associated with a given sentence reduces to what its component terms must refer to for the sentence to be true.

Outline of a nominalist program

If it is to be tenable, a nominalist theory should be able to accomplish (at least) four tasks with respect to the category of linguistic items it deals with: refute the corresponding form of realism and produce an ontology, a semantic theory, and an epistemology. The remaining chapters of this book will be dedicated to showing how Ockham's doctrine purports to do so with respect to general terms, relational terms, and quantitative terms. But in order to appreciate Ockham's contributions to these issues, it must be understood at the outset why these requirements arise for any nominalist approach whatsoever.

The first thing to realize is this: for any recognizable linguistic category, the unreflective presumption is that it corresponds to some special kind of things. Realism is the default position with respect to any category of linguistic items. One reason for this is that whatever these linguistic items are, they should be meaningful in order to play a distinctive role in language, and it seems, therefore, that they should mean something distinctive. Thus Fredegisus of Tours argued in his "Letter on Nothingness and Shadow," written in the early ninth century, that since the word "nothing" means something, nothingness must exist.[42] A second apparent reason is that existential generalization in some form or other usually seems to be a valid form of inference. Socrates is a human being and Plato is a human being, therefore, one might spontaneously reason, there is something that they both are; there is something, in other words, that is common to the two of them. Or again: Socrates is Plato's teacher, therefore there exists a certain relation between them. And so on. If one is to resist transforming such facile inferential moves into specific ontological claims, one has to show first why the result is unsatisfactory. In reply to Fredegisus, for example, one might point out that his admittance of nothingness as a

---

[42] An English translation of this text is to be found in Jun 2003.

distinct entity leads to a contradiction: saying that there is nothing in a certain box would entail that there is something in this box after all. This is generalizable: since realism rests on apparently natural modes of inference from language to reality, nominalism with respect to a given category of linguistic items is committed to showing why the realist interpretation of these items is to be rejected, or at least called into question.

Second, what about ontology? If a nominalist chooses to say that the terms she is interested in refer to nothing whatsoever, she might manage to dispense with ontology altogether. She might be content with showing that no ontological commitment is brought about by the correct use of these terms. But nominalists, as we saw, often adopt a different strategy by claiming that the linguistic items they want to deal with do refer to something, albeit to the very same objects that are referred to by some more basic units. This is Ockham's approach to general terms, relational terms, and quantitative terms. Ontology, then, becomes inevitable. It must be explained to some extent what these objects are, how they are structured (or not), and how many basic categories of them are to be countenanced. The approach, otherwise, would not be informative enough. Even for a nominalist, a referential account of a certain category of linguistic items requires a metaphysical basis.

Third, a crucial part of any nominalist doctrine, obviously, is to propose a semantic account of the linguistic items it is interested in. Even if it claims that these items do not convey any ontological commitment, it should explain what their roles are in our languages and in particular how they affect (or not) the meaning of the linguistic expressions and sentences in which they occur. Ockham, for example, does this in some detail for propositional quantifiers and negations, which he takes to be non-referential units.[43] If a nominalist holds, on the other hand, that the terms he focuses on do have some ontological import, he must explain how it is that no *special* entity is needed. This might be done, as Ockham does, by distinguishing various ways in which different linguistic units refer to the very same things in the world without being

---

[43] This is part of his theory of truth-conditions in *SL* II, 2–20 (transl. Freddoso and Schuurman 1980: 86–154). More on this in chapter 4.

synonymous, various "modes of signification," as Ockham says. Or it might be done by distinguishing a variety of semantic dimensions for the linguistic units under consideration, sense and denotation, for example, as Frege did. This is not to say that the nominalism versus realism issue is merely a linguistic matter. The kind of semantics that nominalism calls for is strongly constrained by the ontology that one adopts, and this ontology might be motivated by all sorts of reasons, including scientific, metaphysical, or religious ones. But the point now is that no nominalist position can dispense with semantics.

Fourth and last, the semantic theory, as Donald Davidson emphasized, must be compatible with the learnability of the linguistic items it deals with.[44] Given his parsimonious ontology, the nominalist philosopher needs some account or other of how we can master a language with such items in it. A theory of mind and cognition is required. Part of it might come from empirical psychology or cognitive science, but philosophy of mind and epistemology are also called for to help provide a coherent description of the relevant cognitive structures. This is especially true if one considers that specific mental states correspond to the linguistic units in question. We regularly use general, relational, or quantitative terms, for example, for stating the content of the thoughts we attribute to each other. I can attribute to Mary, say, the general belief that donkeys are stubborn, or the relational belief that Eve was the mother of Abel, or the quantitative belief that twenty is greater than ten. How can such belief-attributions be correct if their most important component terms do not refer to any distinctive objects that Mary could grasp? Along with many other philosophers and cognitive scientists, Ockham assumes that what is needed here is a theory of concepts considered as combinable mental units, but whether the nominalist takes this route or not, she owes us some explanation of the cognitive processes involved in our ability to use and to understand the terms she deals with. And she must explain how these cognitive processes allow human beings to know anything about the world.

Taken together, these four tasks give rise to a comprehensive program for any nominalist doctrine. We will now ask Ockham how he

---

[44] See Davidson 1984b.

deals with each one of them in his account of general, relational, and quantitative terms. His own developments are not organized with these rubrics in mind, but we find a lot on each of them across his various writings, and his ideas on the matters cohere with one another within a rich nominalist system.

2
Against Realism

The predominant position in Ockham's youth with respect to general terms, relational terms, and quantitative terms was that a special kind of entities in the world corresponds to each of these three categories. Universals (or at least common natures), relations, and quantities were taken to be somehow distinct from singular substances and qualities.[1] As we saw, Ockham disagreed on all three counts. This chapter will be devoted to his criticisms of the realist doctrines he was familiar with. His arguments, though, were quite numerous on each topic and cannot all be presented here, even in a summarized form. I chose a few that in addition to playing an important role in Ockham's own thought seem most philosophically interesting.

Universals

As regards general terms, I will stress four antirealist arguments, each one aimed at a slightly different target. Some of Ockham's most cherished principles will emerge in the process.

---

[1] On universals in the thirteenth century, see in particular De Libera 1996: 229–304, and Piché 2005. The interpretation of the theory of universals of the most important philosopher of the period, Thomas Aquinas, is still a matter of disagreement among commentators. Yet insofar as Aquinas accepts common natures as special components that are "individualized" by something *else* within singular substances, it seems plain to me that he must be labeled a realist with respect to general terms; see, e.g., Galluzzo 2004, Brower 2016. On the predominance of realist theories on relations and the other Aristotelian categories in the thirteenth century, see Henninger 1989: 1–118, Pini 2005: especially 66–73.

Ockham's Nominalism. Claude Panaccio, Oxford University Press. © Oxford University Press 2023.
DOI: 10.1093/oso/9780190078980.003.0003

The argument from numerical unity

Let us start with the basic realist claim that terms like "horse," "animal," and "white" refer in some guise or other to intrinsically general beings that really differ from any singular thing.[2] Ockham counters this position with the idea that whatever can be counted as one is a singular thing. Take any alleged universal you like, Ockham says, and call it *a*.[3] Let us ask now: Are *a* and Socrates, say, different things? If they are not, *a* is a singular thing, since Socrates is indeed a singular thing. If they are different things, on the other hand, as the realist contends, and neither of them is to be identified with a plurality of other things, then there are only two things there: *a* and Socrates. But whenever there are only two things, each one of them is numerically one. And if each is numerically one, it is singular, by the very definition of what it is to be singular. This thing, Ockham says, "is one thing and not many; therefore it is numerically one thing, and therefore it is singular."[4]

What if the alleged universal entity *a* was identified with a plurality of things rather than with one thing only? Well, Ockham asks, will each of these several things be singular or universal? If the former, the alleged universal *a* would not be distinct from singular things after all; it would be identified with a plurality of them. If the latter, then take any one of these several universal things *a* is supposed to be identical with and ask again whether this one in particular is numerically one or not. If it is, then it is singular by the same tautology as before: whatever is numerically one is singular. If it is a plurality of things, on the other hand, we are back at the same question again: is each one of these things singular or universal? Either there will be an infinite regress from then on and we will never reach the entities that the world is made of—which sounds utterly unappealing to Ockham—or we will

---

[2] The idea that there is a *real* distinction between universals and individuals was not very popular in Ockham's time, but it was considered as a possible approach and had to be discussed as such. It soon came indeed to be defended by Walter Burley; see Conti 2010: 651–654, Dutilh Novaes 2013, Wöhler 2013.

[3] *Exp. in libr. Porph*, Prol., 2, *OPh* II: 11–13 (transl. Kluge: 206–208); see also *SL* I, 15, *OPh* I: 50–51 (transl. Loux 1974: 79–80).

[4] *Exp. in libr. Porph.*, Prol., 2, *OPh* II: 13 (transl. Kluge 1973–1974: 267).

have to conclude at some point that nothing in the world is really distinct from singular things, either individually or taken collectively.

The argument from separability

The realist might bite the bullet and say that universals are singular things after all, but things of a very special sort. Think of what Plato's Ideal Forms are generally supposed to be: transcendent individuals that ordinary singular things receive their properties from somehow. Bucephalus is a horse, in this view, in virtue of a special relation of "participation" that it has with some transcendent singular thing, entirely distinct from it, namely the Ideal Form of Horseness; and Bucephalus is white insofar as it also participates in the transcendent Form of Whiteness. In Ockham's time, this variety of realism was quite unpopular. It was identified with Platonism (as it still is today), and Platonism was taken to have been refuted by Aristotle. Ockham himself indeed is sometimes content to reduce a rival position to Platonism as a way of discrediting it.[5] At least one of his arguments, nevertheless, does apply to Platonism, even if it is not primarily intended to. It is the argument from separability.

In Ockham's view, this argument is based on a theological principle about God's omnipotence: God can do anything that does not involve a contradiction.[6] Since "a exists" and "b does not exist" are not contradictories if a and b are distinct from each other, it follows that for any two distinct creatures, God could make it that one of them exists without the other.[7] Despite the theological ring this has in Ockham, the latter point can be reformulated in a purely philosophical fashion: if two things are really distinct from each other, it is possible that one of them exists while the other does not.[8] Let us call this the *principle of*

---

[5] See, e.g., *Ord.*, dist. 2, q. 4, *OTh* II: 117–118 (transl. Spade 1994: 126; Tweedale 1999: 301–302).

[6] See *Quodl.* VI, 6, *OTh* IX: 604: "[. . .] whatever does not involve an obvious contradiction is to be attributed to the divine power" (transl. Freddoso 1991: 506).

[7] See *Ord.*, dist. 9, q. 3, *OTh* III: 310: "any created absolute thing can exist, by divine power, without any other thing whatsoever" (my transl.).

[8] In Ockham's view, this principle does not apply to God, since nothing else could exist without Him. But I will leave this theological restriction aside for the sake of the present discussion.

ontological separability. With the reference to God removed, it comes down to what David Lewis describes as the "Humean prohibition of necessary connections":[9] the existence of a thing does not necessarily require the existence of any other one. We can now see this "prohibition" to have been Ockhamist long before it was Humean.

We are not talking here of *natural* possibility, of course. Ockham is ready to concede that a given effect cannot naturally exist without its cause, or that a given singular quality cannot naturally exist without the substance it is linked to. But as several commentators have remarked, there is a distinction to be drawn in his approach between two kinds of possibilities: natural and absolute. In theological terms, the former corresponds to what can exist in the world as God actually arranged it, while the latter is equated with what God could do in the absolute, that is, anything that is not self-contradictory. Ockham, in other words, accepts two levels of possibility and necessity, just as several contemporary philosophers do when they distinguish between natural and metaphysical possibility.[10] Set in this vocabulary, Ockham's principle of ontological separability has to do with metaphysical possibility only.

Admittedly, if the principle is cut off from its theological foundation, it is left standing on its own in Ockham. This does not prevent it, however, from being philosophically interesting. For one thing, it could be argued for on independent grounds even if Ockham did not do so. David Lewis, for example, sees it as "our best handle on the question what possibilities there are."[11] The separability principle, moreover, seems intimately connected with a notion that lies at the heart of Aristotle's criticism of Plato: the idea, namely, that the substance of each thing is "proper to it."[12] What Aristotle—and many medieval philosophers after him—found difficult to understand in Plato's position is how a relation with something *else* could determine what a substance essentially is. In order to be distinct from something else, they thought, a thing must be determinate *by itself* in the first place.[13] If so,

---

[9] Lewis 2009: 111.
[10] See, e.g., Fine 2002, Kment 2017, sect. 2.
[11] Ibid.
[12] Aristotle, *Metaphysics* VII, 1038b9–10.
[13] See Ockham's formulation of the idea in *Ord.*, dist. 2, q. 5, *OPh* II: 154: "every thing really distinct from some other thing is distinguished from that thing either by its own

it is at least conceivable that any particular thing should exist without any other one. But the step is small from conceivability to metaphysical possibility. Ockham heartily takes it by identifying the realm of the metaphysically possible with whatever it is that is not self-contradictory. This identification, in his view, has theological grounds: God's omnipotence should be restricted only by non-contradiction. But it is a path that is worth exploring anyway, independent of the Christian doctrine about omnipotence.

Once the separability principle is endorsed for some reason or other, Ockham's antirealist argument is straightforward. Everybody admits that there exists something strictly individual in the world. It follows, in virtue of the principle of separability, that these individual elements, whatever they are, could exist without the corresponding common natures or Ideal Forms.

Ockham primarily used this argument against the moderate realists he was acquainted with, who thought of the common nature as an internal component of singular beings: "if in an individual there were two such really distinct items," he argues, "it does not seem to involve a contradiction for one being able to be without the other."[14] But the same argument can *a fortiori* be addressed to Platonists. The only reason why Ockham does not explicitly do so is that he was not primarily concerned with refuting Platonism. Aristotle, he thought, had done that. The relevance of the argument from separability against Platonism is clear nonetheless. Platonists take the concrete individual things to be really distinct from the Ideal Forms they participate in, and external to them. It follows by the separability principle that these worldly individual things could exist, and therefore be what they essentially are, even if the Ideal Forms did not exist. But this is precisely what the Platonists wanted to deny in the first place. If they accept the

---

self or by something intrinsic to itself" (transl. Tweedale 1999: 313; also transl. in Spade 1994: 149).

[14] *Ord.*, dist. 2, q. 5, *OTh* II: 159 (transl. Tweedale 1999: 318; also transl. in Spade 1994: 152). See also *Ord.*, dist. 2, q. 4, *OTh* II: 115–117 (transl. Spade 1994: 124–125; Tweedale 1999: 299–301), where the argument is put in terms of what God can do: God could create an individual without creating anything else. From a philosophical point of view, this comes down to saying that there is no contradiction in supposing a world of mere individuals.

principle of ontological separability, the Platonists are thus caught in a plain contradiction. If, on the other hand, they reject the separability principle, they are left with a rather mysterious conception of what the relation is supposed to be between the Ideal Forms and the worldly individuals, as Aristotle pointed out. It is hard to understand, in particular, how concrete individuals could be in any relation whatsoever with these external Forms if these individuals themselves were not independently determinate in some way or other.

The argument from mereology

As an alternative to Platonism, what most medieval realists explored, sometimes in great detail, was the idea that a common nature is not external to the worldly individual but an internal constituent, a *part*, of it. This is what is often called "moderate realism," and it is what the third Ockhamist argument I want to consider is concerned with. This argument has to do with what we call today "mereology," the theory of parts and wholes. It starts with the idea that parts and wholes must be proportionate to each other in such a way that if one of them is singular, the other is singular, too.[15] Common natures, then, cannot be parts of singular things unless they are singular themselves. But no singular thing, Ockham thinks, can be an *essential* part of several individual substances at once.[16] Human-nature-in-Peter, say, will have to be a different singular thing than Human-nature-in-Mary. If so, however, neither of them would be a *common* nature.

As I just reconstructed it, this argument rests on two mereological principles: a principle of proportionality (a singular whole has only singular parts) and a principle of essential privacy for substances (no essential part of a singular substance can be an essential part of another singular substance). Why should these be accepted? As to the first one, Ockham argues that if Peter, say, had universals as some of his essential parts, he would not be more singular than universal.[17] If generality

---

[15] This principle is explicit in *Ord.*, dist. 2, q. 5, *OTh* II: 153 and 158.
[16] *Ord.*, dist. 2, q. 4, *OTh* II: 108 (transl. Tweedale 1999: 290).
[17] *SL* I, 15, *OPh* I: 51 I (transl. Loux 1974: 80).

creeps into what a thing essentially is, this thing will be intrinsically general. But we want Peter to be a genuinely singular thing, and this is what the proportionality principle guarantees. The principle of essential privacy, on the other hand, is very much Aristotle's idea again that the substance of each thing is proper to it,[18] except that it is expressed now in terms of parts and wholes. An essential part of a certain whole, in this context, is a part without which this particular whole could not exist. In the case of substances, according to the Aristotelian principle, any such part should be proper to the singular substance it is a part of. Taken together, the two principles sketch a plausible and coherent mereology for complex singular substances: all of their parts are singular, and the essential parts of any one of them are proper to it. This mereology, however, is incompatible with the immanent realists' idea that a common nature is an essential part of several singular substances at once.

Immanent realists, of course, could deny either one of the two mereological principles. But since these are intuitively plausible, the burden will then be on the realists to provide an alternate understanding of the part-whole relations within singular things, especially within singular substances. This transfer of the burden of the proof, at any rate, is a significant result.

The argument from the indiscernibility of identicals

John Duns Scotus died in 1308, while Ockham was still a student. Yet his theory of universals can apparently deal with the three Ockhamist arguments we have reviewed so far. Scotus's key idea here is that *real* distinction is not the only kind of distinction to be metaphysically significant. There is also what he calls "formal distinction": two items are formally distinct from one another, in this vocabulary, when neither of them can exist without the other even by God's power, each one thus being an incomplete entity by itself. This is so with common natures, Scotus claims. They cannot exist without being individuated

---

[18] Aristotle, *Metaph.* VII 1038b9–10.

in some singular substance or other. And what individuates a common nature in a given singular substance is taken to be a special constituent of this substance, which Scotus calls an "individual difference." There is no need to delve further here into what exactly these individual differences are supposed to be. What is relevant with respect to the nominalist arguments discussed so far is that the common nature in Mary, say, is not said to be *really* distinct from Mary's individual difference, but only *formally* so. Scotus, then, can grant that anything which is really distinct from a singular thing is itself a singular thing, as shown by Ockham's argument from numerical unity. He can grant that any two really distinct things could be separated from each other in some metaphysically possible world, as the argument from separability assumed. And he can grant that any really distinct essential part of a singular substance is both singular and proper to this substance, as the mereological argument assumed. Yet Scotus is still a realist with respect to general terms insofar as he accepts special entities as counterparts for general terms, namely common natures. The key to his strategy is to endow these entities with a special mode of existence, that of being a formally distinct component rather than being a really distinct entity on its own.[19]

Ockham was very familiar with this position. It is indeed his primary target when it comes to universals. The main argument he offers against it is aimed, as can be expected, at the very idea of formal distinction. One way that Ockham puts it is the following.[20] The common nature, obviously, is not formally distinct from the common nature, even according to the Scotists themselves. But they take the individuating element to be formally distinct from the common nature. Something, then, is true of the individuating element, but not of the common nature. The Scotists, therefore, must admit that the common nature and the individuating element are not identical with each other. But if they are not identical, they must be *really* distinct from one another, which is precisely what Scotism wanted to avoid in the first place.

---

[19] On Scotus on universals, see Tweedale 1999 (where several relevant texts from Scotus are translated in English) and Noone 2003 (for a shorter presentation).
[20] See *Ord.*, dist. 2, q. 1, *OTh* II: 14–16; and *SL* I, 16, *OPh* I: 54–55 (transl. Loux 1974: 82).

The Scotists, of course, would like to say both that the common nature and the individuating factor are not quite identical with one another, and that they are not really distinct, either. The reason why this cannot be allowed, according to Ockham, is that "all way of proving a real distinction or a real non-identity between anything would thus be lost."[21] The only good way we have to prove that two things are really distinct from each other is to show that something is true of one of them but not of the other one. Lest we renounce one of our best rational tools, therefore, admitting that something is true of the common nature but not of the individuating element, as the Scotists do, should lead to the conclusion that they are really distinct entities.

Ockham's strategy in this case rests on what we call today the indiscernibility of identicals: if a and b are identical with each other, whatever is true of a is true of b.[22] Ockham's distinctive point is that this principle provides us with the only good way we have of proving that two things are *really* distinct from one another. Showing that something is true of a but not true of b is the only available method for proving that a and b are really distinct. What the idea of a merely formal distinction jeopardizes in the end is one of the most fundamental modes of inference we use both in science and in everyday life. In Ockham's view, this is a compelling reason to reject it.

It is striking that none of the four Ockhamist arguments we have reviewed against realism with respect to general terms centrally uses the famous "Ockham's Razor." The idea that entities should not be multiplied beyond necessity in our account of what is going on in the world has been called Ockham's Razor since the nineteenth century.[23] Ockham never formulates it quite this way, but he regularly invokes some equivalent principle of parsimony, for example, that "a plurality is not to be posited without necessity"[24] or that "if two or three things are sufficient for the truth of a proposition, then a fourth thing

---

[21] *Ord.*, dist. 2, q. 1, *OTh* II: 16.
[22] For Ockham's version of this principle, see in particular *Ord.*, dist. 2, q. 1, *OTh* II: 14–17.
[23] The phrase "Ockham's Razor" was coined in the 1850s by the Scottish philosopher William Hamilton. On the medieval history of the principle and on Ockham's use of it, see Maurer 1978, 1984, Keele 2010: 89–109.
[24] *Ord.*, dist. 30, q. 2, *OTh* IV: 322 (my transl.).

is superfluous."[25] This principle was not invented by Ockham; it was accepted by virtually everyone in his time. But he did make a more sustained and effective use of it than most of his contemporaries. It is good policy, in Ockham's eyes, to keep ontology to the smallest possible number of basic categories of beings; and this methodological rule does play an important role in his discussion of relations and quantities, as we will see. With respect to general terms, however, the Razor principle remains marginal in Ockham's argumentation. The reason for this is that he sees the rule of parsimony as yielding only "probable" or plausible conclusions. It is a fine guide to the ontology when nothing stronger is available. But in the matter of universals, Ockham thinks, there are more conclusive arguments to be offered: all varieties of realism with respect to general terms conflict with some basic principle of sound scientific reasoning.

Six such principles are invoked by Ockham in the arguments we have looked at so far. Let me list them again in a more systematic order, with the first one having to do with singularity; the next three with identity, distinction, and separability; and the last two with mereology:

(1) anything that is numerically one is singular (by definition);
(2) if a and b are identical with each other, whatever is true of a is true of b (indiscernibility of identicals);
(3) if a and b are not identical with each other, they are really distinct from each other (the only good rule of inference available for proving that any two things are really distinct from each other);
(4) if something is really distinct from something else, either of them can exist while the other one does not (principle of ontological separability);
(5) if a whole is singular, all of its parts are singular (principle of mereological proportionality);
(6) any essential part of a singular substance is proper to it (principle of essential privacy for substances).

---

[25] *Quodl.* VII, 1, *OTh* IX: 704 (transl. Freddoso 1991: 593).

All of these are more fundamental in Ockham's eyes than the Razor principle. Rejecting any one of them clashes with some of our most basic notions and jeopardizes some of our most efficient ways of reasoning. Accepting these principles, on the other hand, leads the realists into contradictions.

Relations

The predominant position in Ockham's time was that relational terms refer to special "respective" entities that are *really* distinct from the "absolute"—or non-relational—things.[26] The fatherhood of Adam with respect to Abel was taken to be something real in addition to Adam and Abel, and the resemblance between them was taken to be yet another real thing. Ockham thought that from a purely philosophical perspective, "countless" arguments can be adduced against this view.[27] Christian theology, admittedly, requires special *respectus* to account for Divine Trinity, Incarnation and the Eucharist,[28] but if we follow only natural reason, he claimed, we have to conclude that "every created thing is absolute and that among creatures there are no relations outside the soul distinct from absolute things."[29] Most of Ockham's critical discussion in this matter is aimed at Duns Scotus and purports to show that the acceptance of relations as really distinct entities is inconsistent with Scotus's own principles and theses.[30] Some of Ockham's main lines of argumentation, however, are still relevant for today's philosophical discussions on the subject. I will focus on two of them: an argument from infinite regress and an argument from parsimony. Both presuppose that there are no universals in the outside world, and that if

---

[26] See Henninger 1989, Brower 2018.
[27] *SL* I, 50, *OPh* I: 162 (transl. Loux 1974: 164).
[28] See *Ord.*, dist. 30, q. 4, *OTh* IV: 366–374.
[29] *Quodl.* VI, 15, *OTh* IX: 636 (transl. Freddoso 1991: 537). Ockham's main discussions of the ontological status of relations are to be found in: *Ord.*, dist. 30, *OTh* IV: 281–395; *Rep.* II, q. 1, *OTh* V: 3–49; *Exp. in libr. Praedic.* 12, *OPh* II: 238–248; *Quodl.* VI, 8–30, *OTh* IX: 611–701 (transl. Freddoso 1991: 512–589); and *SL* I, 50, *OPh* I: 159–162 (transl. Loux 1974: 162–164).
[30] For a detailed discussion of Ockham's criticisms of Scotus on relations, see Adams 1987, ch. 7: 215–277.

relations are real things, they should be singular connections between singular entities, what we call "tropes" in today's philosophy;[31] the resemblance between Socrates and Plato, for example, would be a different singular entity than the resemblance between Paul and Peter.

The argument from infinite regress

While Ockham admitted that a continuously extended thing has an infinity of actual parts, he followed Aristotle in rejecting as impossible the actual existence of an infinite number of different things that are not such spatial parts.[32] But accepting relations as additional real things in the outside world, he thought, leads to just this unwanted consequence. He has different ways of proving this, not all of which are regress arguments. One of them, for instance, has to do with causality.[33] Take a common causal situation, such as the sun heating a certain piece of wood. Since this piece of wood is infinitely divisible, the sun is thus related to an infinite number of parts. If relations are real things, then there will be an infinity of relations holding between the sun and this particular piece of wood. Even in such a simple case, the realist about relations will thus be committed to an actual infinity of real causal relations, none of which can be considered as being a part of an extended continuum. And the same holds for spatial relations: an infinity of them will be needed between any two extended bodies because of the infinity of their parts.[34]

Whatever strength such considerations have against Ockham's opponents, they are not regress arguments, strictly speaking. An infinite regress argument is supposed to show that the thesis it is meant to criticize somehow involves a series in which each member generates

---

[31] On this notion of "trope," see Maurin 2018.
[32] See *Exp. in libr. Phys.* VI, 1, *OPh* V: 458: "[. . .] although the parts of a continuum can be actually infinite in natural reality since a continuum is divisible into parts that are always divisible, it is impossible, however, that there should exist in natural reality an infinity of things that are not parts of some thing or of some things" (my transl.). On Ockham's idea that the parts of a continuum are actually infinite in number, see also *Exp. in libr. Phys.* I, 2, *OPh* IV: 110, and *Quaest. in libr. Phys.* 68–71, *OPh* VI: 587–597.
[33] See *Quodl.* VI, 12, *OTh* IX: 631–632 (transl. Freddoso 1991: 531–532).
[34] See *SL* I, 50, *OPh* I: 159–160 (transl. Loux 1974: 162).

a new one with no end to the process.³⁵ This is not so with the causality argument just reviewed: the causal relations between the sun and the piece of wood turn out to be infinite in number because the piece of wood has an infinite number of parts, and not because each causal connection generates another one. By contrast, the Ockhamist argument I will now consider is a genuine infinite regress argument. It is a version of what is called "Bradley's regress" in contemporary philosophy, an argument that is still widely present in philosophical discussions over the reality of relations and that is usually attributed, as its name indicates, to the nineteenth-century British philosopher Francis H. Bradley.³⁶

Ockham's reasoning is the following.³⁷ If relations are real things distinct from their absolute *relata*, any particular diversity, then, is such a real thing. But—and let me now quote Ockham's own words:

> If a diversity is a thing distinct from absolute things, then that diversity is distinct from its absolute subject [. . .]; and, as a result, it is itself really related to that absolute thing. Therefore, it is related to it by another relation. And consequently, this second relation [of diversity] is really diverse from the first relation. Therefore, it is diverse from it by another relation, and this third relation is diverse from the second by still another relation, and so on ad infinitum, with the result that in each thing there will be infinitely many really distinct things.³⁸

This is a result that Ockham takes to be "absurd," as he bluntly says in the *Ordinatio*.

Duns Scotus, who held the realist thesis that Ockham attacks here, anticipated this objection. His reply was that the regress can be halted early on in the process since the second relation of diversity is really identical with the first one. Scotus's principle is that if it is a contradiction to say that a certain thing exists without having a certain property,

---

³⁵ See Cameron 2018.
³⁶ See Perovic 2017.
³⁷ See *Ord.*, dist. 30, q. 1, *OTh* IV: 292, and *Quodl.* VI, 11, *OTh* IX: 625–626 (transl. Freddoso 1991: 525).
³⁸ *Quodl.* VI, 11, *OTh* IX: 625–626 (transl. Freddoso 1991: 525).

this property must really be identical with the thing in question. Consider two distinct human beings, Socrates and Plato. Since each one of them can exist without the other, each can exist without having the property of being related to the other one by a relation of diversity. The diversity of Socrates with respect to Plato, then, is really distinct from Socrates, and the diversity of Plato with respect to Socrates is really distinct from Plato.[39] It would be a contradiction, however, to suppose that the diversity of Socrates with respect to Plato exists without being related to Socrates. Its relation to Socrates, consequently, is not an additional entity, according to Scotus. The regress is blocked at this point not by denying that the second relation of diversity is real, but by identifying it with the original diversity of Socrates with respect to Plato. What Scotus rejects in the argument from infinite regress is the assumption that on the realist view any relation of diversity must be related to its subject by *another* relation of diversity.[40]

Ockham knew this reply, but found it unsatisfactory. His point is simple: if two relations have different terms, the realist cannot identify these relations with each other. "Whenever the termini of given relations are distinct, then there are distinct relations," he says.[41] But the first relation of diversity relates Socrates to Plato, while the second diversity is supposed to relate Socrates to the first diversity, which, according to the realist, is a real thing, entirely different from Plato. If they are real things, then, the two diversities must be distinct from each other. And the same must be said about the third, the fourth, etc. ad infinitum. A Scotist might try to evade this rebuttal by saying that there is indeed some ontological distinction to be drawn between the first and the second diversity, but only a *formal* distinction, not a real one. This would allow the two diversities to be really identical with each other after all while nevertheless relating different entities. As we have seen,

---

[39] Like all medieval realists with respect to relations, Scotus thought that a relational property always inheres in a single substance while being directed at another one: Socrates's diversity with respect to Plato inheres in Socrates, and Plato's diversity with respect to Socrates inheres in Plato. Although "correlative," these two relations of diversity were thus taken to be really distinct from each other. See on this Henninger 1989, Brower 2018.

[40] This point is made in Scotus's own *Ordinatio*, II, dist. 1, q. 4–5, n. 239 (Ed. Vaticana vol. VII: 119).

[41] *Quodl.* VI, 11, *OTh* IX: 626 (transl. Freddoso 1991: 525).

however, Ockham rejects the very concept of formal distinction. For him, whenever something is true of *a* but not true of *b*, *a* and *b* must be *really* distinct from each other.

A slightly different way out of the infinite regress argument is widespread in contemporary discussions over relations. It rests on a distinction between internal and external relations. Scotus already used a similar vocabulary to distinguish, just as contemporary philosophy does, between those relations that cannot but hold when the *relata* exist, and those that could hold or not.[42] Socrates and Plato, for example, could not both exist without being of the same species or without being distinct from each other; co-specificity and distinction are thus said to be internal relations. Socrates and Plato, on the other hand, could exist without being friends, or without being spatially close to each other; friendship and spatial proximity, consequently, count as external relations. Now several contemporary philosophers claim that only external relations have to be posited as real entities. An internal relation, by contrast, is an ontological free lunch, they say; it "supervenes" on its *relata* in such a way that it adds nothing new to the ontology.[43] If this is so, Ockham's regress cannot even start, since the diversity between Socrates and Plato is an internal relation. Contrary to what we had in Scotus, not even this first diversity would be accepted as a real entity of its own. A typical external relation such as spatial proximity, on the other hand, could be countenanced as a real entity without any regress ensuing, since any relation that holds between this proximity and either Socrates or Plato would be an internal relation: it could never be the case that this particular proximity between Socrates and Plato exists without being connected to the two of them.

Ockham, however, would reject the idea that the distinction between internal and external relations has ontological significance. If there was a good reason to accept any relation whatsoever as a real thing, he claims, diversity and distinction would have to be posited as real things for the very same reason.[44] Conversely, then, if you can dispense with internal relations in the ontology, you can dispense with

---

[42] Ockham quotes Scotus on this in *Rep.* II, q. 2, *OTh* V: 48.
[43] See Lewis 1986: 62, Armstrong 1989: 43.
[44] *Ord.*, dist. 30, q. 1, *OTh* IV: 292.

external relations, as well. The point, I gather, is that a relational term can plausibly be denied to refer to a special entity if one can provide a good semantic account of the true sentences in which this relational term occurs, without postulating any such special entity. This is precisely what Ockham's semantics for relational terms is designed to accomplish, as we will see in chapter 4. Ockham's contention is that if this semantics works for such relational terms as "diversity" and "distinction," it equally works for all relational terms.

This, of course, is what some realist philosophers would deny. There is a good semantic reason, they think, why a special ontological status should be attributed to external relations but not to internal relations. It rests on the so-called Truthmaker principle: if a certain sentence is true about the world, there must exist a certain entity in virtue of which this sentence is true.[45] This entity, according to the Truthmaker principle, should be such that if it exists, the sentence in question *must* be true. For sentences about internal relations such as "Socrates and Plato are distinct from each other," the truthmakers simply are Socrates and Plato themselves: whenever they both exist, the sentence is true. But sentences about external relations are not made true by the sole existence of their *relata*: Socrates and Plato might both exist, and the sentence "Socrates is spatially close to Plato" could still be true or false. The truth of this sentence, these philosophers reason, requires a truthmaker that is different from both Socrates and Plato. The external relation of spatial proximity, therefore, has to be accepted as an additional entity in the ontology. No regress follows, however, since the relation between this particular spatial proximity and its *relata* is not itself an external relation and does not, therefore, have to be posited as an entity of its own. This rejoinder, obviously, is highly relevant for the assessment of Ockham's regress, but it is effective against it only if the Truthmaker principle is endorsed. The question is: does it need to be? Ockham is actually committed to rejecting this principle, as we will see presently in discussing the next argument.

---

[45] See Armstrong 2004, Lowe and Rami 2009, MacBride 2020.

The Razor argument

The argument I now want to consider has two steps to it.[46] The first one rests on a restricted version of the principle of ontological separability: whatever is essentially prior to something else can exist, by divine power, without the posterior thing. But a relation, if it was something real, would be essentially posterior to its absolute *relata*, it would be dependent on them, just as a quality is dependent on the substance it qualifies. The *relata*, therefore, could exist without the existence of this particular relational thing. Suppose, then, that Peter and Mary are similar to each other in some respect—they are both two-legged, for example—and suppose that this similarity is something real, as the realist contends. Since Peter and Mary are both essentially prior to this similarity, they could both exist without it. Yet they would still be two-legged, since *ex hypothesi* the only thing that would have been removed from the world is this relational thing that is supposed to exist in addition to the two of them. And consequently, they would still be similar to each other. It follows that two things can be similar to each other without the existence of any special relational entity.

The second step of the argument is based on the Razor principle: when two things are sufficient for a good account, there is no point in postulating a third one. But the first step has shown that two absolute things can be related to each other without a special relational entity in addition to the two of them. It is vain, therefore, to postulate the existence of such relational entities.

This calls for a couple of remarks. First, it might seem that the argument would have been both simpler and stronger if Ockham had used the unrestricted principle of ontological separability that we met with when discussing realism with respect to general terms. Why doesn't he argue, for example, that if a similitude was a real thing, it could exist by itself without its *relata*? Realism about relations would thus be shown not merely to bring about a superfluously rich ontology, but to lead straightforwardly to the absurd notion that the similitude between Peter and Mary could exist even if Peter and Mary did not.

---

[46] See *Ord.*, dist. 30, q. 1, *OTh* IV: 291–292, and *Quodl.* VI, 8, *OTh* IX: 614 (transl. Freddoso 1991: 515).

The reason why Ockham does not go this way, I take it, is that his argument, like many others that he offers when discussing the status of relations, is directed at Scotus. And Scotus would surely deny that the unrestricted principle of ontological separability holds for relational entities. Relational things in Scotus's view are sharply contrasted with "absolute" things, and they are taken to be ontologically dependent on the latter. Even Ockham, in fact, sometimes formulates his principle of separability with reference only to absolute entities: "every *absolute* creature," he writes in the *Ordinatio*, "can exist by divine power without any other one."[47] In Ockham's eyes, this is not a genuine restriction, since only absolute things exist anyway among creatures, according to him. But he could hardly assume when discussing realism about relations, that only absolute things exist, since this would beg the question. Scotus, on the other hand, does accept the restricted separability principle. He acknowledges that some things are ontologically prior to others—a substance with respect to its accidents, for example—and that God could make it that in such cases the prior thing exists without the posterior one.[48] Ockham simply points out that this should apply to absolute things with respect to merely relational things, and that if God were to keep two absolute things in existence while removing the relational things, then these absolute things would still be similar to each other, or distinct from one another, and so on. The argument, then, does not lead to the strong conclusion that relational things are impossible, but only that they are superfluous. In the context of this particular discussion, this is the most efficient use that Ockham could make of his separability principle.[49] This is why the Razor is needed to round off the argument.

But now comes another worry: does the argument really show that *all* relational things are superfluous? This might work for similitude or distinction, one can object, because they are internal relations, but it is less convincing when it comes to external relations such as spatial proximity. The point of this rejoinder is that the existence of a

---

[47] *Ord.*, dist. 9, q. 3, *OTh* III: 310 (my italics).
[48] See Henninger 1989: 79–82.
[49] Ockham, anyway, did not think that merely respective entities are absolutely impossible, since he accepts them in theology; see *Ord.*, dist. 30, q. 4, *OTh* IV: 366–374.

particular spatial relation between Peter and Mary, say, is necessary for the truth of a sentence such as "Peter and Mary are spatially close to one another." Peter and Mary alone do not suffice to make this sentence true, since they could both exist while being far away from each other. Should God destroy or modify this particular spatial relation, it would no longer be true that Peter and Mary are spatially close to one another, even if nothing else is taken out of existence. Ockham's opponent could thus accept both the restricted separability principle and the Razor principle, while denying that external relations could be destroyed without any change in the truth-values of relational sentences.

This brings us back to the Truthmaker principle: the truth of a sentence about the world, this principle asserts, requires the existence of one or more truthmakers. But in the case of external relations, the *relata* alone cannot serve as truthmakers. External relations, consequently, have to be posited as real extra entities. Ockham was familiar with this way of reasoning. In the *Ordinatio* and in the *Tractatus de quantitate*, for example, he considers an argument based on the idea that no sentence can change from true to false, or conversely, without some thing ceasing to exist or something new coming to exist, which is indeed a medieval version of the Truthmaker principle.[50] Yet Ockham sees no reason to endorse such a principle:

> And if it is said that it is impossible to pass from a contradictory to a contradictory without some novelty—if, therefore, this is first true: "This substance is of such a quantity," and afterwards it is false, there must be some novelty, or at least the destruction of some old thing—, it must be replied that this is not true [...][51]

One drawback of the principle, in particular, is that when applied to spatial distances, it entails the actual existence of an infinite number of additional real things: any particular object in the universe is distant from a large number of continuous bodies, each one of which is divisible into an infinity of actual parts; the thing in question, therefore,

---

[50] *Ord.*, dist. 30, q. 1, *OTh* IV: 282, *Ord.*, dist. 30, q. 2, *OTh* IV: 320), *Tract. de quant.*, q. 3, *OTh* X: 74.
[51] *Tract. de quant.*, q. 3, *OTh* X: 74 (my transl.).

must have a different spatial relation with each one of these parts. Whenever something moves, moreover, its distance from any one of these parts will change and at every moment, therefore, an infinity of real things will be destroyed while an infinity of new ones will come into existence.[52] As we saw, Ockham took such actual infinities to be naturally impossible (except for the parts of a continuum), but whatever we think about this, the argument shows at least that the acceptance of spatial relations as real things extraordinarily enriches the ontology. The good news is that this profligacy can be avoided by simply renouncing the Truthmaker principle. Ockham sides with those among our own contemporaries who reject it.[53]

According to the Truthmaker principle as it is usually understood, if a sentence is true in a certain situation but false in another situation, there must be an entity that exists in one of these situations but not in the other one.[54] In Ockham's view, by contrast, local movement or the mere passage of time often suffice for a sentence to change from true to false or conversely,[55] and nothing forces us to think that local movement and the mere passage of time involve any other real things in the world beyond the things that are mobile themselves.[56] As Peter gets farther away from Mary, no real thing ceases to exist and no new thing comes into existence; it is just that Peter and Mary are now differently related in space than they were before. The intuition here is that the truth of such relational sentences does not require special truthmakers. Things in the world are spatially—or temporally—related to one another, yet neither these relations nor space itself nor time need to be reified. Such a view, of course, requires a semantic account of the truth of the sentences in question that dispenses with the Truthmaker principle, and this is just what Ockham purports to offer with his idea of

---

[52] See, e.g., *Ord.*, dist. 30, q. 2, *OTh* IV: 325.
[53] See, e.g., Hornsby 2005, MacBride 2005.
[54] See, e.g., Rami 2009, MacBride 2020.
[55] See, e.g., *Rep.* IV, q. 6, *OTh* VII: 85: "I say that sometimes there can be a passage from a contradictory to a contradictory in virtue of the sole passage of time, either actual or potential, or in virtue of local movement" (my transl.).
[56] See, e.g., *Brev. summ. libr. Phys.* III, 1 *OPh* VI: 40: "[. . .] we should note that motion is not a distinct and definable entity in itself, and if it does signify things, it signifies nothing but present, past, or future things" (transl. Davies 1989: 40); or *Quaest. in libr. Phys.* 37, *OPh* VI: 494: "[. . .] the word 'time' does not refer to something absolutely distinct from past, present, and future permanent things" (my transl.).

connotation, as we will see in chapter 4. Insofar as this approach is successful, it allows for a much more parsimonious ontology.

The discussion of the last paragraphs has come to focus on spatial relations, and Ockham indeed does put special insistence on these. He wrote extensively on physics, and a large part of his developments in this field are intended to show that neither place nor space nor void nor movement—nor time, for that matter—are to be counted as additional entities in the world.[57] But can all external relations be dealt with in the same way? Ockham himself expresses doubts about two relations in particular that are central to Aristotelian metaphysics: hylomorphic composition, on the one hand, which Ockham sees as holding between singular chunks of matter and singular substantial forms, and the inherence relation, on the other hand, that holds between singular qualities and the substances they are attached to. An Aristotelian philosopher, he contends, should hold both that a singular substantial form hylomorphically informs a given chunk of matter if and only if they occupy the same place, and that, similarly, a given quality inheres in a given substance if and only if they occupy the same place.[58] A Christian, however, might believe that God could make it true that a substantial form and a chunk of matter, or a quality and a substance, are spatially compresent without this substantial form informing this chunk of matter, or this quality inhering in this substance. What must happen in such a situation, according to Ockham, is that God creates a special relational entity that *prevents* the natural connection to hold.[59] The point of this original solution is that it allows Ockham to maintain that in the natural world spatial compresence suffices for a substantial form to inform a certain chunk of matter and for a quality to inhere in a certain substance. Additional entities are needed only in cases of miraculous divine interventions.

Ockham's insistence on the ontological innocuity of spatial and temporal relations paved the way for a conception of nature that became

---

[57] These points are lengthily discussed in, e.g., *Exp. in libr. Phys.* IV, *OPh* V: 3–313, *Summ. phil. nat.* III–IV, *OPh* VI: 247–394, and *Quaest. in libr. Phys.* 8–22 and 72–78, *OPh* VI: 412–453 and 597–611. For detailed commentaries, see Goddu 1984, ch. 4–5: 112–158, and Adams 1987, ch. 19–20: 799–899. More on this in chapter 3.

[58] See *Ord.*, dist. 30, q. 4, *OTh* IV: 369–372, and *Sum. phil. nat.* I, 19: *OPh* VI: 208.

[59] See *Quaest. var.* 6, art. 2, *OTh* VIII: 210–211.

predominant in the seventeenth century, and according to which *all* natural phenomena can be accounted for in terms of the local motion and spatial arrangement of material bodies.[60] Ockham himself, however, was not that radical. He countenanced qualities as real things in addition to substances, and he endorsed Aristotelian hylomorphism. Yet his strategy with respect to spatial and temporal relations is a genuine philosophical breakthrough insofar as it allows for a typical group of relational sentences to change from true to false or conversely without the need for any real thing to be added to or subtracted from the ontology. Once this is accepted in the case of spatial and temporal relations, as Ockham repeatedly does, there is no reason why the same could not hold for other external relations, whether they are reducible or not to spatial and temporal relations. External relations, in such a perspective, are just as ontologically innocuous as internal relations are usually taken to be. The basic idea is this: real things can be mind-independently ordered in the world, without such orderings being reified. If a good semantic account of relational terms can be provided along these lines, as Ockham thinks it can, Ockham's Razor generally tells against the Truthmaker principle as it is understood today.

To sum up, the key presuppositions in the Ockhamist arguments I have reviewed against the reality of relations are the following three:

- finitism with respect to the number of real things in the actual world (except for the parts of an infinitely divisible continuum);
- a restricted principle of ontological separability;
- the Razor principle.

For a contemporary assessment of these arguments, the last of these principles should be the one to focus on. Finitism is not taken to be compelling anymore, as it used to be in the Aristotelian tradition, but we might still want to avoid an infinite regress with respect to relations for parsimony reasons. And as we have seen, restricted separability only works, in Ockham's own eyes, when it is supplemented by the Razor. Now why should the Razor principle be endorsed?

---

[60] Pasnau 2011 calls this view "corpuscularianism," and he insists on Ockham's role in its development in the late medieval and early modern periods.

This is currently debated in philosophy,[61] but Ockham himself never discussed the point. All else being equal, the more ontologically parsimonious theory is more likely to be true, in his view, than the less economical one, and not only more easily manageable: the Razor has a bona fide epistemic value for him rather than a merely pragmatic one. And since he frequently uses it in philosophy proper, he must not have seen it as an essentially theological principle based on the Christian belief in a benevolent God. Although he did not take the Razor to yield decisive conclusions, but only "probable" ones, he treated it in practice as a sound principle for rational enquiry.

Quantities

To be a quantity (or a quantum) for Ockham is "to have parts outside of parts and to have parts that are distant in position from parts."[62] Following Aristotle, he distinguishes two main kinds of quantities:[63]

(1) continuous quantities, the parts of which are contiguous with each other and taken together constitute a naturally unified whole, what Ockham calls a "unity *per se*"; paradigmatic examples for him are material substances such as a horse or a given volume of water, and single qualities (or "tropes" in modern language) such as the whiteness of this horse or the heat of a certain fire;

(2) discrete quantities, the parts of which do not constitute a naturally unified whole and are not always contiguous to one another, such as a herd of horses or a forest.

All of them are real in Ockham's view since anything that has parts has to be real. A material substance such as a horse, for example, really *is* a quantity for him. But he disagreed with most of his contemporaries by

---

[61] See Sober 2015, Baker 2016.
[62] *Quodl.* IV, 23, *OTh* IX: 407 (transl. Freddoso and Kelley 1991: 336).
[63] On this distinction, see in particular *Quodl.* IV, 27, *OTh* IX: 439 (transl. Freddoso and Kelley 1991: 361–362).

denying that quantities involve extra things in addition to substances and qualities. Let us briefly see why, first for continuous quantities, and then for discrete ones.

Extension

Ockham dedicated two short treatises to the ontological status of continuous quantities,[64] and he discussed the matter at length in several other works.[65] The reason why this meant so much to him is that delicate issues about the Eucharist were involved. The common view was that pure extension—often simply called "quantity" in the context of these debates—was a real accident in-between the substance and the qualities. It was thought to "inhere" in the substance and to serve as a substratum for qualities. This was supposed to explain how it is that the qualities of the bread and the wine in the Eucharist were still extended after the consecration even if their original substances were no longer there. Ockham's rejection of extension as a special kind of being was thus suspected of making the Eucharistic transubstantiation seem impossible. Many of his arguments on the matter, however, are philosophically intriguing independent of these theological intricacies.

One way he approaches the question is by showing first that points are not distinct entities with respect to lines, that lines are not distinct entities with respect to surfaces, and that surfaces are not distinct entities with respect to three-dimensional bodies.[66] He offers quite a number of arguments for this. One of them, for instance, rests on the impossibility of actual infinities: if points were spatially indivisible entities, there would have to be an actual infinity of them in any particular body, and the same holds for lines. Other arguments rest on the principle of separability: if points were distinct entities with respect to lines, they could be destroyed by God while the lines would remain exactly as they were before; if so, however, the postulation of points

---

[64] *Tract. de quant.* (*OTh* X: 1–85) and *Tract. de corp. Christi* (*OTh* X: 87–234).
[65] See *Rep.* IV, q. 6, *OTh* VII: 71–78, *Exp. in libr. Praedic.* 10, *OPh* II: 205–212, *Quodl.* IV, 18–28: *OTh* IX: 388–445 (transl. Freddoso and Kelley 1991: 319–367), *SL* I, 44–45, *OPh* I: 132–145 (transl. Loux 1974: 142–151).
[66] *Tract. de quant.*, q. 1–2, *OTh* X: 5–51.

as distinct entities is superfluous, since points, by definition, are supposed to be the limits of lines;[67] and the same holds *mutatis mutandis* for lines with respect to surfaces, and surfaces with respect to bodies.

Once this result is reached, what remains to be shown is that extension in general is not ontologically distinct from either substances or qualities.[68] With respect to the extension of substances, Ockham's main line of reasoning invokes again both the principle of separability and the Razor. As in the discussion of relations, he uses the restricted principle of separability in this context because this version was accepted by his opponents: any absolute thing which is ontologically prior to another absolute thing can be maintained in existence, at least supernaturally, without that other thing.[69] But a substance is ontologically prior to any of its real accidents. If the extension of a given material substance was an accident distinct from its underlying substance, then, it could in principle be destroyed while the substance would remain intact. Would the substance still have parts outside of parts in this case, or not? The realist at this point faces a dilemma. If the substance still has parts outside of parts, it is still extended, by the very definition of what it is to be extended. The postulation of extension as a distinct entity would thus turn out to be superfluous and should be renounced in virtue of the Razor principle. If, on the other hand, the substance is supposed not to have parts outside of parts anymore when its extension is destroyed, it is a complete mystery where the parts have now gone.

Ockham vividly illustrates the latter problem with the following thought experiment.[70] Take a two-meter-long piece of wood. Each half of it, then, is one meter long and is said by the realist to be a substratum for a one-meter length. Now suppose that one of these one-meter lengths is suddenly destroyed. What happens, Ockham asks, to the corresponding underlying part of the original piece of wood? It must

---

[67] Ockham rejects the suggestion that points could be the parts of lines: each point being spatially indivisible, no finite amount of them could add up to a continuous line; see *Quodl.* I, 9, *OTh* IX: 50–61: "Is a line composed of points?" (transl. Freddoso and Kelley 1991: 46–55).
[68] See in particular *Tract. de quant.*, q. 3, *OTh* X: 51–85.
[69] See, e.g., *Tract. de corp. Christi* 15, *OTh* IX: 120.
[70] See *Tract. de corp. Christi* 15, *OTh* X: 120–121.

still exist *ex hypothesi*, and since its matter has not been destroyed, it must still be somewhere. Yet there is no place for it to be. It cannot have moved away, since it has by itself no capacity to do so. And it cannot be reduced to an indivisible point at the surface of the other half of the piece of wood (or anywhere else for that matter), for there is no reason for it to be at one such point rather than at any other. Ockham here implicitly uses a principle of sufficient reason that he often turns to: in the course of nature, if there is no more reason for something to occur rather than some alternate possibility, and vice versa, neither of them occurs. The only remaining option is that the supposedly dequantified half of the piece of wood stays in exactly the same place where it was before. And the same must be true, accordingly, for any material substance whatsoever if its supposedly distinct extension is instantaneously destroyed. We thus return to the first horn of the realist's dilemma: if the extension of a material substance were destroyed, this substance would remain in the same place where it was before and therefore it would still be extended. This does not show, admittedly, that the postulation of extension as a distinct entity leads to contradiction or to outright logical impossibility, but it neatly exposes the superfluity of this postulation in the case of material substances: any such substance has to be extended by itself, anyway. The Razor does the rest.

What about qualities? What is their connection with extension? Ockham sees only three possibilities.[71] Either (1) qualities are the substrata of certain distinct extensions, or (2) qualities inhere in distinct quantitative extensions as in their substrata, or (3) qualities are extended by themselves just as substances are. The Razor principle tells against the first option: for any material substance, there would then be several simultaneous extensions in the same place in addition to the substance and the qualities, namely one extension for each of the substance's qualities, and this would amount to a useless multiplication of entities. The second hypothesis was favored by many of Ockham's contemporaries in order to secure a common substratum for the qualities of the bread and the wine in the Eucharist: the whiteness of the Eucharistic bread, for example, was supposed to be extended in virtue

---

[71] See *Tract. de corp. Christi* 17–24, *OTh* X: 124–144.

of the fact that it inheres in a distinct extension, unreducible either to the substance of the bread (which is not there anymore) or to the body of Christ (which is allegedly present, but in an unextended way). As Ockham remarks, however, this postulated extension would thus be left without a substratum. But if we have to posit an accident without a substratum anyway in the case of the Eucharist, why wouldn't that be the qualities themselves? This is metaphysically possible in Ockham's view: he accepts qualities as being really distinct from substances, and therefore they can be miraculously maintained in existence without the underlying substances. The postulation of distinct extensions thus turns out to be superfluous again. Only the third possibility remains: qualities are extended by themselves just as substances are. Even leaving aside the miraculous case of the Eucharist, the resulting picture provides a much more economical account of what goes on in the natural world. Think of the whiteness of a certain snow bank: being a material substance, the snow bank is extended by itself, in Ockham's view, and so is its whiteness in such a way that for each extended part of snowy stuff there is a correspondingly extended part of its whiteness. Nothing more is needed but the snow bank and its whiteness. As Ockham succinctly puts it:

> [. . .] it is vain to do with more what can be done with less. But everything that can be saved with such a quantity distinct from substance and quality can be saved without it, as it inductively comes out, therefore such a quantity distinct from substance and quality is not to be posited.[72]

Numbers

In Ockham's metaphysics, each singular substance, even when it is intrinsically complex, is said to have a unity by itself (*per se*), and the same is true of each singular quality. Those are the basic individuals

---

[72] *Tract. de quant.*, q. 3, *OTh* X: 58 (my transl.).

of the world. Several of them together, on the other hand, do not constitute such an intrinsic unity. They amount to what Aristotle called a "discrete quantity," such as a plurality of horses, of fires, of whitenesses, or of things in general for that matter; and each such quantity, whatever its constituents are, can be numbered. Are these numbers distinct entities in addition to the individual substances and qualities? Ockham's answer, as can be expected, is a resolute "no." In one sense, the term "number" refers to the mental concepts that we count things with, the concepts "two," "three," etc., and while these are certainly distinct from the things that are numbered, they are taken to be mental qualities in Ockham's later theory and do not add any special sort of entities to the substance-quality ontology. In another sense, a number is normally something external to mind and language, but it is then to be identified with the numbered things themselves. Ockham argues for this in various passages.[73] Let us look at two of his main arguments.

The first one has two steps to it. It starts with the idea that the unity of an individual thing is nothing in addition to the thing which is one. This is clear in virtue of the separability principle again: if the unity of a horse were distinct from the horse itself, it should be metaphysically possible for the horse to exist while its unity does not. But this is obviously impossible: whenever the horse exists, it must count as one thing and must therefore retain its unity whatever else happens in the world.[74] Ockham then asks us to consider a situation in which entities *a*, *b*, and *c* are distinct from one another while nothing else exists.[75] Since each one of them has its unity by itself, we thus have three entities and there is no point in postulating an additional numerical property of threeness to account for this. And the equivalent must hold *mutatis mutandis* for all finite positive integers, which are the only numbers Ockham cares about.

The second argument I want to consider is this.[76] Take any plurality of things, such as a trio of horses, and suppose that their being three is

---

[73] See, e.g., *Ord.*, dist. 24, q. 2, *OTh* IV: 96–121, *Quaest. in libr. Phys.*, q. 107–112, *OPh* VI: 679–697, *SL* I, 44, *OPh* I: 138 (transl. Loux 1974: 146).

[74] For a slightly more elaborate version of this argument about unity, see *Ord.*, dist. 24, q. 1, *OTh* IV: 78.

[75] *Ord.*, dist. 24, q. 2, *OTh* IV: 96.

[76] See *Ord.*, dist. 24, q. 2, *OTh* IV: 100–101.

an additional entity, distinct from each singular horse. What sort of entity might this be? Obviously not a substance, Ockham says. It should therefore be a singular accident. But what, then, would its bearer be? Being an accident, it does need to have a bearer, since the situation under consideration is a purely natural one and no accident can stand alone without a substratum in the natural world. Yet the bearer in this case cannot be any single one among the numbered horses: none of the horses taken individually has the property of being three. Should the numbered horses, then, collectively be the bearer of this numerical property? Ockham at this point makes use of a principle of proportionality between an accident and its bearer which would have commonly been endorsed in his time: "any accident that is one *per se* has a bearer that is one *per se*."[77] The three horses, however, do not constitute such a unity. They cannot therefore collectively be the bearer of a singular unified accident. Since there is no plausible possibility for anything else to be the bearer of the threeness of the horses, the conclusion must be that no such property exists as an entity in addition to the three single horses. And this conclusion must be generalized to all numerical properties. The argument presupposes a certain metaphysics, of course, but it is not an especially weird one. Once the general substance-accident picture is accepted and extramental universals are excluded, the idea that a singular accident in the natural world requires one and only one singular bearer seems plausible.

The outcome of it all is that in each particular situation a number is always to be identified with the numbered things themselves: the threeness of our trio of horses is nothing in addition to these horses. Ockham would thus reject the idea—defended by Nelson Goodman, for one—that any collection of singular things is itself a singular thing.[78] A singular substance or a singular quality certainly can be complex, in his view; it can have intrinsic parts while retaining its unity per se (as will be explained in chapter 3), but no collection of such individuals can be said to have a unity per se. A trio of horses is not a new singular thing in the world, it is but the three horses themselves. And a plurality of whitenesses that are discontinuously apart

---

[77] *Ord.*, dist. 24, q. 2, *OTh* IV: 101 (my transl.).
[78] See Goodman 1956.

from one other (the whitenesses of three different snow banks, for example) do not constitute a distinct entity, either, they are just three distinct whitenesses. One should say, therefore, "that many men constitute a number and that many animals constitute a number"[79], in the sense in which we can truly assert that these horses are three, or that the Apostles were twelve. The approach, admittedly, requires that the subjects of such sentences have special uses there, in virtue of which they collectively, rather than distributively, refer to certain individuals in the world. But this is something Ockham is ready to integrate in his semantic theory. From "The Apostles were men," for example, we can normally infer that each Apostle was a man, but we should not similarly infer from "The Apostles were twelve" that each one of them was twelve. In Ockham's approach, this difference requires no special enrichment of the ontology, but only a semantic account: in certain contexts, general terms can be attributed a collective reference.[80]

The Ockhamist arguments we have reviewed against the ontological distinctness of quantities, whether continuous or discrete, thus make use of the same three principles Ockham resorted to in his discussion of relations: the rejection of actual infinities, a restricted principle of separability, and the Razor; plus the following two that we had not yet encountered:

- a principle of sufficient reason: in the natural world, if there is no more reason for one or the other of two alternate possibilities to be actualized, neither of them is actualized;
- a principle of proportionality between accidents and substances: in the natural world, the bearer of a singular accident is always a singular substance.

Both of these new principles are supposed to hold only in the natural order of things, but in different ways. The first one is restricted to what naturally happens as opposed to what a free agent can do. A free

---

[79] *SL* I, 9, *OPh* I: 34 (transl. Loux 1974: 69).
[80] See, e. g., *Quaest. in libr. Phys.* 107, *OPh* VI: 681. More on this in chapter 4.

agent, Ockham thinks, is able to act in certain ways rather than others without any compelling reason to do so. This indeed is exactly what the freedom of the will amounts to.[81] Everything else, however, requires a sufficient reason or cause. The point is controversial, of course. One might think, for example, that in certain circumstances two alternate possibilities can each objectively have a fifty percent chance of being actualized and that, nevertheless, one of them will randomly come to be without any free agent intervening in the process.[82] But Ockham does not. With the notable exception of the freedom of the will, the course of nature, for him, is entirely deterministic.

The proportionality principle between accidents and substances, on the other hand, is restricted to the natural world as opposed to what is supernaturally possible, since an accident can supernaturally be made to exist, for Ockham, without any substratum at all (as in the Eucharist). Whether he would be ready to accept faraway possible worlds where accidents are naturally free-floating or naturally inhere in other accidents or in collections of substances is an open interpretative question, but he probably should, since the hypothesis does not seem to involve any contradiction.

Adding to this list of principles those concerning singular identity, distinction, and mereology that Ockham used in his discussion of universals as shown in the first part of this chapter, it is clear that a whole metaphysics is involved in his attacks on the various forms of realism he wanted to reject. Even if the point is to show in each case that the correct use of certain terms—namely, general terms, relational terms, and quantitative terms—do not require the position of special entities as referents for them, Ockham's arguments mostly rest on a complex view of the world, rather than on merely semantic considerations. All the components of this view could (and should) be further scrutinized, of course, but this is something

---

[81] See *Quodl.* I, 16, *OTh* IX: 87 (transl. Freddoso and Kelley 1991: 75). On Ockham's theory of the freedom of the will, see Maurer 1999: 510–515.

[82] The principle of sufficient reason was introduced under this appellation by Leibniz and was the object of philosophical debates in the eighteenth century, as it still is today; see Melamed and Lin 2020.

I cannot engage in here. Suffice it to accept at this point that the metaphysical and methodological principles Ockham invokes so far have some plausibility. The next challenge is to show how thought, language, and knowledge are possible in such a world. And for this, a coherent positive ontology must first be elaborated with only singular substances and qualities in it.

3
Ontology

Although Ockham is a nominalist with respect to general terms, relational terms, and quantitative terms, his general ontology remains quite complex. The focus in this chapter will be on the exposition of his various theses on the matter, while, for the sake of brevity, the arguments he offers in support of them will be mentioned only in salient cases. Ockham, as we saw, acknowledges two kinds of basic individuals: substances and qualities. I will first explore this distinction by explaining, in particular, how substances and qualities are related to each other in Ockham's view, how material substances are composed of matter and form, how complex qualities are composed of simpler qualities, and how Ockham deals with artifacts. The second part of the chapter will explain how it is that the world can be mind-independently ordered for Ockham even though relations are not extramental entities. The third section, finally, will argue that despite his nominalist inclinations, Ockham is committed to the ontological acceptance of merely possible beings.

Individuals

Substances and qualities

Aristotle famously distinguished ten basic categories: substance, quantity, quality, relation, place, time, position, possession, action, and affection.[1] What these are supposed to be categories of, however, was the subject of a long controversy in the Aristotelian tradition. Ockham's position is that Aristotle's list is a classification not of external things

---

[1] Aristotle, *Categories* 4.

but of first-order signs: signs that refer to things that are not signs themselves.[2] Real things, on the other hand, are of only two basic sorts: substances and qualities. This is not to say that Aristotle's classification is a mixed one in which two categories are of real things while the other eight are of signs only. As it occurs in logic, the whole taxonomy is about signs for Ockham. What Aristotle meant, Ockham claims, is that first-order terms can be divided into ten groups: substantial terms, quantitative terms, qualitative terms, relational terms, and so on. The words "substance" and "quality," however, have a special status in this taxonomy: they are the more general terms for answering "What is this?" questions when raised about individuals. The point is that natural kind terms are ordered according to increasing generality and the top terms along these lines are either "substance" or "quality." Starting with "this is a horse," for example, we can move up to "this is an animal" or "this is a body," but we must stop at "this is a substance." Nothing more general can be said of the thing in question along this line except "this is a being." Starting with "this is a whiteness trope," alternatively, we can move up to "this is a color trope," but the more general thing that can be said now along the same line is that the thing in question is a quality. By contrast, none of the other eight labels for the categories—"quantity," "relation," "place," "time," etc.—can occur at the top of such hierarchies of natural kind terms.[3] The most general truth about our world is that everything in it essentially is either a substance or a quality.

In his earlier works, Ockham admitted concepts as an exception. The reason for this was that he implicitly assumed for a while that a mental act of understanding must always have a single object. Since he rejected the real existence of universals out there, he was led to

---

[2] See *SL* I, 40 (transl. Loux 1974: 126–128) and *Exp. in libr. Praedic.*, Prol., *OPh* II: 135–136.

[3] The reason for this varies according to cases. "Relation," for example, is a second-order term for Ockham, as we will see in chapter 4. "Quantity," on the other hand, is not a natural kind term, and the less general terms under it, such as "two-meter length" or "trio," cannot be used to answer questions about what a real thing essentially is. "Action" and "affection" as they occur in the Aristotelian list of categories serve as general labels for groups of verbs according to Ockham, while "time" and "place" serve as general labels for groups of adverbs, etc.; see *SL*. I, 44–54 and 57–62 (transl. Loux 1974: 142–177 and 180–188).

conclude that the understanding of general concepts such as "human being" or "horse" required special kinds of objects that are neither real substances nor real qualities, but mere fabrications of the mind with a purely ideal or intentional mode of existence.[4] Later on, however, he came to realize that no ontological distinction needed to be drawn between the act of understanding and its mental object and that general concepts, consequently, could be identified with the acts of understanding themselves considered as mental signs simultaneously referring to several real external things. The concept of "horse" in this view is nothing but the intellectual act by which all singular horses are simultaneously represented in a given mind. Since mental acts were taken by everybody at the time to be real qualities of the mind, no special intentional entity had to be postulated anymore to account for understanding in addition to the substance of the thinking subject and its mental qualities.[5] This later theory of Ockham is known in the secondary literature as the *actus*-theory of concepts. I will stick to it in the rest of this book.

There is yet another notable breach that Ockham admits, albeit reluctantly, to the principle that everything is a substance or a quality. He thinks that some essentially relational entities—that he calls "*respectus*"—have to be posited in order to account for some revealed articles of faith such as the Divine Trinity or the union of divine and human natures in Christ.[6] This admission is not inconsistent with Ockham's criticism of realism with respect to relational terms, since, as we saw, relational entities are not a metaphysical impossibility for him. Their actual existence, however, is not supported by any philosophical reason in Ockham's eyes. I will consequently leave them aside and restrict my discussion to substances and qualities.

But why not simplify the ontology even further? Couldn't we do with only one basic sort of things rather than two? No, we can't, Ockham claims. His argument for this rests on the following principle:

---

[4] See *Ord.* dist. 2, q. 8, *OTh* II: 271–289 (transl. Spade 1994: 218–229; partial transl. Boehner 1990: 41–43).

[5] See in partic. *Quaest. in libr. Phys.* 1–7, where this new position is argued for. Ockham's change of heart on this is well documented; see Boehner 1958: 96–110 and 156–174, Adams 1987: 73–75, Panaccio 2004: 23–27.

[6] See, e.g., *Ord.*, dist. 30, q. 4.

[...] it is impossible for a thing to pass from a contradictory to a contradictory without acquiring something or losing something, when [this transition] is not accounted for either by the [mere] passage of time or by local motion.[7]

But, Ockham remarks, a typical substance such as a human being can become white after not having been white and this, he thinks, cannot be accounted for by the mere passage of time or spatial movement. In accordance with Aristotelian science, he disregards here the possibility that the appearance of being white might be caused in the perceiving subject by some corpuscular motion within the object, and he concludes from the above principle that a real whiteness must have been acquired by the substance that becomes white. But a whiteness trope, he takes it, is not itself a substance: it requires a substratum in order to exist, and Aristotle indeed mentions whiteness as a paradigmatical example of a quality. Certain qualities, therefore, are needed in the ontology in addition to substances.

Why Ockham thought that neither the mere passage of time nor local motion requires the production or destruction of some entities is something we will come back to later on in this chapter. What is important at this point is that some accidental changes cannot be accounted for in his eyes without accepting the reality of certain qualities. This by no way means that a special quality must be postulated as a real correlate for every qualitative term. In David Lewis's terminology, real qualities are "sparse" in Ockham's ontology rather than "abundant": many qualitative terms in language or thought do not refer to special qualities.[8] It must be decided in each case whether a qualitative term F does refer to real singular qualities or not. The Ockhamist test for this is whether the transition from being (or having) F to not being (or not having) F, or the converse, can be accounted for merely by local motion or the passage of time. If not, a real quality has to be postulated.

---

[7] *Quodl.* VII, 2, *OTh* IX: 707 (transl. Freddoso 1991: 597). See also *SL* I, 55, *OPh* I: 180–181 (transl. Loux 1974: 178). The clause about the passage of time is meant to cover such sentences as "Today is the first of July" or "Peter is 40 years old," that can change from true to false or conversely for no other reason than the passage of time. Those are marginal cases, however, which I will leave aside in the rest of this discussion.

[8] For the distinction between sparse and abundant ontology, see Lewis 1986: 59–60.

All such real qualities, in Ockham's world, are singular properties—what contemporary philosophers call "tropes"—such as a particular patch of redness or a particular emotional state in a given person. And they are individuated by themselves, just like anything is. Yet they are dependent on substances. The connections between substances and qualities are governed by a number of principles, that I will call the "substance-quality principles" ("SQ principles," for short). Ockham does not systematically enumerate them, but they can be gathered from scattered remarks across his writings. Here are the most salient of them, with a few explanations on each one.

(SQ1) Everything is either a substance or a quality.

As I have insisted all along, neither relational terms nor quantitative terms are taken by Ockham to denote special things in the natural world that would not essentially be either substances or qualities, and although I will not develop the point here, this holds as well for all terms from the categories of place, time, possession, position, action, and affection. SQ1, on the other hand, must be understood so as to leave room for the essential parts of material substances in Ockham's ontology, as we will see shortly.[9]

(SQ2) Nothing is both a substance and a quality.

This is not something Ockham bothers to make explicit. Once he has explained what the criterion is for positing certain qualities in addition to substances, he takes it for granted along with Aristotle that the two sorts of entities are mutually exclusive. Their respective characteristics, anyway, are incompatible, as will emerge from the remaining SQ principles.

(SQ3) Every quality naturally inheres in a substance.

"Inherence" is the technical term Ockham uses for indicating that a quality trope naturally depends on a particular substance. This does

---

[9] These essential parts of substances are substantial forms and prime matter, both considered by Ockham to be real "things" (*res*), albeit incomplete ones, as we will see in the next section.

not mean that the quality is an intrinsic part of the substance. Although substance and quality are so closely connected with each other in the empirical world that they normally occupy the same place, qualities are ontologically distinct from substances. And since it is so, God can supernaturally maintain any quality in existence without its underlying substance. Yet no such separation is naturally possible. There are no naturally free-floating qualities. And no quality can inhere in another quality, either. Insofar as it inheres in something at all, that will have to be a substance. No quality is a substratum for anything else.[10] Substances, on the other hand, do not inhere in anything.

(SQ4) Every quality inheres in at most one substance.

There are no collective qualities.[11] This is what I have called in the previous chapter the principle of proportionality between accidents and substances. Any apparently collective quality such as the noise made by a crowd must really be a collection of distinct quality tropes, each one of which inheres in a single substance.

(SQ5) Qualities are accidents.

Qualities can usually come and go without the identity of the underlying substance being affected. A brown horse can become white and still remain the same thing, and any thinking subject can stop having a certain thought without ceasing to exist. This has to be qualified, though. Ockham admits what Porphyry called inseparable accidents, the traditional example being that of crows, which, both Porphyry and Ockham thought, are always black and cannot naturally change color. Yet the blackness of a crow is nevertheless an accident, Ockham explains, because other substances can first be black and then non-black, or conversely.[12]

---

[10] See *Exp. in libr. Praedic.* 9, *OPh* II: 199: "[...] the opinion that an accident is immediately in another accident as in a subject is false and contrary to Aristotle's opinion" (my transl.).

[11] See *Rep.* III, q. 4, *OTh* VI: 133: "What is by itself an accident [i.e., real qualities] has only one subject which is a thing by itself" (my transl.).

[12] See *Exp. in libr. Porph.* 5, 3, *OPh* II: 87–89 (transl. Kluge 1973-1974, ch. 6.3: 339–342).

Since blackness tropes are accidents in these other cases, they must have the same ontological status in crows. It is just that there is something about crows that naturally necessitates that they are black (see SQ7).

(SQ6) Qualities are not naturally transferable.

A quality trope is always bound to a given substance in such a way that it cannot naturally be detached from it without ceasing to exist. If the horse Brunellus loses its original color, this particular color trope just goes out of existence. Note that what is involved here is *natural* necessity again, as it was in SQ3: "No accident which is numerically one," Ockham writes, "can successively be in different first subjects *by the action of a natural cause*."[13] This formulation suggests *a contrario* that trope transferability is nevertheless a metaphysical possibility: God could supernaturally move a certain quality trope from one substantial substratum to another. The ban on transferability concerns only the natural order of the world.

(SQ7) Substances naturally impose constraints on the kind of qualities that can inhere in them.

Intellectual acts, for example, are qualities in Ockham's ontology, but they cannot naturally inhere in just any kind of substance: a tree cannot naturally have a thought. All flowers, on the other hand, must have some color or other. This is generalizable: there are some kinds of qualities that water, fire, or horses must naturally have and some that they cannot have. This is how the world is made.

(SQ8) Substances never admit of variation in degrees, but qualities often do.

This is something Aristotle had pointed out. While a horse, for example, cannot be said to be more or less a horse than any other horse, it can be said to be more or less white, and a human being can be said to be more or less generous than another one. The latter is due, Ockham

---

[13] See *Tract. de corp. Christi* 19, *OTh* X: 130 (my transl. and italics).

explains, to the fact that various quality tropes of the same sort can be added to one another so as to form a new and more intense trope of the same sort.[14] I will come back to this mode of composition later in this chapter.

As one can now surmise, the distinction between natural and metaphysical possibility (or necessity) that was introduced in chapter 2 is crucial to Ockham's conception of how substances and qualities are connected to each other. Most of the SQ principles just listed have to do with the natural order of the world rather than with the whole array of metaphysical possibilities. Despite SQ1, Ockham's God can create merely relational *"respectus"* that are neither substances nor qualities. Despite SQ3, SQ6, and SQ7, He can detach any quality from its natural substantial substratum and leave it free-floating or transfer it to some other substance, even if the latter could not naturally have a quality of this kind. The only clear metaphysical necessity in our list is that of SQ2: anything which is a substance is essentially a substance and anything which is a quality is essentially a quality. Ockham cannot admit any metaphysically possible world in which something is both a substance and a quality. As to SQ4 (no quality inheres in more than one substance), SQ5 (qualities are accidents), and SQ8 (substances do not admit of degrees, but many qualities do), their modal status is unclear, but I will not further speculate about this here. The outcome, at any rate, is that the connections between substances and qualities are governed by a natural order in the world we inhabit in such a way that the range of naturally possible worlds is much more restricted than that of metaphysically possible worlds.

The composition of material substances

There are simple substances in Ockham's world, namely God and the angels.[15] Material substances, on the other hand, are always complex.

---

[14] *Exp. in libr. Praedic.* 15, *OPh* II: 290–292.
[15] On Ockham's God, see Adams 1987, ch. 23–31: 1011–1347, and Maurer 1999, ch. 4–5: 184–265. On his conception of angels, see Maurer 1999: 339–374.

Following Aristotle, Ockham endorses hylomorphism: material substances are internally composed of form and matter. The form accounts for what specific natural kind a given substance belongs to, for its being a horse, for example, or a tulip, or a diamond. The matter accounts for the fact that this substance is a spatially extended mass.[16] Distinguishing form and matter within substances is how Ockham—following Aristotle again—explains natural substantial change. In the generation of plants or animals, for example, certain singular substances come into being. But, Ockham argues, no material substance can naturally be created out of nothing (*ex nihilo*). Any naturally generated material substance, therefore, presupposes the pre-existence of something.[17] And this presupposed entity cannot be extrinsic to this substance, for if it were, the newly generated substance would still be created *ex nihilo*: if a lamb, say, was exclusively produced by an extrinsic cause while no part of it pre-existed, the lamb would have been created *ex nihilo* by the extrinsic cause in question, a feat Ockham takes to be naturally impossible. Something intrinsic to the lamb, therefore, must have pre-existed its generation. But since the lamb is a new substance in the world, some other part of it must come into existence when it is generated. The pre-existing part is the matter, the basic stuff this substance is made of, and the new part is the form.[18] Since both are needed for a material substance to exist, they are said by Ockham to be the "essential parts" of the resulting substance.[19]

In Ockham's version of the theory, form and matter are both strictly singular. Contra Aquinas, he firmly rejects the idea that substantial forms are individuated by the chunks of matter they combine with.

---

[16] See *Summ. phil. nat.* I, 13, OPh VI: 191–194. It should be noted that the matter of a singular substance does not determine it to have a precise length, height, or width, according to Ockham, but only that it is extended in accordance with such dimensions. In his view, the same quantity of matter can occupy more or less space according to how much it is "rarefied" or "condensed." Ockham's conception of rarefaction and condensation, however, remains underdeveloped; see Adams 1987: 178–179.

[17] Note that Ockham confines the argument here to naturally created substances. He adheres to the Christian notion of creation ex nihilo, however, for substances created otherwise than through natural means, that is, by God's divine actions.

[18] See *Summ. phil. nat.* I, 1, OPh VI: 155–158.

[19] The essential parts of a substance are to be sharply distinguished from its "integral parts," such as arms, legs, or pieces of flesh in the case of human beings. On medieval mereology, see Arlig 2019.

Everything in Ockham's ontology is individuated by itself. The substantial form, admittedly, accounts for what natural kind a particular substance belongs to, but this by no way requires for Ockham the existence of a real common component shared by all the individuals of the same kind. It suffices that their respective singular substantial forms exactly resemble one another. And neither is matter individuated by the form it combines with or by the substance it is a part of. Prime matter—or "pure matter," as Ockham sometimes calls it—has a reality of its own. It is not pure potentiality, as Aquinas thought: "matter," Ockham writes, "is a thing [res] actually existing in nature."[20] It never exists all by itself admittedly, since it always combines in nature with some substantial form or other, but it has its own reality all the same: how could anything be a part of something real, as matter is a part of material substances, Ockham asks, if it was not itself real?[21] Pure matter has the potentiality of being combined with any substantial form whatsoever to compose a new singular substance, but it is a real singular and distinct component of any substance that it is truly a part of, and its distinctive singularity is not conferred upon it by anything else.

Another important aspect of Ockham's conception of the composition of material substances is the doctrine of the plurality of the forms: some material substances—human beings and animals in particular—are endowed with several substantial forms. There was indeed a lively controversy in the thirteenth and fourteenth centuries over whether certain material substances have more than one substantial form.[22] Aquinas, most saliently, was a unitarianist: even a human being, he thought, has only one substantial form. Ockham disagrees. In all animals, he argues, the form of corporeity must be distinguished from the sensory form.[23] Consider the body of a dead horse. It can retain its original color, at least for a while. But quality tropes, as we saw, are not transferable from one substratum to another, according to Ockham. The substratum of the color trope, then, must remain the

---

[20] *Summ. phil. nat.* I, 9, *OPh* VI: 179 (my transl.).
[21] *Summ. phil. nat.* I, 10, *OPh* VI: 181.
[22] For a short overview, see Pasnau 2010a: 644–646.
[23] See *Quodl.* II, 11, *OTh* IX: 162–164 (transl. Freddoso and Kelley 1991: 136–139).

same when the horse is dead as when it was alive. Since the horse is dead, however, some essential part of it must have been destroyed. It follows that when the horse was alive, there were at least two distinct formal components to its singular substance: a form of corporeity and a sensory form, each one being able—in combination with matter—to serve as substratum for different quality tropes, for example, color tropes in the case of the former and acts of sensory perception in the case of the latter. Human beings, in Ockham's view, even have a third substantial form, namely an intellectual form. His argument for this is that while contrary acts cannot coexist in the same substratum, a human being can intellectually will something that she does not sensitively desire; the intellectual substratum, then, must differ from the sensory one in human beings.[24]

That there can be several substantial forms within the same substance suggests that Ockham's substantial forms are "tropes" in today's sense. Tropes in this sense are particular instances of properties that combine with one another, thus constituting concrete objects such as human beings, horses, or tables.[25] According to D. C. Williams, who introduced the term in contemporary metaphysics, each trope is an "incomplete" or "partial" entity; it has no autonomous existence if not incorporated somehow into complex wholes.[26] As we have seen, it is quite uncontroversial that Ockham's qualities are tropes in Williams's sense: they are singular entities that cannot exist without being attached to a substance—at least in the natural world. We can now gather that pretty much the same holds for substantial forms. "Such a form," Ockham writes, "is a certain thing that cannot be by itself [*per se*], but is always within a composite, informing a pre-existing matter, without which it cannot be."[27] Substantial forms can thus be seen as

---

[24] See, e.g., *Rep.* IV, q. 9, *OTh* VII: 161–164. While Ockham usually takes the substance as a whole to be the *substratum* (or subject) of the qualities, he sometimes specifies that a substantial form can be the "primary subject" (*subiectum primum*) of certain simple qualities. The latter holds at least for substances with several substantial forms, i.e., animals and human beings; see, e.g., *Ord.*, Prol., q. 4, *OTh* I: 144–145 (transl. Longeway 2007: 253), *Quaest. In libr. Phys.* 59, *Oph* VI: 557.
[25] See Campbell 1990, Ehring 2011, Maurin 2018.
[26] Williams 1953.
[27] *Summ. Phil. Nat.* I, 15, *OPh* VI: 196 (my transl.).

particular property instances: the substantial forms of an animal, for example, are its singular corporeity (*corporeitas*) and its singular sensitivity (*sensitivitas*). And if substantial forms are tropes when several of them coexist within the same substance, this must hold as well when only one substantial form is present, as Ockham took to be the case for non-living substances such as a diamond or a certain volume of water. Leaving matter aside for a while, what we find in Ockham, then, is a variety of what Peter Simons calls a "nuclear theory of tropes."[28] A concrete substance in this approach is composed of a *nucleus* of essential tropes—one or more substantial forms in Ockham's doctrine—externally supplemented by a number of accidental tropes of various kinds—qualities in Ockham's ontology. This allows for more ontological structure than simply putting all tropes on a par, and most saliently, for a crucial distinction between what is essential to a given substance and what is accidental to it.[29]

What about matter? A first thing to be pointed out about it is that prime matter for Ockham is not a unique substratum for all substantial forms to be received in, as it is often thought to be in Aristotle. If it was such a universal substratum, Ockham argues, it would simultaneously receive forms that are incompatible with one another, such as the substantial forms of a horse and those of a human being, which is impossible.[30] The matter of any singular substance is numerically different for him from the matter of any other substance and it is an actual individual: Socrates has his own matter, I have mine, and so on. Admittedly, different chunks of matter can combine into larger ones or be divided into smaller chunks by natural causes, but in all cases the resulting piece of matter is a numerically distinct singular entity.[31]

Ockham, on the other hand, thought of each chunk of matter as a distinct substratum for one or more substantial forms. He says that the forms are "received" in matter, or that matter is the "subject" of the

---

[28] Simons 1994.
[29] I have argued for this tropist interpretation of Ockham's ontology in Panaccio 2015a.
[30] *Summ. Phil. Nat.* I, 12, *OPh* VI: 189.
[31] See *Summ. Phil. Nat.* I, 9, *OPh* VI: 180: "different matters of exactly the same sort can merge into a matter that is one in number, in the same way that two waters that are separate from one another can be united and merge into a water that is one in number" (my transl.).

corresponding forms.³² Yet a singular substratum of this sort can be seen as a trope, too, it seems to me, as much as qualities and substantial forms can. It is true that trope theories are often contrasted in contemporary philosophy with "substratum theories," according to which the properties of a concrete object are attached to a common substratum rather than constituting a mere bundle. But the substratum is usually seen in these discussions as a "bare particular" that underlies the properties and holds them together.³³ A bare particular in this perspective—or a "thin particular" in David Armstrong's terminology—is conceived of as a singular entity "taken apart from its properties."³⁴ For those who accept it, the bare particular is supposed to be the bearer of all the properties of a given individual, including the essential ones such as being human or being extended, and it is taken to be distinct somehow from any one of these properties. Ockham's matter, by contrast, is not such a bare substratum. It has an intrinsic nature of its own and, in particular, it is extended *by itself*. Its being spatially extended, in other words, is not a property that is distinct from it. Matter, in addition, is said by Ockham to be a "partial" or incomplete entity, just as substantial forms are and as tropes are supposed to be according to D. C. Williams's characterization. The only theoretical role played in Ockham's theory by the idea that matter is a substratum is to emphasize what Ockham calls its natural priority over any particular substantial form: "What is prior by nature," he writes, "is that which can exist without the posterior but not conversely," and this is the case with prime matter with respect to any particular substantial form in his view.³⁵ Prime matter for him indeed is "unengenderable" (*ingenerabilis*) and uncorruptible by any natural power,³⁶ and the natural production of a new material substance always requires the pre-existence of the relevant matter. But being a substratum in this sense is not incompatible with being a trope. Seeing it as a trope makes it clear that the matter of a substance is not a portion

---

³² See, e.g., *Summ. Phil. Nat.* I, 9, *OPh* VI: 181, and *Summ. Phil. Nat.* I, 17, *OPh* VI: 199.
³³ See, e.g., Simons 1994: 565–567.
³⁴ Armstrong 1989: 95. The phrase "bare particular" was introduced by Bergmann 1967: 24–25. There is an ongoing debate about whether such bare particulars are to be countenanced; for an introductory discussion, see Moreland 2001: 148–157.
³⁵ *Ord.*, dist. 9, q. 3, *OTh* III: 298 (my transl.).
³⁶ *Summ. phil. nat.* I, 11, *OPh* VI: 186–188.

of a universal continuous stuff for Ockham; it is the distinct singular materiality of this particular substance.

The resulting picture, admittedly, is not that of a mere "bundle" of tropes. Each material substance is intrinsically composed out of a variety of nuclear elements, one of which is a materiality trope that serves as a substratum for one or more substantial forms. When combined with one another, these nuclear tropes are a substratum for a variety of accidental quality tropes that can usually come and go without the identity of the underlying substance being affected. The destruction of the substantial form, by contrast, annihilates the substance in question and forces its indestructible matter to combine with some other substantial form, as it happens, for instance, when the body of an animal rots away or when a piece of wood is burnt.

Intensive qualities

Qualities, too, can have parts according to Ockham, and in more than one way. A central idea in his mature view on mental language is that the intellectual act of forming a mental proposition, which he takes to be a quality, is really composed of simple conceptual acts, as we will see in chapter 5. The qualities of material substances, on the other hand, are spatially extended by themselves for him, which means that they have "parts outside of parts," just as material substances do,[37] and that they are infinitely divisible into smaller spatial parts.[38] What we will be interested in in this section, however, is yet another mode of composition. As we have seen, many qualities, whether in the physical or the mental world, admit of variation in degrees, while substances never do. This is what I have called Principle SQ8, that Ockham inherited from Aristotle.[39] A certain volume of water can become warmer or colder

---

[37] See, e.g., *Quodl*. IV, 33, *OTh* IX: 465: "every extended quality is truly a quantity [. . .] by its own proper and intrinsic quantity" (transl. Freddoso and Kelley 1991: 383).

[38] Ockham firmly rejects atomism about the material world; see *Exp. in libr. Phys.* VI, 1, *OPh* V: 449–462, and *Quodl*. I, 9, *OTh* IX: 50–61 (transl. Freddoso and Kelley 1991: 46–55).

[39] See above, pp. 69–70.

than it was before, and a human being can be more or less in love than she was before. This distinctive feature of qualities gave rise to a lively discussion among medieval philosophers about how to understand what is going on when such variations in qualitative intensity occur.

Some, such as Walter Burley, held that the previous quality simply disappears and is replaced by a more or less intense one of the same kind, while others, such as Albert the Great, claimed that a quality increases or intensifies insofar as it is progressively purified from its contrary, warmness from coldness for example, or generosity from selfishness. Ockham thinks differently.[40] When a quality intensifies, according to him, a quality trope is added to a previously existing one of the same sort and combines with it into a newly unified qualitative whole of still the same sort.[41] When a piece of wood is progressively warmed up by a fire, say, new heat tropes are successively caused in the piece of wood, and as each one comes into existence it merges with the previous ones into a more and more intense heat trope. This process differs significantly from the piling up of wood logs on top of one another. In the wood logs case, the resulting stack is a mere aggregate of different material things. When a quality intensifies, by contrast, the new components are added to the pre-existing ones within a single qualitative whole having what Ockham calls a "unity *per se*." While the piling up of logs does not amount to a single log, the combination of several heat tropes constitutes a genuine singular unit of the same sort as each one of its components. The process, Ockham says, is similar to what happens when we pour a certain volume of water into another one: they merge with one another into a new unified volume of water. In this respect, the qualities that admit of degrees are more like substantial stuffs such as water, fire, or air, than like plants or animals: they are homogeneous wholes. In the case of extended qualities, moreover, all of the parts end up occupying the same place as one another and as the qualitative whole that they are parts of: as a certain surface becomes more intensely white, each new whiteness trope spreads across the

---

[40] For a general presentation of this debate and a detailed discussion of Ockham's arguments, see Adams 1987: 697–740.
[41] See in particular *Ord.*, dist. 17, q. 6–7, *OTh* III: 495–545.

same spatial extension as all of its predecessors, and nobody can perceive any one of them separately. While each new component quality trope is a real part of the whole, its addition changes neither the nature of the whole nor its extension, but only its intensity.

Conversely, when the intensity of a quality is reduced by some external cause, what happens in this view is that the qualitative whole loses some of its parts. Consider a cup of hot water. The water contained in it constitutes a numerically distinct substance for Ockham. It is distinct as a substance, in particular, from any other separate volume of water and it has its own qualities. The water in the cup, then, is the substratum for a singular heat trope located in the same place as itself and any decrease in the temperature of this particular watery substance is accounted for by the loss of parts of this unified heat trope. As long as some parts of it remain, the water is still hot, albeit less than it was before; and when all the parts are gone, the water is not hot anymore. As to whether there is a minimal degree of heat such that no smaller part of it can be lost without the underlying substance ceasing to be hot, Ockham's answer is no.[42] And this claim holds as well for all qualities that similarly admit degrees: they all are infinitely divisible into further homogeneous parts.[43]

Ockham's ontology, in short, countenances two kinds of individuals in the natural world: substances (and their parts) and qualities, and their connections are governed by a number of principles. Each kind, on the other hand, has a distinctive mode of composition: complex substances are composed of form(s) and chunks of matter, all of them strictly individual, while the qualities that admit of degrees are infinitely divisible into homogeneous parts of the same sort as the qualitative whole itself. This approach, as I have argued, can be seen as a "nucleus theory of tropes" in Peter Simons's sense, one that draws a distinction between accidental tropes (i.e., qualities) and essential tropes (i.e., substantial forms and chunks of matter). For every unit

---

[42] See *Quaest. in libr. Phys.*, 150, *OPh* VI: 806–809, where Ockham variously argues in favor of this position.

[43] Whether such qualities have a maximal degree is another question. Ockham's position is that God can always increase the intensity of a given quality, but that in the natural world, each kind of substance imposes a limit to the intensification of the qualities that inhere in it. See, e.g., *Rep.* III, q. 8, *OTh* VI: 268–269.

in this arrangement, whether substances, quality tropes, substantial forms, or chunks of prime matter, Ockham subscribes to what contemporary metaphysicians call "primitivist individuation":[44] each entity is individuated by itself. None of them, on the other hand, is a "bare particular." They all have certain characteristics in virtue of what they essentially are, rather than in virtue of something that is superadded to them. A certain substantial form, for example, is an intellective one rather than a sensory one in virtue of what it essentially is, a certain quality is a whiteness trope rather than a heat trope in virtue of what it essentially is, and matter is essentially extended, without anything but singular entities being involved.

Artifacts

What about artifacts? A house, a bed, or a shoe are singular things, too. But what is it exactly that newly comes into existence when such things are produced? As in all other cases, the matter must have pre-existed obviously, but is any new substantial form or qualitative trope created when a craftsperson manufactures something? Ockham discusses the point in various places in his physical works.[45] His insistence, then, is always the same: no new ontological constituent is ever involved in artifacts. Manufactured objects are nothing but natural substances and qualities re-arranged in certain ways. Ockham distinguishes three basic modes of such re-arrangements: subtraction, transfiguration, and conjunction.[46] In the first case, parts of a natural thing are removed by the craftsperson as when a sculptor carves a figure in a rock. In the second case, the external configuration of something is modified as when a piece of clay is molded into a statuette. In the third case, various pre-existing objects are combined, as when a house is built out of wood and stone. Ockham's point is that all three kinds of modifications can be accounted for by

---

[44] See Maurin 2018, sect. 2.3.
[45] *Exp. in libr. Phys.* II, 1, paragr. 2–4, *OPh* IV: 214–237, *Summ. phil. nat.* I, 20, *OPh* VI: 208–213, *Quaest. in libr. Phys.* 118–122, *OPh* VI: 716–729.
[46] *Exp. in libr. Phys.* II, 1, *OPh* IV: 217.

mere spatial movements. And spatial movement never involves any special thing in addition to the moving bodies, as will be explained in the next section. The building of a house, for example, might involve the cutting of trees, the removal of their bark, the carving of stones, and the putting together of the parts according to a certain arrangement. And the destruction of the house is nothing but a displacement of its parts. All of this boils down in the end to moving natural things around. In all cases, moreover, the principle of movement stems from nothing but natural things, the moving power of the craftsperson, for example, or the weight of a piece of wood, the malleability of clay, the force of the wind, and so on.[47] Saying that a house or a bed or a shoe has been generated is just to say that certain natural things have been re-arranged in certain ways.[48]

In certain cases, admittedly, the work of a craftsperson might lead to the generation of new substances or new qualities. The farmer produces carrots and potatoes; and the blacksmith brings about the existence of new heat tropes. Yet what the craftsperson does in such situations is merely to move certain things around. The farmer puts a seed in the ground and eventually pours water upon the growing plant; and the blacksmith moves the horseshoe near a fire. Natural causality then takes over. The carrot is really generated by the action of the seed, the water and the Sun; and the heat of the horseshoe is really caused by the fire.[49] Since neither spatial movement nor natural causation are additional entities for Ockham (as we will shortly see), none of the real things involved in craft requires anything in the ontology but human beings and their mental qualities on the one hand, and natural substances and qualities on the other hand. Strictly speaking, artifacts in the end are nothing but natural things that have been spatially arranged in special ways.

---

[47] The point is discussed in detail in *Exp. in libr. Phys.* II, 1, paragr. 4, *OPh* IV: 216–237.
[48] *Exp. in libr. Phys.* II, 1, *OPh* VI: 220–222.
[49] *Summ. phil. nat.* I, 20, *OPh* VI: 209.

An ordered world

It is clear by now that Ockham's world has a lot a structure to it. How is this to be understood if no special relational entity is to be admitted in the ontology? This is what I will address in this section by discussing four kinds of worldly arrangements: (1) spatial and temporal structure; (2) inherence and information; (3) essential similarity; and (4) causation.

Motion, space, and time

A crucial claim in Ockham's ontology is that the motion of a body from one place to another—local motion, as he calls it—does not require the addition of any new entity nor the destruction of any pre-existing one. If you move from one side of a column to the other side, the supply of real things in the world has neither increased nor decreased. Motion, Ockham insists, is no distinct entity with respect to the moving body. One of his main arguments for this is that if local motion was a thing, that thing would have to be composed of parts that would not be simultaneous with one another. At any particular moment, then, some of these parts would not exist. But "what does not exist cannot be a part of any being: no being is composed of non-beings."[50] Motion, therefore, cannot be a distinct entity. It should not be concluded, however, as Zeno did, that local motion is an illusion and that nothing really moves from one place to another. According to Ockham, what is going on when a body is moving is that it "acquires one place after another."[51] That requires no real entity except the body itself and the various places it successively occupies.[52]

What about these places, then? Ockham, unsurprisingly, refuses to countenance them as extra entities, either. He turns to Aristotle's definition: a place is "the innermost boundary of a containing body."[53]

---

[50] *Summ. phil. nat.* III, 5, *OPh* VI: 262 (my transl.).
[51] *Summ. phil. nat.* III, 6, *OPh* VI: 264.
[52] *Summ. phil. nat.* III, 10, *OPh* VI: 282–283.
[53] Aristotle, *Physics* IV, 212a20. The definition is quoted and commented upon by Ockham in various passages; see in particular *Exp. in libr. Phys.* IV, 6, *OPh* V: 50–79.

Consider a trout in a lake. Its immediate location at any moment in this perspective is the inside surface of the surrounding water that is contiguous to the trout. But the surface of a material substance for Ockham, as we saw when discussing realism about quantitative terms, is no extra entity in addition to this material substance itself. The place—or location—of a certain body a is just the surrounding body b certain parts of which are contiguous to a.[54] The immediate place of the trout is the water in the lake that immediately surrounds the trout. Saying that this place changes as the trout swims is just to say that the surrounding parts of the lake change accordingly. If the trout moves from the lake to an adjacent brook, the immediate place of the trout is now the brook, or some part of it. No extra real entity is required to account for local motion except the moving bodies and the containing bodies, all of which are but singular substances.

A place, on this approach, can itself be in a place and move from one place to another: "a place," Ockham writes, "truly moves and truly is in a place."[55] The point is that a surrounding body is usually surrounded by another one—or by a combination of other ones. If I hold an apple in my hand, my hand can be said to be the immediate place of this apple, but as I move from one house to another with the apple in my hand, the apple will also have moved along. In a sense, then, location and motion are relative. Any particular body is immediately located in the body that immediately surrounds it, but it can also be said to be mediately located in the larger place that surrounds this body. It follows that a body can be at rest with respect to a surrounding body while in motion with respect to a larger or smaller one. Locating a given object in a certain place thus requires that we pick a surrounding body—or combination of bodies—as the term of reference. Ockham is clearly aware of this relativity: "a place," as he puts it, "is motionless by equivalence [*per aequivalentiam*]," which he explains by saying that for something to count as a place, it must be treated "*as if* it really was motionless."[56] If there is a last bodily reality that surrounds every other one, as the ultimate heaven is supposed to do in Aristotelian physics, everything is

---

[54] *Exp. in libr. Phys.* IV, 6, *OPh* V: 56–57.
[55] *Exp. in libr. Phys.* IV, 7, *OPh* V: 88.
[56] Ibid., *OPh* V: 85 (with my italics).

ultimately located with respect to it at every moment in an unqualified way. But the existence of an ultimate and motionless term of reference is not logically required by Ockham's theory. His conception of spatial order is basically a relational one. Space for him is not an absolute all-embracing medium. The place of a given body is nothing but another body, and ordinary material things are located in several places at once, depending on the chosen term of reference. Since motion is nothing but a body that changes place, motion also turns out to be relative to a term of reference temporarily considered as fixed. None of this requires enriching the ontology in any special way.

Another important component of Ockham's conception of motion is that "motion has a prior and a posterior."[57] When something moves, it is first in a certain place and afterward in some other place. Local motion, in other words, takes time. Time, however, is not to be seen as a special entity of its own. Ockham's main argument here is the same as in the case of motion. If time were such an entity, it would have to be composed of past and future parts that do not presently exist, but nothing can be composed of non-beings.[58] Measuring the temporal duration of something is actually a mind-dependent activity that consists in comparing the measured phenomenon with a certain uniform movement. The best term of reference for this, Ockham thinks, is the motion of the first mobile, that is, of the first celestial sphere that is put in motion by the unmoved mover according to Aristotelian cosmology. In practice, however, any uniform movement will do, such as that of the Sun.[59] Saying that "time exists" is shorthand for a longer sentence such as "Something is moved from which the mind can know how much something else is moved."[60] No other entity is required for temporal measurement than the uniformly moving object that serves as a reference, the objects the movement or the persistence of which is being measured, and the measuring mind. Those are all independently accepted substances, parts of substances, or qualities.

---

[57] *Summ. phil. nat.* III, 7, *OPh* VI: 271.
[58] *Summ. phil. nat.* IV, 5, *OPh* VI: 355–356.
[59] *Summ. phil. nat.* IV, 7, *OPh* VI: 357–359.
[60] *Exp. in libr. Phys.* IV, 18, *OPh* V: 199. In *Summ. phil. nat.* IV, 5, Ockham proposes an even more elaborate analysis of "time exists" (*OPh* VI: 356).

This analysis of temporal statements assumes that a mobile is first in one place and afterward in another place. "First" and "after" (*prius et posterius*), however, are not names of anything. They are adverbs, Ockham insists. Their function is to indicate that things are ordered in certain ways, but they convey no additional ontological commitment.[61] This is a prominent theme in Ockham's nominalism: material things are spatially arranged with respect to one another and they can move or be moved so as to be differently arranged, but such spatial and temporal orders are not to be reified.

Inherence and information

In Ockham's vocabulary, qualities are said to "inhere" in substances, and substantial forms are said to "inform" prime matter. These are two other ways, then, in which certain things are ordered with respect to others. Do we need special relational entities to account for them? Ockham's principle, as we saw when discussing the status of qualities, is that entities are to be posited when a change in the truth-value of a sentence cannot be accounted for either by local movement or by the mere passage of time.[62] How does this principle apply to qualitative inherence and to the information of matter? When a substance becomes white, a new entity indeed comes into existence, namely a whiteness trope. And when a chunk of matter receives a new substantial form, the form in question comes into existence. So far, the only entities involved are substances, qualities, and the essential parts of substances (matter and form), as usual.

Is that all there is to it? Isn't an explanation needed for the fact that the newly produced quality inheres in a certain substance rather than in another one, and that the newly produced substantial form informs a certain chunk of matter rather than another one? Ockham's answer is that in the natural world, spatial colocation suffices for this, "compresence" in other words, as contemporary metaphysicians say. If we

---

[61] *Summ. phil. nat.* III, 7, *OPh* VI: 269–270.
[62] See *Quodl.* VII, 2, *OTh* IX: 707 (transl. Freddoso 1991: 597; text quoted above, p. 66), and *Ord.*, dist. 30, q. 4, *OTh* IV: 369.

leave religious faith aside and stick to natural philosophy, it is impossible, Ockham claims, that a quality should be in the same place as a substance while not inhering in it, or that a substantial form should be in the same place as a certain chunk of matter while not informing it. And it is similarly impossible that a quality that inheres in a substance should not be exactly where this substance is, or that the substantial form that informs a certain chunk of matter should not be exactly where this chunk of matter is.[63] Only spatial connections are involved, and spatial connections are not additional things, as we have just seen. A quality, moreover, cannot naturally move away from the substance it inheres in without ceasing to exist,[64] and presumably, a substantial form that normally informs a chunk of matter cannot naturally move away from it without ceasing to exist. Ockham does not think that any special explanation is required for the adhesion of a quality to a substance when the latter moves from one place to another, or for the adhesion of a substantial form to a chunk of matter when the substantial whole moves from one place to another. This is just how qualities and substantial forms behave: they naturally cling to their underlying substance or chunk of matter without the need for any additional glue.

Ockham's God can cut off a quality from its underlying substance, as in the Eucharist, or separate a substantial form from its underlying chunk of matter while maintaining this quality or this substantial form in existence, since both qualities and substantial forms are counted as things in the Ockhamist ontology. Yet these supernatural feats do not require any enrichment of the ontology: given the principle of ontological separability, only qualities, substances, and their parts are required for God to do this. A more troublesome difficulty arises, however, as Ockham admits that God might supernaturally make it so that a certain quality be in the same place as a certain substance while not inhering in it, or that a certain substantial form be in the same place as a certain

---

[63] *Summ. phil. nat.* I, 19, 207–208.
[64] See above, principles SQ3 and SQ6 (pp. 67–69): qualities cannot naturally be free-floating, and they are not naturally transferable from one substance to another.

chunk of matter while not informing it.[65] Doesn't this supernatural—or metaphysical—possibility show that compresence does not suffice after all for a quality to inhere in a substance or for a substantial form to inform a certain chunk of matter? Ockham's way out is ingenious.[66] Since special relational entities are required anyway by certain articles of faith such as the Divine Trinity or the divine incarnation, but can utterly be dispensed with in natural philosophy, Ockham conjectures that in the supernatural cases we are now interested in, such entities are especially created by God only when He wants to neutralize the ordinary course of nature. The idea is that if God wants a quality to be located in the same place as a certain substance without inhering in it, He creates a special "*respectus*," some kind of stopper that interferes with the ordinary course of nature by preventing this quality from inhering in this substance as it would naturally do; and the same holds *mutatis mutandis* if God wants a substantial form not to inform a compresent chunk of matter. In the natural world, though, compresence is both necessary and sufficient for qualitative inherence and for the information of matter by substantial forms. And compresence is not an additional entity.

Essential similarity

Across Ockham's writings, three varieties of similarity play significant philosophical roles. One of them is the resemblance between a mental representation and what it represents, between a concept, in particular, and the things it stands for in the intellect. Ockham, to say the least, is not very clear about what this amounts to. I will briefly address this point in chapter 5. Second, there is qualitative similarity, as in Aristotle:[67] a substance is similar to another one in this sense if one of its qualities is of the same sort as a quality of the other substance. The horse Silver and a snow bank are similar to one another by both being

---

[65] *Ord.*, dist. 30, q. 4, *OTh* IV: 369–370.
[66] See *Quaest. var.* 6, art. 2, *OTh* VIII: 210–211.
[67] See Aristotle, *Categories* 8, 11a15–19.

white, and given that psychological moods are qualities for Ockham, Peter and Mary are similar to one another by both being in a joyous mood. Third, a thing is similar to another one by being of the same species or the same genus as this other thing. Two horses are similar to each other in this sense, and so are two snow banks with respect to each other. This third kind of similarity is what I call *essential similarity*. It differs from the previous variety, since two substances can be qualitatively similar to one another without being essentially similar: Silver the horse and the snow bank are both white, but they belong to different species and genera. Qualitative similarity, nevertheless, is ultimately reducible to essential similarity insofar as it requires that the qualities that make two substances qualitatively similar should themselves be essentially similar to each other: Silver and the snow bank are qualitatively similar because one of the quality tropes that inhere in Silver is essentially similar to one that inheres in the snow bank: these are both whiteness tropes. My focus here, consequently, will be on essential similarity.

A first point to be noted about essential similarity is that it comes in degree, for Ockham. Two horses, for example, are of the same ultimate species as each other—the *species specialissima*—just as two roses are with respect to each other, or two whiteness tropes. A horse and a dog, on the other hand, are of the same genus—they are both animals—but not of the same ultimate species. The essential similarity between two horses, then, is of a greater degree than the essential similarity between a horse and a dog, or between a horse and a rose. When two things are of the same ultimate species, Ockham says that they are "maximally similar" to each other (*simillimus*).[68] How lesser degrees of essential similarity are assessed is something he is not quite explicit about, but it can be inferred from his theory of real definitions. By contrast with nominal definitions that are meant to unfold the linguistic meaning of a term, real definitions in Ockham are expected to provide

---

[68] See *Ord.*, dist. 2, q. 9, *OTh* II: 311: "only individuals of the same ultimate species are maximally similar to one another" (my transl.).

adequate descriptions of the essential structures of things.[69] The most complete way to do so, according to him, is first to identify the most general genus that these things belong to (i.e., substance or quality) and then to successively enumerate the essential parts of the things in question from the most generic to the most specific.[70] The real definition of human beings, for example, should first specify that they are substances (this being the most general genus that human beings belong to), and then that they are material (since matter is an essential part of human beings as well as of every other material substance), that they are corporeal (since human beings have a "form of corporeity" as one of their essential parts), that they are sensory (since human beings have a sensory substantial form as a part of them), and finally that they are intellectual (since human beings have an intellect as one of their substantial forms).[71] It can be gathered from this that human beings essentially resemble animals (they have a sensory substantial form, just like animals do), but to a lesser degree than they resemble other human beings; and that they essentially resemble all material substances, too, but to a still lesser degree.

Essential similarity among substances thus depends on the similarity of (some of) their respective essential parts. Since these essential parts can be seen as tropes, as I have argued, essential similarity among substances ultimately comes down to essential similarity among tropes. And the same holds *a fortiori* for quality tropes. In their cases, Ockham says, no real definition is possible, since all of their parts are of the same sort.[72] However intense it is, a whiteness trope is composed of nothing but whiteness tropes, as we have seen. Yet any whiteness trope, of whatever degree it is, essentially resembles any other whiteness trope: "a more intense and a less intense [qualitative] form," Ockham writes, "are of the same ultimate species."[73] Whether between substances or qualities, all essential similarity in the end is grounded in essential similarities between tropes.

---

[69] On the distinction between real and nominal definitions, see *SL* I, 26, *OPh* I: 84–89 (transl. Loux 1974: 105–108).
[70] See *Ord.*, dist. 8, q. 6, *OTh* III: 251–258.
[71] *SL* I, 26, *OPh* I: 85 (transl. Loux 1974: 105).
[72] *Exp. in libr. Porph.* 3, 3, *OPh* II: 61 (transl. Kluge 1973–1974, ch. 4.3: 312).
[73] *Ord.*, dist. 17, q. 7, *OTh* III: 543 (my transl.).

No infinite regress ensues, because essential similarities are not tropes themselves. They are not things at all. Suppose Socrates and Plato are both white. They are thus qualitatively similar to one another, and this is because a quality that inheres in Socrates is essentially similar to one that inheres in Plato, both being whiteness tropes. Now it is true for Ockham that the only way that Socrates and Plato can cease to have this particular similarity between themselves is that some new entity emerges or some pre-existing entity is destroyed. But these are none other than color tropes in this case. The destruction of Plato's whiteness, say, and its replacement by an emerging blackness trope will do the job. This holds for substantial forms, too: the only way that two substantial forms can cease to be essentially similar to each other is that one of them ceases to exist. And consequently, the only way that two substances—two horses, say—can cease to be essentially similar to each other is that one of them ceases to exist.[74] Conversely, two things that are not essentially similar to one another can never become so. A whiteness trope can be replaced by a blackness trope in a certain bundle, but it can never be changed into a blackness trope while remaining identical to itself. A sensory substantial form can never be changed into an intellectual form while remaining identical to itself. To put it in modern philosophical language, essential similarities merely supervene on qualitative and substantial tropes.[75]

Tropes, moreover, are not what they are in virtue of resembling other tropes. Even if there was only one whiteness trope in the world, it would still be a whiteness trope on Ockham's view. The attribution of a species or a genus to an individual is not ultimately made true by tropes in resemblance as in certain contemporary trope theories.[76] Sameness of species between Socrates and Plato holds because

---

[74] A word about matter: all chunks of matter are essentially similar to one another in Ockham's ontology, and they can never naturally cease to be so, since prime matter is naturally indestructible.

[75] See, e.g., *Ord.*, dist. 30, q. 1, *OTh* IV: 310: "someone who has an intellectual grasping of Socrates and Plato and their whitenesses, without intellectually grasping anything else, will straight away say that Socrates is similar to Plato" (my transl.). The similarity between Socrates and Plato in this example is a qualitative one, but as we saw, it is reducible to the essential similarity between Socrates's and Plato's whitenesses.

[76] See, e.g., Campbell 1990.

Socrates is a human being and Plato is a human being, too,[77] and sameness of color between them holds because a whiteness trope inheres in Socrates and another whiteness trope inheres in Plato, or a blackness trope in Socrates and another blackness trope in Plato.[78] Ockham simply denies that sameness of type requires a special ontological ground over and above the individuals themselves. Every single entity is individuated by itself, he contends, and whatever it essentially is, it is so by itself as well.

Causation

Following Aristotle, Ockham acknowledges four kinds of causes: material, formal, final, and efficient. Speaking of a material cause, however, is but to point to the presence of a chunk of matter in a material substance, and speaking of a formal cause is but to point to that of a form,[79] and we have already dealt with both of these. Final causes, on the other hand, are mind-dependent. Saying that a certain thing a is the final cause of b is to say that b was produced because an intentional agent wanted a to come into existence by way of b. Ockham's—somewhat violent—example is that of a punch given to an adversary: the final cause of the punch, he says, is the suffering of the adversary, since this suffering is what the puncher intended to be produced as a result of the punch.[80] In the actual sequence, though, only efficient causes are effective: the desire for the suffering of the adversary is the efficient cause (or at least part of it) of the act of punching, and this act of punching

---

[77] *Ord.*, dist. 2, q. 6, *OTh* II: 211: "the intellect can abstract something common to Socrates and Plato which will not be common to Socrates and whiteness. Neither should we seek any cause for this other than that Socrates is Socrates, Plato is Plato, and each is a human being" (transl. Tweedale 1999: 375–376; also transl. in Spade 1994: 181).

[78] See *Ord.*, dist. 30, q. 1, *OTh* IV: 310: "Strictly speaking, the term 'resemblance', as it applies to Socrates and Plato, imports nothing but that Socrates is white and Plato as well, or that each of them is black etc." (my transl.). For a similar point in recent philosophy, see Melia 2015.

[79] *Quodl.* IV, 1, *OTh* IX: 293 (transl. Freddoso and Kelley 1991: 245).

[80] Ibid.: 296.

in turn efficiently causes the suffering that was aimed at. From a purely philosophical point of view, there is no final cause to be searched for where no intentional agent is involved.[81] And even when an intentional agent is involved, the actual production of the effect—the act of punching in the above example—hangs on desires and acts of will being efficient causes of external actions. Material and formal causality having already been dealt with, then, and final causality being ultimately reducible, what remains for us to look at in order to understand what the causal order amounts to in Ockham is efficient causality.[82]

A first point to note is that Ockham's focus when dealing with efficient causality is the causation of objects. What he is interested in is the natural advent of new singular things, whether they be substances as in the generation of an animal, or quality tropes as in the production of heat in a piece of wood. He does acknowledge that in a wide sense of "cause," we can say that an object is caused to move although no real thing then newly comes into existence, but he has nothing much to say about this kind of case.[83] In the strict sense, a cause, he says, is "that to the real existence of which something entirely distinct from it owes it to newly exist."[84] Both causes and effects in this perspective are singular substances or qualities rather than events or states of affairs.

Efficient causality for Ockham, as the above definition also makes clear, is a relation of dependence: the effect *owes* its existence to that of the cause. This is not a matter of temporal succession. Ockham insists, on the contrary, that strictly speaking an efficient cause is always simultaneous with its effect: what does not exist anymore when a certain effect is produced cannot be its cause.[85] Nor is causal dependence reducible to constant conjunction. Ockham is no forerunner of Hume in this matter. Causal connections hold between singular entities, for him. That a certain fire is the cause of a heat trope in a piece of wood does not depend on whether their connection instantiates a regularity or not. It would still be a causal connection even if it were the

---

[81] Ibid.: 299.
[82] An excellent discussion of Ockham on efficient causality is to be found in Adams 1987: 741–798.
[83] *Summ. phil. nat.* II, 3, *OPh* VI: 217–218.
[84] Ibid.: 218 (my transl.).
[85] See, e.g., *Rep.* II, q. 3–4, *OTh* V: 61.

only one of its kind. Ockham is a proponent of what is called today a "singularist" conception of causation.[86] Causal dependence, moreover, is a necessary connection for him: if something causes something else to exist in the actual world under certain conditions, it would cause it in all naturally possible worlds under the same conditions as well.[87] Ockham's God, of course, can supernaturally prevent any natural cause from having its normal effect and He can produce any effect whatsoever without the mediation of anything, but in the natural order of things, efficient causes necessitate their effects when the right conditions are in place.

None of this, however, requires for Ockham the existence of special relational entities. For one thing, each causal relation, if it existed as a distinct entity, would be a singular trope, since there can be no universal things out there. If so, however, there would have to be an actual infinity of such causality tropes even in a very simple situation such as that of the Sun heating a piece of wood. The point is that the piece of wood is a continuously extended thing and thus has an infinity of spatial parts for Ockham. The Sun, consequently, would have to be related to each one of these parts by a different causal relation, and we would have to admit an actual infinity of real things that are not themselves parts of a spatial continuum, which is impossible, he thinks.[88]

There is no independent reason, anyway, for postulating such causality tropes as distinct from substances and accidents. An entity must be posited, according to Ockham, when a change in truth-values cannot be entirely accounted for by local motion or by the mere passage of time.[89] When it becomes true that a certain thing a efficiently causes another thing b that it did not cause before, both a and b must be posited of course, but they are either substances or qualities in the kind of cases Ockham is dealing with, like a parent and a child, for example, or the heat of a fire and the resulting heat of a nearby piece of wood. Most of the time, some local motion is also needed in the

---

[86] See Moore 2009, Psillos 2002: 57–79.
[87] The point is forcefully argued for in Adams 1979 and 1987: 741–758.
[88] *Quodl.* VI, 12, *OTh* IX: 631–632 (transl. Freddoso 1991: 531–532), *Ord.*, dist. 30, q. 1, *OTh* IV: 301–302.
[89] *Quodl.* VII, 2, *OTh* IX: 707 (transl. Freddoso 1991: 597). See above, n. 7 of the present chapter.

natural world, since most natural causes are effective only within limited distance (a fire can produce a heat trope in a piece of wood only if it comes to be close enough to it somehow),[90] but local motions, as we saw, are not to be countenanced as additional entities. Other concurrent conditions must usually hold as well, but these, Ockham thinks, always reduce to local motion or to the presence or absence of some substance or quality (a fire can be prevented from heating a piece of wood, for example, by the insertion of some fireproofing material between them). Everything else being equal, in other words, the existence of the cause suffices to bring about the effect.[91]

Ultimately, the causal powers of a thing, for Ockham, are grounded in what that thing essentially is: "[. . .] it pertains to the notion of a cause that it could by its own power (*virtute propria*) be followed by the effect, by the nature of the thing and naturally."[92] Ockham here uses "could" rather than "must" to indicate that the effect might not be produced if the right concurrent conditions are not satisfied, but whenever they are, the cause is essentially such that it brings about the effect. It is a crucial component of his view on efficient causality that two things that are essentially similar to each other to the highest degree have maximally similar causal powers: "all agents of the same most specific species are able to produce effects of the same kind."[93] An agent who would not be able to sin, for example, would not be of the same species as the human beings we are familiar with, whatever other resemblances she would have with them.[94] Having maximally similar causal powers is constitutive of what it is to be of the same most specific species. This is not, of course, because the individuals in question all instantiate some real ideal form or really share a common nature, since there are no such things. Similarity in causal powers is grounded in what each individual thing essentially is by itself, just as all essential similarities are. Such individual causal powers, moreover, are nothing over and above the things that have them. To be able to produce a

---

[90] For a cause to produce its effect, Ockham says, they must be "duly placed and close enough" (*Summ. phil. nat.* I, 1, *OPh* VI: 158).
[91] See *Quodl.* VII, 3, *OTh* IX: 710 (transl. Freddoso 1991: 600).
[92] *Rep.* IV, q. 1, *OTh* VII: 17 (transl. in Adams 1987: 752).
[93] *Ord.*, Prol., q. 2, *OTh* I: 92 (transl. in Adams 1987: 754; see also Longeway 2007: 225).
[94] *Ord.*, dist. 44, q. 1, *OTh* IV: 652–654 (transl. Bosley and Tweedale 1997: 89–90).

thought, for example, is nothing in human beings but to have an intellectual substantial form as one of their intrinsic essential parts. And heat tropes have it in themselves to produce other heat tropes under the right circumstances. No additional causal glue is ever needed.

Ockham's natural world, then, is mind-independently structured in various ways, and yet no purely relational entity finds any place in it, and no states of affairs either, if the latter are seen as a special sort of things, as they are in David Armstrong's metaphysics, for example.[95] Ockham is comfortable with the idea of "real relations," admittedly, but only insofar as it implies no more than that things are truly related with one another in various ways "in the absence of any operation of the intellect."[96] True relational statements, however, require no special addition to the substance-quality ontology. The matter is especially clear for him when it comes to spatial order and local motion. It can very well be true that Socrates was first to the left of Plato, and then to his right, without any change in the stock of existent things. This is actually one of the core intuitions of his thought about ontology. As I pointed out in the previous chapter when discussing his criticism of realism with respect to relational terms, this position is incompatible with the admission of what is called today the "Truthmaker principle," according to which any change in the truth-value of a sentence requires the advent of a new thing or the removal of a previously existing one, but Ockham happily bites this bullet.[97] A very similar principle was advocated by his confrere Walter Chatton, and Ockham rejected it as needlessly uneconomical.[98]

When spatial arrangement and local motion do not suffice to account for the truth of a relational sentence, on the other hand, Ockham thinks that some real things do need to be posited. Yet these are always singular substances or singular qualities. The relevant connections in such cases are grounded in what these things

---

[95] See, e.g., Armstrong 1997.
[96] *Quodl.* VI, 25, *OTh* IX: 678 (transl. Freddoso 1991: 572).
[97] See the discussion above, pp. 49–50.
[98] Walter Chatton, *Lectura super Sententias* I, dist. 3, quest. 1, ed Wey and Etzkorn 2008: 7–8; and Ockham, *Quodl.* I, 5, *OTh* IX: 32–34 (transl. Freddoso and Kelley 1991: 30–32). On this debate, see Maurer 1984, Keele 2007.

essentially are. Beware: the essence of a substance or of a quality must not be taken here to be something in addition to these things themselves. "*Essentia*," Ockham insists, is but a nominalized form of the verb "*esse*" (to be).[99] When we speak of what a thing essentially is, we are simply referring to what that thing could not cease to be without ceasing to exist. Socrates could not cease to be a human being without ceasing to exist, and neither could Plato; this is why we can say that they essentially resemble each other. As to the connections between substantial form and prime matter, between quality and substance, or between cause and effect, Ockham's God, admittedly, can always block them without destroying the entities in question. What He cannot do, however, is prevent a substantial form from being disposed to inform matter, or a quality trope from being disposed to inhere in a substance, or a cause from being disposed to bring about an effect of a certain sort. Such dispositions characterize these entities in all metaphysically possible worlds where they exist. God can prevent these dispositions from being actualized, even in circumstances in which they would normally be actualized, but special interventions on His part are necessary for this to happen. To prevent a substantial form from informing a compresent chunk of matter, or a quality from inhering in a compresent substance, He must introduce a special blocking "*respectus*," as we have seen. And to prevent a cause from producing the sort of effect it is disposed to produce, when the right concurrent conditions hold, He must exceptionally suspend his causal collaboration in the process.[100] While remaining in the severe framework of his nominalist substance-quality ontology, Ockham thus endorses a strong form of essentialism. Not only are things ordered in precise ways in all naturally possible worlds, but certain fundamental organizational features hold among them in all metaphysically possible worlds.

---

[99] See, e.g., *SL* III-2, 26, *OPh* I: 553–555 (transl. Longeway 2007: 190–192).
[100] In Ockham's view, God is the primary cause of everything and his collaboration is always needed for the action of any secondary cause; see, e.g., *Rep.* II, q. 4, *OTh* V: 60–66.

Possible beings

By using the language of possible worlds to express Ockham's thoughts on necessity and possibility, I do not want to suggest that Ockham would have countenanced possible worlds in today's sense as additional things in his ontology. He does indeed argue that God could have created other worlds than the actual one, with more or fewer beings in them,[101] but his understanding of what a possible world is, is not that of recent modal logic. A world for him is an aggregate of things.[102] Consequently, a counterfactual situation in which some of the actually existing things were spatially arranged in a way that never was nor will be realized in the actual world, would not suffice to characterize a different possible world in Ockham's sense, since the supply of existing things would not be different in this situation from those that actually exist. Speaking of possible worlds in such cases, as I have done, is only a convenient way of transposing Ockham's frequent use of counterfactual statements.

What does raise a genuine problem, though, for an examination of his ontology is that some of Ockham's counterfactual statements do seem to refer to entities that do not actually exist, that never existed, and that never will exist. The question we must face is whether mere possible *things* are to be accepted in the ontology. Consider, for example, Ockham's distinctive doctrine of the intuition of non-existents, that is, the claim that God can supernaturally make us have a direct and truthful perceptual apprehension of something that does not exist, in virtue of which we would immediately know that this thing does *not* exist.[103] A prophet could be made to see a temple, say, of which he would thereby immediately know that *this* temple does not exist. What would the object of such an intuition be? Ockham's answer is that it is the one determinate thing that would

---

[101] *Ord.*, dist. 44, q. 1, *OTh* IV: 650–661 (partial transl. Bosley and Tweedale 1997: 89–91). Contrary to Leibniz, Ockham thinks that God could have created worlds that are better in various respects than the actual one.

[102] Ibid.: 651.

[103] See, e.g., *Ord.*, Prol., q. 1, *OTh* I: 30–39 (partial transl. Boehner 1990: 18–25) and *Quodl.* V, 5, *OTh* IX: 495–500 (transl. Freddoso 1991: 413–417). On Ockham's theory of the intuition of non-existents, see, e.g., Panaccio and Piché 2010.

have caused this very perceptual apprehension if the latter had been naturally caused.[104] Since this thing does not exist, though, what is referred to here is a determinate entity that is merely possible. Ockham thus seems to be committed to countenancing mere *possibilia*. This is still a controversial issue among commentators, admittedly, but my own understanding is that he is indeed so committed.

My reason for thinking so is the following.[105] Although Ockham is not quite explicit about his criterion of ontological commitment, we can spell out the one he implicitly endorses by looking at how he typically proceeds when he wants to show that the statements he takes to be true do not commit us to anything but singular substances and qualities. We will thus find that Ockham's analysis of modal statements commits him by this very same criterion to the acceptance of merely possible beings in his ontology. Let us look at this more closely.

Ockham's implicit criterion of ontological commitment has to do with the referential import of words and concepts in true sentences. This is precisely why semantics is so important to his nominalist project: it is by way of semantics that the substance-quality ontology can ultimately be shown to be sufficient for whatever it is that we take to be true about the world, as we will see in some details in chapter 4. Ockham typically wants to claim that the terms of the statements he takes to be true need not be semantically connected to anything but singular substances and qualities. Marilyn Adams proposed the following formulation of the criterion he implicitly uses for this:

> for Ockham, we may say, a theory has an ontological commitment to entities of a certain sort if, in order for the theory to be true, a term

---

[104] *Rep.* II, q. 13, *OTh* V: 287–289. Ockham holds the very strong thesis that in the natural order of things, any given singular effect can be caused by only one cause (or combination of causes) rather than by any other. If a certain heat trope is actually caused by a certain fire, for example, the very same trope could not have been caused by any other fire in the natural order. How exactly to understand this claim is at the heart of an ongoing discussion I have with Susan Brower-Toland; see Brower-Toland 2007a, 2017, Panaccio 2010. What matters in the present context, however, is only that it clearly involves a reference to a determinate non-actual thing, a point on which we agree, Brower-Toland and I.

[105] For a more elaborate presentation of this argument and more references to the secondary literature, see Panaccio 2019b.

must be taken to supposit or stand for such entities in a proposition included in the theory.[106]

Actually, supposition, in the medieval technical sense, is not the only semantic feature of terms that carries ontological commitment for Ockham; this is so with signification and connotation as well.[107] But supposition certainly is the most important one, and I will limit myself to it here, as suggested by Adams. That a term should supposit for certain things in a true sentence is in general sufficient from an Ockhamist point of view for showing that these things must be admitted in the ontology.

Supposition, as Ockham understands it, is the referential function of a term within a sentence. To say that a term supposits for something in a given sentence is to say that it stands for that thing in that sentence.[108] For any given term, its supposition can vary according to context. In "all cherry trees are in blossom," for example, the subject term "cherry tree" supposits for presently existing cherry trees; in "the cherry trees were in blossom," by contrast, it would supposit for past cherry trees; in "cherry tree is a two-word phrase," it would supposit for the corresponding linguistic expression; in "cherry tree is a natural kind concept," it would supposit for the concept of cherry tree, and so on. More will be said about this in chapter 4. The point now is that showing that a term must supposit for certain things in a sentence normally comes down to showing that these things must be attributed some sort of reality, for Ockham. For an affirmative present-tense sentence such as "a cherry tree is in blossom" to be true, there must presently exist at least one thing that the subject term "cherry tree" supposits for: a real cherry tree. For an affirmative past sentence such as "a cherry tree was in blossom" to be true, there must have existed at least one cherry tree at some point in the past. And so on. That Ockham thus attributes

---

[106] Adams 1987: 81.
[107] See Panaccio 2019b. Note that Adams's formulation of the criterion uses "if" rather than "if and only if": this criterion provides in her view a sufficient condition for ontological commitment, not a necessary one.
[108] *SL* I, 63, *OPh* I: 193 (transl. Loux 1974: 189).

ontological import to supposition is especially clear in his treatment of such sentences as "man is a species," that he takes to be true. "Man" there, he says, cannot supposit for a real extramental universal, since there is no such thing. What it must supposit for, instead, is the concept of "man," which is a mental quality. As a general policy, when Ockham wants to show that entities of a certain sort can be dispensed with, he typically holds that no accepted truth requires such things to be supposited for. There would be no point to this Ockhamist approach if supposition was not taken by him to carry ontological commitment.

Now, Ockham repeatedly admits that merely possible beings are sometimes supposited for in modal contexts. He has it, for example, that even in a situation in which no man exists, the sentence "A man can smile" is true when the subject term "man" is taken to supposit for merely possible men.[109] In a sentence such as "A man can be white," the subject term, he says, can supposit for things that can exist.[110] And it is a general rule for him that the predicates of modal sentences about possibilities supposit not only for what does exist, but also for what can exist.[111] It straightforwardly follows that Ockham is committed to countenancing mere *possibilia* in his ontology.

This is not to say that *possibilia* are a ghostly sort of actual beings. They are not actual at all. We should not say, Ockham insists, that "something that does not exist in nature, but could exist, is a real being."[112] This passage and others like it *prima facie* seem to support an actualist interpretation of Ockham, where only actual beings are attributed any ontological status. His point there, however, as the context makes clear, is that when we say of anything that it *is* a real being, we are restricted by the present-tense verb to refer only to presently existing actual things.[113] A term can supposit for merely possible beings only when it occurs in a sentence with a modal copula, such as "A man can be white." We should not say, therefore, that merely possible things

---

[109] *SL* III-3, 2, *OPh* I: 593.
[110] *SL* III-1, 23, *OPh* I: 420.
[111] *SL* I, 72, *OPh* I: 218 (transl. Loux 1974: 206).
[112] *SL* I, 38, *OPh* I: 108 (my transl.); see also *Exp. in libr. Phys.* III, 2, *OPh* IV: 415–416.
[113] For a thorough analysis of this passage, see Karger 1981: especially 390–394.

are real, but only that they *can be* real. This is what has been aptly labeled as Ockham's "purely modal" conception of possible beings.[114] Mere *possibilia* are not hidden somehow in the actual world. Yet they can be distinctively referred to ("supposited for") in true sentences. They must, therefore, be attributed a special ontological status, as reflected in Ockham's mention of a wide sense of "being" which applies to anything whatsoever that could exist, even if it actually does not exist.[115] And what is ontologically special about mere *possibilia* is precisely that they do not actually exist, but they *could*. Ockham in the end takes the notion of possibility as a primitive one.

All such *possibilia* must be individuals in Ockham's nominalism, since extramental universals are deemed to be metaphysically impossible. God, on the other hand, could create purely relational entities (*respectus*, as Ockham says) and distinct quantitative tropes, but there can be no such things in the natural world that we inhabit. Nothing is naturally possible in it but substances (and their parts) and qualities. As we have seen, this restricted array of ontological categories is compatible for Ockham with quite a lot of structure in the natural world: substances are composed of matter and form, qualities inhere in substances, some individuals essentially resemble one another, all of them have causal powers, they are all spatially arranged in precise ways, and they constantly move from one location to another. The challenge for Ockham's nominalism at this point is to explain how language and thought can be truthful in such a world. This is what the next two chapters will be about.

---

[114] See Karger 1981: 394, and Knuuttila 1993: 147.
[115] *Ord.*, dist. 36, q. 1, *OTh* IV: 538. Ockham adds that this sense of "being" is rarely used in practice. As I see it, this only makes it all the more significant that he should feel the need for it.

4
Semantics

Ockham readily acknowledges that many affirmative sentences with general terms, relational terms, or quantitative terms are true. How can that be, if every real thing we ever talk about is either a singular substance or a singular non-relational quality? This is what Ockham's elaborate semantic theory is designed to clarify. His general strategy is to base the meaning of sentences on the semantic properties of their component terms (the *proprietates terminorum*, as the medievals said) and to resolve the latter into several direct or indirect ways of referring to singular substances and qualities. In addition to being nominalist, Ockham's approach is a variety of semantic atomism: simple words are taken to be independently endowed with meaning, and the truth-conditions of sentences are generated on this basis.[1]

I will first explain how semantic generality is accounted for in this perspective by focusing on the terms that were at the heart of the medieval discussion of universals, namely natural kind terms. Relational and quantitative terms are general, too, of course, and much of what will be said about natural kind terms carries over to them, but both categories also present special features that will next be surveyed in some detail.

Natural kind terms

Porphyry's famous questions about universals were coined by him as being about genera and species: Do genera and species exist in themselves or in concepts only? Are they corporeal or incorporeal? Do they exist apart or in sensible objects? Ockham, as we saw, squarely

[1] On the notion of semantic atomism, see Fodor and Lepore 1992: especially 1–35, and Jackman 2017.

denies that genera and species are extramental things. They are but signs in his view. Genera are nothing but genus-terms such as "animal" and "flower", and species are nothing but species-terms such as "horse" and "tulip." Such natural kind terms are called "absolute terms" by Ockham.[2] In his approach, then, a sound theory of universals crucially requires a plausible account of the semantics of these absolute terms: how can they meaningfully occur in true sentences about the world if genera and species do not exist outside of language and thought?

Signification

At the very beginning of his *Summa of Logic*, Ockham distinguishes three sorts of meaningful terms that are liable to occur in three corresponding sorts of sentences: written, spoken and mental terms.[3] The first two are conventional, while the latter are natural signs. At all three levels, furthermore, there is a distinction to be drawn between categorematic and syncategorematic terms, the difference being that categorematic terms are individually endowed with a "signification" (*significatio*), while *syncategoremata* are not.[4] The point is that the latter—quantifiers, connectors, prepositions, etc.—do not refer to anything in the world. They are merely functional units that connect categorematic terms with one another into syntactically well-formed sentences with specific truth-conditions, and they determine what reference these categorematic terms are liable to have in each particular sentential context. Whether in written, spoken, or mental discourse, the connection with reality is secured by the units that do have a signification in Ockham's technical sense, namely, the categorematic terms.

How mental categorematic signs naturally acquire their signification is something we will deal with in chapter 5. Spoken words, on the other hand, receive their signification by being "subordinated" (*subordinatus*) to previously existing mental terms or "concepts"

---

[2] *SL* I, 10, *OPh* I: 35–36 (transl. Loux 1974: 69–70).
[3] *SL* I, 1, *OPh* I: 7–9 (transl. Loux 1974: 49–51).
[4] *SL* I, 4, *OPh* I: 15–16 (transl. Loux 1974: 55).

(*conceptus*), and written terms acquire their signification by being subordinated in turn to previously existing spoken terms.[5] Subordination, on Ockham's understanding of it, is a conventional operation in virtue of which a term inherits the signification of the pre-existing meaningful unit that it is subordinated to. When a group of speakers agrees to subordinate a certain spoken word to the concept of "horse," say, the result is that this spoken word will from then on be conventionally considered by this group of speakers to signify the same as what the concept of "horse" naturally signifies, whatever that is. Accordingly, when a written mark is subordinated to the spoken word "horse," it thereby conventionally acquires the same signification again.[6]

Whether natural or conventional, categorematic signification is further subdivided by Ockham into primary signification (or signification *tout court*, as I will sometimes say) and secondary signification (or connotation). The distinctive feature of absolute terms is that they have only a primary signification, while those that also have a secondary signification are called "connotative" terms.[7] What we are interested in now, consequently, is primary signification, since it constitutes the whole meaning of natural kind terms. We will return to secondary signification when discussing relational terms.

In Ockham's vocabulary, a term is said to primarily signify what it is true of. A spoken word, most saliently, does not primarily signify the concept it is subordinated to, as Aquinas and many other medieval philosophers would have said, but the individual things that this concept also signifies. According to Ockham, the word "horse" primarily signifies singular horses, just as the concept of "horse" does, and the word "animal" primarily signifies singular animals, just as the concept of "animal" does.[8] Primary significates, consequently, are always singular things. In the case of the terms "horse" and "animal," these significates are singular substances, but there are absolute terms that

---

[5] *SL* I, 1, *OPh* I: 7–8 (transl. Loux 1974: 50).

[6] Conventional terms can thus turn out to be equivocal if they are subordinated to different concepts by the speakers of a given language; see *SL* I, 13, *OPh* I: 44–47 (transl. Loux 1974: 75–77).

[7] *SL* I, 10, *OPh* I: 35–38 (transl. Loux 1974: 69–71).

[8] On the medieval debate as to whether words signify concepts or things, see Panaccio 2017a: 140–158.

signify singular qualities, such as "whiteness" and "heat," which primarily signify whiteness tropes and heat tropes, respectively. It is a central idea of Ockham's semantics that primary signification relates each general term to several singular things at once. Ockham would have rejected what Rudolf Carnap called the "principle of univocality," according to which any denoting sign denotes one and only one entity.[9] He would have endorsed instead the idea of "multiple denotation" as proposed, for example, by the nominalist philosopher Richard M. Martin, according to whom general terms "denote the objects to which they apply."[10]

Since the meaning of absolute terms is nothing but their primary signification, they convey no description of their significates and they have no nominal definitions that could unwrap their semantic content.[11] One can say that Ockham reduces the signification of natural kind terms to their extension, provided that extension is not counted as an additional entity like a set might be in contemporary discussions. Strictly speaking, we should not say that an absolute term signifies the set of everything that it is true of, but that it distributively signifies all these singular things; it signifies each of them separately. Ockham insists, moreover, that it signifies each of them equally: "horse" signifies each horse in exactly the same way as any other horse, "whiteness" signifies each whiteness trope in exactly the same way as any other whiteness trope, and neither term calls anything to mind in virtue of its signification but horses or whitenesses, respectively. For something to be signified by a certain absolute term, it must merely be essentially similar to whatever else this term signifies. Ockham's approach to natural kind terms is thus closely related to that of Hilary Putnam in the 1970s:[12] when one singular significate is fixed in some way or other for a given absolute term, its other significates are thereby automatically fixed, too; they are all the individuals that essentially resemble the original exemplars.[13] Since the signification of spoken and written

---

[9] Carnap 1956: 98.
[10] Martin 1958: 99. A similar idea is to be found in Black 1971, Hintikka 1971, and Goodman 1984: 48–50.
[11] *SL* I, 10, *OPh* I: 35–36 (transl. Loux 1974: 69–70).
[12] See Putnam 1975, 1981.
[13] Since there are degrees of essential similarity, as we saw earlier (pp. 87–88), the required degree must be fixed in each case by whether we are dealing with a very narrow

words is derived from that of concepts through subordination, what is left for the theory to explain at this point is how the original primary significates are determined in the case of natural kind concepts. This, we will discuss in chapter 5.

A last point to be mentioned about primary signification is that Ockham distinguishes two varieties of it. In one sense of "to signify," he says, a term signifies the individuals that it is presently true of, while in a wider sense it also signifies past, future, and possible things.[14] In the wider sense, then—which Ockham usually favors—a natural kind term such as "horse" signifies not only the horses that presently exist, but all past, future, and even merely possible horses as well; none of them, of course, being anything but individuals.

Supposition

When a categorematic term is inserted in a sentence as its subject or predicate, it acquires a new semantic property called "supposition" (*suppositio*), according to Ockham. It is the referential function that this term has in the context of this particular sentence: "when a term stands for something in a proposition in such a way that we use the term for the thing [...]", Ockham writes, "the term supposits for that thing."[15] It is one of the central ideas of medieval semantics, and of Ockham's in particular, that it distinguishes the semantic properties of a term considered in itself from those that it acquires in sentences. This nicely accommodates two apparently competing intuitions that we easily have about the meaning of a term: that it varies according to sentential context, on the one hand, and that the meaning of sentences depends on the prior meaning of their component terms, on the other hand. In Ockham, signification is the paradigmatic pre-propositional property, while supposition is the contextual one. The latter derives

---

species-term such as "horse" or a very general genus-term such as "substance" or something in between ("animal," for instance, is a species-term with respect to "substance" but a genus-term with respect to "horse").

[14] *SL* I, 33, *OPh* I: 95 (transl. Loux 1974: 113).
[15] *SL* I, 63, *OPh* I: 193 (transl. Loux 1974: 189).

in general from the former in ways that vary according to the syntax of the sentence and the surrounding categorematic and syncategorematic units.

Ockham identifies three main varieties of supposition: personal, material, and simple.[16] Personal supposition is what he calls the "significative" use of a term: it occurs when the term stands for its significates, or for some of them, as does "horse" in "horses are animals" or "a horse is running." Material supposition, roughly, is when the term stands for itself as a spoken or written word, as "horse" does in "horse is a word."[17] Simple supposition is when the term stands for the corresponding concept, as in "horse is a natural kind concept." Personal supposition is thus the normal use of a categorematic term, and Ockham takes it to be semantically possible in any context whatsoever.[18] Even a sentence such as "Horse is a word" could mean that a real singular horse is a word.[19] That would be false in this particular case, but it would still be a possible interpretation. Material supposition, by contrast, is considered possible only when the term occurs in a sentence of which the other extreme (the predicate or the subject, as the case may be) is a second-order term that primarily signifies words, what Ockham calls a "term of second imposition."[20] In "horse is a word" or "horse is a noun," for example, the term "horse" can be taken in material supposition since the predicates "word" and "noun" are terms of second imposition: the things they are true of—their primary significates—are spoken or written units. Similarly, simple supposition is possible only when the other extreme is a second-order term that signifies concepts, what Ockham calls a "term of second intention."[21] In "horse is a natural kind concept," for example, "horse" can have simple supposition and stand for the concept of "horse," because the things that the complex predicate "natural kind concept" primarily signifies are mental units.

---

[16] SL I, 64, OPh I: 195–197 (transl. Loux 1974: 190–191).

[17] Note that quotation marks could not be used as markers for material supposition in the Middle Ages, since they were only invented in the sixteenth century.

[18] SL I, 65, OPh I: 197 (transl. Loux 1974: 191–192).

[19] Remember that there is no article in Latin. There is no conspicuous syntactical difference consequently between sentences such as "*Equus est nomen*" (Horse is a noun) and "*Equus est animal*" (A horse is an animal').

[20] SL I, 11, OPh I: 38–41 (transl. Loux 1974: 72–73).

[21] SL I, 12, OPh I: 41–44 (transl. Loux 1974: 73–75).

Although Ockham is not explicit about it, the reason why material and simple suppositions are not acceptable when the other extreme is a first-order term presumably is that no such sentence could ever be true. If "horse" was in material or simple supposition in "horse is an animal," for example, the sentence could never be true, since the predicate "animal" does not signify words or concepts. Certain sentences with a second-order term in them, on the other hand, can be true when the other extreme is in personal supposition, such as "(A) noun is a word." Personal supposition, consequently, must always be an open alternative, even if it sometimes leads to falsehoods.

A striking result of this Ockhamist rule is that all sentences in which the subject or the predicate is a second-order term—a term of second imposition or of second intention—are ambiguous, since the other extreme in such sentences could be taken to have either personal supposition or one of the other two, as the case may be. This particular kind of ambiguity, as it turns out, is highly relevant for the debate on universals. In "horse is a species," for example, the subject-term "horse" can have personal supposition (since this is always allowed) and the sentence would then mean that some equine reality out there is a species, as realist philosophers think; or it could be taken in simple supposition (since the predicate "species" is a term of second intention), and it would then mean that the concept "horse" is a species-term. The former interpretation yields a falsehood for Ockham in this particular example, while the latter corresponds to a truth. This frequently happens, Ockham thinks, in the philosophical discussion over universals as in sentences like "Man is a universal," "Man is predicated of many," and "Risible is distinctive of man." What is meant on any particular occasion depends on the intention of the speaker, that is, on which supposition he or she intended to use.[22] Realists, most saliently, often intend to take terms in personal supposition when they should be in simple or material supposition, according to Ockham's nominalist perspective. This is one of their more pervasive errors.

The crucial point for Ockham is that whether in personal, simple, or material supposition, a term always supposits for individuals. This

---

[22] *SL* I, 65, *OPh* I: 197 (transl. Loux 1974: 191–192). For more details on how such sentences are disambiguated in Ockham, see Panaccio 2013.

is clear for personal supposition, since the referents of the term, then, are among its primary significates, and the primary significates of a categorematic term are but singular substances or singular qualities, as was insisted on in the previous section. Personal supposition is nevertheless to be distinguished from primary signification because in most sentential contexts a term in personal supposition does not stand for all its primary significates, but for some of them only. In a present-tense sentence such as "The cherry trees are in blossom," for example, the subject-term "cherry tree," according to Ockham, is restricted by the present-tense verb to supposit for presently existing cherry trees only, while in past-tense or future-tense sentences such as "The cherry trees were in blossom" or "The cherry trees will be in blossom," it might supposit for past or future things, respectively.[23] It is only in modal sentences with a verb of possibility, such as "Cherry trees can be in blossom," that a term can personally supposit for everything that it primarily signifies (in the wide sense of "to signify"), all possible cherry trees in our example. Past things, however, were just as singular as presently existing things are, and the same holds *mutatis mutandis* for future and merely possible beings.

When taken in simple supposition, as "horse" should be in "Horse is a species" for the sentence to be true, a term stands for a concept. Yet concepts for Ockham are no special abstract entities, as in Gottlob Frege. In his mature theory, they are singular qualities of the mind. My concept of "horse" is a mental quality of mine, while your concept of "horse" is a quality of your own mind: they are distinct tropes. In practice, Ockham often expresses himself as if a term in simple supposition stood for something like *the* concept of horse, but since there is no such thing outside of singular minds, a term in simple supposition, strictly speaking, never imports anything but singular mental tokens. Similarly, a term in material supposition can never refer to anything but spoken or written tokens. Even if he does not develop the

---

[23] See *SL* I, 72, *OPh* I: 215–218 (transl. Loux 1974: 204–206). Note that in the latter cases, the subject term might also supposit for presently existing things. All sentences with past-tense or future-tense verbs thus interestingly turn out to be ambiguous for Ockham: "All the cherry trees were in blossom last year" might mean that all the cherry trees that presently exist were in blossom last year, or that all the cherry trees that existed last year were then in blossom (whether they still exist or not).

point in much detail, Ockham is committed to what is called today "inscriptionalism," the theory according to which there are no such things as linguistic or conceptual types, but only spatiotemporally located tokens.[24] Whether in personal, in material, or in simple supposition, then, the *supposita* of a term are but singular objects.

Truth-conditions

No less than twenty-eight chapters of Ockham's *Summa of Logic* are dedicated to the truth-conditions of various kinds of assertive sentences—or "propositions," as he calls them (*propositiones*).[25] This special interest in truth-conditions was a striking innovation with respect not only to Aristotle, but also to the most famous thirteenth-century handbooks of terminist logic, such as Peter of Spain's *Summulae logicales* and William of Sherwood's *Introductiones in logicam*. Ockham was quite self-conscious about the requirements of his nominalism: his main concern in these developments is to make it clear that the sentences we accept as true do not commit us to the existence of anything but singular substances and qualities. The basic strategy he adopts for this is to spell out "what is necessary and sufficient" (*quid requiritur et sufficit*) for the truth of the most elementary propositions in terms of the supposition of their subject and predicate terms.

The first distinction Ockham draws among propositions is between the categorical and the hypothetical.[26] This roughly corresponds to our distinction between atomic and molecular sentences. The former, he says, are composed of a subject, a copula, and a predicate, while the latter are composed of several such categorical propositions linked together by logical connectors such as "and," "or," "if," "because," and "when." The truth-conditions of hypothetical propositions are briefly

---

[24] See Scheffler 1979: especially 8–9, Parsons 2016: 163–184.
[25] *SL* II, 2–20, *OPh* I: 249–317 (transl. Freddoso and Schuurman 1980: 86–154) and *SL* II, 30–37, *OPh* I: 345–356 (transl. Freddoso and Schuurman 1980: 184–196). Note that in conformity with Ockham's vocabulary, I will often use "proposition" as a synonym for "assertive sentence."
[26] *SL* II, 1, *OPh* I: 241–242 (transl. Freddoso and Schuurman 1980: 79).

dealt with in the last chapters of Part Two of the *Summa*, but Ockham is much more interested in categorical propositions, and those are the ones I will concentrate on here. It is in their treatment that we most clearly see how the ontological commitments of sentences are reduced to the referential scope of their categorematic terms.

As is well known, Aristotelian logic identifies four basic sorts of general sentences: universal affirmative, universal negative, particular affirmative, and particular negative. In all four cases, the truth-value of the proposition depends, according to Ockham, on what the subject-term and the predicate-term supposit for. A universal affirmative is true if and only if "the predicate supposits for all those things that the subject supposits for."[27] "Every horse is an animal" is true, for instance, because the predicate term "animal" in it supposits for everything that the subject-term "horse" supposits for. A particular affirmative such as "some horses are white" is true if and only if "the subject and predicate supposit for some same thing."[28] Accordingly, a universal negative proposition is true if and only if the subject and the predicate do not share any *supposita*, while a particular negative is true if and only if the predicate does not supposit for everything that the subject supposits for. As to singular propositions such as "Brunellus is a horse," the principle is the same: the affirmative ones are true if and only if the predicate supposits for what the singular subject-term supposits for, and the negative ones are true if this is not the case.[29]

None of this might seem very informative. After all, it is not obviously easier to decide if the predicate term "animal" stands for everything that the subject-term "horse" stands for in "every horse is an animal" than it is to directly make up our mind as to whether every horse is an animal or not. The point of the Ockhamist truth-conditions, however, is not to provide an epistemic test; it is to make it conspicuous that the only things we are committed to accept in our ontology by the categorical sentences we take to be true are the *supposita* of the subject and predicate terms. And those *supposita*, as was argued in the previous section, are always singular substances or qualities. Here is what

---

[27] *SL* II, 4, *OPh* I: 260 (transl. Freddoso and Schuurman 1980: 96–97).
[28] *SL* II, 3, *OPh* I: 255 (transl. Freddoso and Schuurman 1980: 92).
[29] *SL* II, 2, *OPh* I: 249–254 (transl. Freddoso and Schuurman 1980: 86–91).

Ockham writes, for example, when discussing singular propositions with natural kind terms as their predicates:

> [...] by means of propositions like "Socrates is a man" and "Socrates is an animal" it is not asserted that Socrates has humanity or animality. Nor is it asserted that humanity or animality is in Socrates, or that man or animal is in Socrates, or that man or animal are of the essence or the quiddity of Socrates, or that animal is part of the quidditative concept of Socrates. Rather it is asserted that Socrates is truly a man and is truly an animal [...] it is asserted that Socrates is a thing for which the predicate "man" or the predicate "animal" stands or supposits.[30]

The same point *mutatis mutandis* is insistently made by Ockham with respect to particular and universal propositions.

Put in modern language, these truth-conditions can be said to be purely extensional. The only features that are relevant for the truth or falsity of standard categorical propositions are the extensions of their subject and predicate terms. These extensions, of course, are not to be seen as extra things in addition to individuals, such as sets are sometimes taken to be. Just like primary signification, the supposition of a general term is a kind of multiple denotation: when it occurs as subject or predicate of a proposition, a general term simultaneously supposits for several individuals at once. This holds for natural kind terms as it does for all other general terms.

What about intensional contexts, then? The extensional approach to truth-conditions implies that if we replace a term in a sentence by a term that is coextensive with it, the truth-value of the resulting whole remains unchanged. Given that the phrases "the Morning Star" and "the Evening Star" really denote the same thing, to take Frege's famous example, replacing one by the other in a sentence should not modify its truth-value: "The Morning Star is a planet" has the same truth-value as "The Evening Star is a planet." It is well-known, however, that there are contexts in which such substitution does change the truth-value: The

---

[30] *SL* II, 2, *OPh* I, 250 (transl. Freddoso and Schuurman 1980: 87—slightly amended).

sentence "The Chaldeans thought that the Morning Star was not the Evening Star" changes from true to false when "the Evening Star" is replaced by "the Morning Star," the sentence "The Chaldeans thought that the Morning Star was not the Morning Star" being most certainly false. These contexts are called "intensional" or "opaque" in today's semantics. Their existence is generally considered to constitute a powerful objection against a purely extensional approach to truth-conditions, and their semantics is often thought to require the postulation of special abstract objects.[31]

Ockham's approach to such contexts is based on a distinction between modal and non-modal (or *de inesse*) propositions. The former are defined as those propositions in which a modal term occurs, and a modal term is defined by Ockham as a term that can be predicated of a whole proposition.[32] This yields a wider range of modal propositions than was usually acknowledged in medieval logic. Ockham counts among modal terms not only "possible," "necessary," "contingent," and "impossible," as everybody did, but also "true," "false," "known," "ignored," "uttered," "written," "believed," "doubted," and so on, since all of these can be predicated of whole propositions in sentences of the form "p is true," "p is known," "p is uttered," "p is believed," etc. For a proposition to count as a modal one, however, the modal term need not be actually predicated of a whole proposition. It must only be present in such a way that it qualifies a proposition somehow. Ockham distinguishes between those cases in which the modal term is indeed applied to a whole proposition, as in "p is necessary" and "it is necessary that p," and the cases in which the modal term is merely attached to the copula, as in "a necessarily is F" and "a is believed to be F." He describes the former as being modal propositions with a *dictum* (the *dictum* being the proposition that the modal term is predicated of, the one that would occupy the place "p" in the above examples), and the latter as being modal propositions without *dictum*.[33]

Modal propositions with a *dictum*, he further points out, are generally ambiguous between "the sense of composition" and "the sense

---

[31] A *locus classicus* for this antinominalist argument is Church 1951.
[32] *SL* II, 1, *OPh* I: 242–243 (transl. Freddoso and Schuurman 1980: 80–81).
[33] *SL* II, 9, *OPh* I: 273 (transl. Freddoso and Schuurman 1980: 108–109).

of division." When taken in the sense of composition, a modal proposition with a *dictum* asserts that the mode is truly predicated of the proposition represented by the *dictum*: "it is necessary that every horse is an animal" then means that the proposition "every horse is an animal" is a necessary one. In the sense of division, by contrast, the modal proposition with a *dictum* is equivalent to the corresponding modal proposition without *dictum*: "It is necessary that every horse is an animal" when taken in the sense of division is equivalent to "every horse necessarily is an animal." This is a way of rendering what is often conveyed by the distinction between *de dicto* and *de re* modalities:[34] taken in the sense of composition, Ockham's modal propositions with a *dictum* are *de dicto*, they say something about a proposition as a whole, while both the modal propositions without *dictum* and the modal propositions with a *dictum* taken in the sense of division are *de re*, they apply a certain predicate (e.g., "animal") to certain things (e.g., horses) under a certain modality (e.g., necessarily). Accordingly, their truth-conditions are dealt with in different ways.

In the *de dicto* cases, the *dictum* is taken to be the subject of the modal proposition, while the predicate is the modal term. Taken in the sense of composition, the sentences "It is necessary that horses are animals" and "It is believed that horses are animals" really have the form "*horses are animals* is necessary" or "*horses are animals* is believed." The subject-term in such cases is a proposition taken in material or simple supposition, while the predicate is a second-order term applicable to propositions. The beauty of this approach is that the truth-conditions of such modal propositions are the same as those of any subject-predicate sentence: the affirmative ones are true if the predicate supposits for what the subject supposits for, and the negative ones are true if the predicate does not supposit for what the subject supposits for.[35] Admittedly, the fact that the subject is in material or simple supposition raises a special difficulty: what is it exactly that the subject-term supposits for in *de dicto* modal propositions? Ockham, as we saw, is committed to inscriptionalism in this regard: only tokens can

---

[34] See Gallois 1998, Nelson 2019. The *de re* / *de dicto* distinction seems to have been introduced by Peter Abelard in the twelfth century; see Dutilh Novaes 2004.

[35] *SL* II, 9, *OPh* I: 274 (transl. Freddoso and Schuurman 1980: 109).

be supposited for in such cases. But which tokens exactly would that be is not something he cares to clarify. If pushed on the matter, he would presumably have said that these tokens vary according to context. In some cases, they would be all the tokens that are morphologically similar to the one that occurs as subject in the modal proposition with *dictum*. In "*horses are animals* is a three-word sentence," for example, the subject-term presumably stands for all the English tokens that are morphological replicas of "horses are animals." In "*horses are animals* is necessary"; by contrast, the subject-term would normally stand for all the tokens in whatever language that are *semantically* equivalent to "horses are animals." There is a bundle of interesting questions here that Ockham does not address and that a complete inscriptionalist semantics should deal with, but what is important for us at this point is that the truth-conditions of *de dicto* modal propositions are formally the same in the end as those of any other categorical subject-predicate sentence, and that the required *supposita* are nothing but singular entities.

That the subject-term is in simple or material supposition, on the other hand, explains in this account why coextensive terms cannot always replace each other without a change in truth-value. In the sentence "*The Morning Star is not the Evening Star* was believed by the Chaldeans," the subject-term is the proposition "the Morning Star is not the Evening Star" taken in simple supposition, and the reason why it cannot be replaced *salva veritate* by "the Morning Star is not the Morning Star" is that the two phrases are not coextensive at all: when taken in simple supposition, they do not supposit for the same mental tokens.

Things are somewhat more complicated when it comes to *de re* modal propositions such as "it is necessary that every horse is an animal" taken in the sense of division. The correct logical form in such cases, according to Ockham, is that of the modal proposition without *dictum*: "every horse necessarily is an animal" in our example, where both the subject-term "horse" and the predicate term "animal" are in personal supposition, while the modal adverb "necessarily" modifies the copula. This proposition is true, he explains, if and only if the relevant modality ("necessary" in this case) is rightly predicated of every corresponding singular proposition of the form "this is an animal" where the singular subject "this" designates one of the *supposita* of "horse."[36] For "every horse necessarily is an animal" to be true it must be the case, when designating any single horse, that "this is an animal" is necessary. If the original subject-term is accompanied by a particular quantifier, on the other hand, such as in "Some horse is believed by Mary to be an animal," the sentence is true if and only if at least one singular sentence of the form "this is an animal" where "this" designates a horse, is believed by Mary.[37] And so on *mutatis mutandis* for negative *de re* modal propositions.

The truth-conditions of *de re* modal propositions are thus reduced to those of the *de dicto* modal propositions that attribute the relevant modality to certain singular sentences, such as "*This is an animal* is necessary" and "*This is an animal* is believed," etc. Yet Ockham is explicit that both the subject and the predicate terms of the original *de re* modal proposition do have a supposition. In "every horse necessarily is an animal," the subject-term "horse" supposits for horses while the predicate term "animal" supposits for animals. This is clear for the subject, since Ockham expressly requires that each singular proposition that has to be taken into account in such cases be such that its own subject ("this") designates one of the *supposita* of the subject-term of the original proposition, that is, singular horses in our example. "Horse" consequently supposits for singular horses in "every horse necessarily is an animal," just as it does in non-modal propositions. This should come as no surprise: *de re* modal propositions are about things, after all, and these in Ockham's semantics must be the singular things that the subject-terms of such propositions stand for, real horses in our example. What is more problematic, however, is what happens on the predicate side. The predicate of a *de re* modal proposition normally has personal supposition for Ockham,[38] but the problem, then, is that while the replacement of the subject-term by a coextensive one does not affect the truth-value of such modal propositions (if "Tullius" and

---

[36] *SL* II, 10, *OPh* I: 276–279 (transl. Freddoso and Schuurman 1980: 111–115).

[37] Note that on Ockham's analysis the copula of the original belief-sentence "Some horse is believed by Mary to be an animal" must be "is believed by Mary to be," since Ockham considers "horse" and "animal" as the subject and predicate terms, respectively; see on this Panaccio 2012a: especially 143–150.

[38] See, e.g., *SL* I, 72, *OPh* I: 218 (transl. Loux 1974: 205–206).

"Cicero" designate the same person, "Cicero is believed by Mary to be a good author" must have the same truth-value as "Tullius is believed by Mary to be a good author" when both sentences are construed as being *de re*), this is not so on the predicate side: "Cicero is believed by Mary to be the author of the *Cataline Orations*" might change from true to false when the predicate is replaced by a coextensive one, as in "Cicero is believed by Mary to be the author of the *Hortensius*." How does Ockham account for this referential opacity on the predicate side if the predicate of a modal *de re* proposition supposits for things out there just as the subject does?

Ockham is well aware of the limitations that the modal contexts impose on substitutivity on the side of the predicate in *de re* modal propositions. He insists indeed that the predicate of the singular sentences that need to be mentioned in the truth-conditions of a *de re* modal proposition should be the very same predicate (*ipsummet predicatum*) as in the original sentence and "under its proper form."[39] The truth of "some Roman is believed by Mary to be the author of the *Catiline Orations*" (understood as a *de re* modal proposition) requires that a singular proposition of the form "this is the author of the *Catiline Orations*," where "this" designates a Roman, is believed by Mary. Whether any singular proposition of the form "this is the author of the *Hortensius*," where "this" also designates a Roman, is believed or not by Mary is entirely irrelevant, even though "the author of the *Catiline Orations*" and "the author of the *Hortensius*" are in fact coextensive. That the predicate should thus remain precisely the same from the original modal proposition to each one of the relevant singular ones is due, Ockham explains, to the fact that the predicate "appellates its form."[40]

The appellation of the form here should be understood as a special kind of contextual connotation.[41] When used as a predicate, a term is endowed with a new semantic property, that of indirectly calling to mind the tokens that are morphologically (and semantically,

---

[39] *SL* II, 10, *OPh* I: 276 (transl. Freddoso and Schuurman 1980: 112).
[40] See, e.g., *SL* I, 72, *OPh* I: 216 (transl. Loux 1974: 204–205) and *SL* III-1, 43, *OPh* I: 474.
[41] This account of Ockham's appellation of the form is argued for in Panaccio 2012a. More on connotation in the next section.

I suppose) similar to itself. This holds for natural kind terms, according to Ockham, as well as for any other: even though "horse" has no connotation when considered in itself, it acquires one when it occurs as the predicate of a sentence. This appellation of the form does not play any significant role in non-modal present-tense sentences, but it does in *de re* modal contexts: the singular propositions that need to be turned to according to the Ockhamist truth-conditions of *de re* modal propositions should all have as their predicates a token of precisely the same form as the predicate of the original modal sentence. A coextensive but morphologically different one will not do, and this is why the substitution of coextensive terms for one another is not always possible *salva veritate* in such contexts.

Appellation of the form, however, does not prevent the predicate of a true affirmative *de re* modal sentence to supposit for some things. What would these things be? The question is important for Ockham's nominalism, since supposition for him is so closely associated with ontological commitment. In order to establish what the acceptance of a *de re* modal proposition commits us to, we need to be clear about what its terms supposit for, and we still have to clarify that point with respect to the predicates of such propositions. A good clue here is that Ockham repeatedly insists that the semantics of modal propositions closely parallel that of tensed propositions.[42] In a past-tense proposition, for instance, the predicate is restricted by the past-tense verb to supposit for the things it truly applied to in the past period indicated by the verb. In "dinosaurs were animals," for example, the predicate "animals" supposits only for past animals. Similarly, Ockham says, "the predicate in propositions concerning the possible [supposits] for things that can be."[43] This is to say that an affirmative modal copula such as "can be" or "possibly is" determines the predicate to supposit for possible things, just as the past-tense verb determines the predicate to supposit for past things. An adverb of necessity, presumably, would similarly restrict the predicate to stand for things that it necessarily applies to. And so on. It turns out, then, although Ockham does not care to mention it, that such sentences are true after all under exactly the same conditions as

---

[42] See, e.g., *SL* I, 72, *OPh* I: 215–218 (transl. Loux 1974: 204–206).
[43] *SL* I, 72, *OPh* I: 218 (transl. Loux 1974: 206).

any other affirmative categorical proposition: "All men can be animals" is true if and only if the things that the subject-term "men" supposits for in this sentence are among the possible animals that the predicate supposits for.[44] And "All men necessarily are animals" is true if and only if the things that "men" supposits for in this sentence are among the things that are necessarily animals.

This result, admittedly, is a bit odd in the case of *de re* belief sentences. On our reconstruction, the predicate-term "animals" in "some plants are believed to be animals" should be determined by the epistemic modal copula "is believed to be" to supposit only for things that are believed to be animals. And some of those, of course, might not be animals at all. A monkey face orchid might be mistakenly believed by someone to be an animal. Although Ockham does not discuss this kind of case, he has to bite the bullet, it seems to me. This consequence is in keeping with the parallel he often draws between *de re* modal sentences and tensed sentences: the modal term is part of the copula in the former just as the tense of the verb is in the latter, and it must determine what the predicate supposits for just as the tense of the verb does in tensed sentences.[45] Even in such cases, though, what the predicate supposits for are but singular things: on a *de re* construal, the things that are believed to be animals—certain plants, for example—must be singular substances or qualities. Despite the well-known limitations that modal contexts impose on the replacement of terms by

---

[44] Note that every such modal sentence is ambiguous for Ockham as to whether the subject-term supposits for all possible men or for presently existing men only, just as every past-tense sentence is ambiguous as to whether the subject-term supposits for the things that it presently applies to or for the things that it applied to in the past. The corresponding predicates, however, always supposit for what is required by the tense or modality of the copula, according to Ockham; see *SL* I, 72, *OPh* I: 215–217 (transl. Loux 1974: 204–206) and above n. 23 of present chapter.

[45] An alternative option would have been to see the modal modifier as part of the predicate. On this analysis, the predicate of the sentence "Some plants are believed to be animals" is "believed to be animals" rather than "animals" *tout court*. It would then supposit for the singular things that are believed to be animals, just as "animals" turns out to do in the Ockhamist approach. That Ockham associated the modal term with the copula rather than with the predicate is largely due, I suppose, to a desire to keep his semantics as close as possible to ordinary surface grammar (think of the sentence "Horses can be white," in which the modal term is clearly part of the verb), and to the parallel he wanted to maintain with tensed sentences, in which the tense is usually indicated by the verb in Indo-European languages.

coextensive ones, the truth-conditions of *all* modal sentences, whether *de dicto* or *de re*, turn out to be formally the same as that of standard categorical sentences, and no special entities are ever needed for their truth in addition to singular substances and qualities.

Natural kind terms, in short, have but one semantic feature when considered alone: each one of them distributively signifies a number of individuals that are essentially similar to one another and it does not carry any other information about these individuals. When inserted into propositions as subjects or predicates, these terms, like any other categorematic term, acquire a supposition, which is the particular referential function they happen to have in the context of these propositions. The supposition of a natural kind term, as that of any categorematic term, is normally derived from its primary signification in ways that vary according to the propositional contexts and the intentions of the speakers. In its most usual occurrences, the term has personal supposition and stands for its singular significates or some of them. In some special cases, when the context allows, it can have material or simple supposition if the speaker intends to, and it will then stand for certain linguistic or mental tokens, all of them being singular qualities in Ockham's view, either of the mind or of some physical substratum, such as air or paper. The truth-conditions of the categorical sentences in which these terms occur entirely depend, then, on the suppositions of their subject and predicate terms, given the logical form of the sentence. In *de re* modal sentences, an additional semantic property is called for in order to explain certain limitations to the substitutivity of coextensive terms—the appellation of the form—yet no additional ontological commitment is thus introduced. The bottom line is that no true categorical sentence, whether modal or non-modal, that has a natural kind term as subject or predicate requires the existence of anything in the world but singular substances and qualities.

Relational terms

Let us turn now to the semantics of relational terms. All such terms are connotative according to Ockham.[46] We must first examine, therefore,

---

[46] *SL* I, 10, *OPh* I: 37 (transl. Loux 1974: 71).

what connotation amounts to and how it affects relational terms in particular. We will then discuss Ockham's proposal that the term "relation" itself should be seen as a second-order term and that relations, consequently, are nothing but signs. And we will finally seek to understand how relational statements can nevertheless be mind-independently true and what their role is in the description of the world for Ockham.

Connotation

Much of what we have said in the previous section holds for connotative as well as for absolute terms. "White," for example, which is a paradigmatic connotative term for Ockham, primarily signifies all singular white things, just as "horse" primarily signifies all horses. In personal supposition, the term "white" supposits for these primary significates (or some of them), and in material or simple supposition, it supposits for certain linguistic or mental tokens, as "horse" does. The truth-conditions of the categorical sentences that "white" occurs in as subject or predicate parallel those of the categorical sentences in which absolute terms occur: just like "Bucephalus is a horse," "Bucephalus is white" is true if and only if the predicate supposits in it for what the subject-term "Bucephalus" supposits for; "some white [things] are animals" is true if and only if the predicate "animal" supposits in it for some of the things that the subject-term supposits for, just as in "some horses are animals," etc.

Connotative terms, however, have an additional semantic property, namely, a secondary signification, also called "connotation." In addition to their primary significates, they call to mind certain other things that they might not be true of. "White" primarily signifies all white things and connotatively calls to mind the whiteness tropes that are attached to these white things, even though the whiteness tropes are not white themselves.[47] "Mother" primarily signifies mothers and

---

[47] Only substances can rightly be said to be white in the natural world, for Ockham, since something is white for him only if a qualitative whiteness trope inheres in it, and qualitative tropes inhere only in substances (see principle SQ3, see above, pp. 67–68).

connotatively calls children to mind. "Horseman" primarily signifies horsemen and connotatively calls horses to mind. And so on. Being semantically complex, all connotative terms have a nominal definition according to Ockham.[48] This definition, he explains, usually contains one categorematic term in the nominative case and one or more categorematic terms in "oblique" cases (genitive, dative, ablative, and accusative in Latin). The former indicates a general category of things that the primary significates of the term belong to, while the latter designate the *connotata* of that term. "White," for example, can be defined as "a substance that has a whiteness," thus making it explicit that the things it primarily signifies are substances while the things it connotes are whiteness tropes. Similarly, "mother" could be defined as "a female animal that has a child," making it clear that its primary significates are female animals while its *connotata* are their children. In all cases, the things that are connoted are singular substances or singular qualities, just as the primary significates are: the *connotata* of "white," "mother," and "horseman" are whiteness tropes, children, and horses, respectively, and none of them is a universal entity or an intrinsically relational one. This is what nominal definitions are for in Ockham: they spell out the ontological commitments associated with connotative terms, making it conspicuous in the process that these terms do not require any enrichment of the ontology beyond the familiar categories of substance and quality.[49]

As their nominal definitions reveal, all connotative terms have a relational aspect to them. "White," for example, primarily signifies those substances that are related in a certain way with whiteness tropes, and "horseman" primarily signifies the human beings who are related in certain ways with horses. Neither "white" nor "horseman," however, properly count as relational terms. What distinguishes relational terms from other connotative terms is a syntactical feature, according to Ockham. Relational terms are such that if they are true of something, it is always possible to add a nominal complement to them that will designate some of their *connotata*. Take "mother," for example. We can use this term without mentioning any nominal complement: we can

---

[48] *SL* I, 10, *OPh* I: 36 (transl. Loux 1974: 70).
[49] On the role of nominal definitions in Ockham, see Panaccio 2004: 85–102.

say "Mary is a mother" just as we can say "Mary is white" or "Mary is a horsewoman." What qualifies "mother" as a relational term is that a nominal complement can *always* be added to "mother" in such sentences: if Mary is a mother, she must be someone's mother. If somebody is a mother, in other words, it always makes sense to ask who she is the mother of. This is generalizable *mutatis mutandis* to all relational terms: "no one is a father," Ockham writes, "unless he is someone's father, nor is anything similar unless it is similar to something."[50] Non-relational connotative terms, by contrast, behave differently: the truth of "Mary is white" does not require the truth of a parallel sentence in which "white" is accompanied by a nominal complement, and it does not make much sense to ask what Mary is white of, or white to.[51]

This difference in syntactical behavior, though, carries no additional ontological commitment. The correct application of "mother" requires the existence of nothing but a mother and a child, just as the correct application of "white" requires the existence of nothing but a substance and a whiteness trope. Neither the primary significates nor the *connotata* of a relational term are anything but substances and non-relational qualities.

Relations as signs

Ockham admits, however, that there are real things of which it can truly be said "This is a relation." What are they if there are no special relational entities? Raising this question is tantamount to asking what the term "relation" itself signifies. What does it mean to say, for example, that a relation holds between Socrates and Plato, or that motherhood and similitude are relations? Ockham's answer is to distinguish

---

[50] *SL* I, 52, *OPh* I: 172 (transl. Loux 1974: 172).

[51] Ockham admits, nevertheless, that non-relational connotative terms can usually be accompanied by the corresponding abstract term as a nominal complement. If something is white, we can say, according to him, that it is white by some whiteness, and if someone is a horseman, we can say that he is a horseman by some horsemanship. But Ockham expressly excludes this particular feature when specifying what the distinction is between relational terms and other connotative terms. The former, he says, "cannot be truly predicated of anything unless it is possible to add to them names *which are not their abstract forms*" (*SL* I, 52, *OPh* I: 172 [transl. Loux 1974: 171]; my italics).

two senses of the term "relation," neither of which involves any special entity.[52] In one sense, "relation" collectively designates the singular things that happen to be related to one another in some way. We can simultaneously point at Socrates and Plato, according to Ockham, and truly say "this is a relation," just as we can say of the two of them taken together, "this is a similitude" or "this is a friendship." In this sense, "relation" is a first-order term, like "mother," "friend," or "similar": it signifies things out there that are (usually) not signs themselves, and as in all other cases, these things are substances or qualities. The distinctive semantic feature of "relation" in this sense with respect to "mother," "friend," or "similar" is that it *collectively* signifies certain substances or qualities, rather than distributively, just as the term "people," for instance, signifies several men taken together. This is an important difference in the mode of signification, but no special *significata* are involved.[53]

The second sense of the term "relation" is the one Ockham generally favors, and it is, he claims, the one that Aristotle used as well.[54] "Relation" in this sense is a second-order term. It designates signs. These signs can be conventional words (and thus taken, "relation" is what Ockham calls a "name of second imposition") or concepts (and thus it is a "name of second intention").[55] There is an additional ambiguity here in the meaning of the term "relation" as to whether it refers to conventional words or to concepts, but in either case the *significata* of the term "relation" are significant units—either words or concepts— and this is what really matters at this point.[56]

In this sense of the word, relations, then, are signs. This might sound like a rather extreme view, but Ockham's position is much more moderate than it seems. "Relation" in the relevant sense is simply

---

[52] See, e.g., *Ord.*, dist. 30, q. 1, *OTh* IV: 314. The same distinction is drawn with respect, in particular, to "real relation" and "relation of reason"; see *Quodl.* VI, 25, *OTh* IX: 678–679 (transl. Freddoso 1991: 571–572), *Ord.* dist. 35, q. 4, *OTh* IV: 470–471.

[53] More on collective names when we come to quantitative terms later on in this chapter.

[54] See, e.g., *SL* I, 49, *OPh* I: 155–159 (transl. Loux 1974: 158–161), *Quodl.* VI, 22, *OTh* IX: 666–669 (transl. Freddoso 1991: 562–564).

[55] *SL* I, 49, *OPh* I: 155–156 (transl. Loux 1974: 159).

[56] Whether "relation" is used as a term of second imposition or as a term of second intention or as both at the same time must depend on the context and on the intention of the speaker.

synonymous with "relational term" for him. We can truly say "This is a relation" when pointing at some real thing only if this thing is a sign, and what we are saying then is that this sign is a relational term. This is true, for example, if we point (physically or mentally) at a spoken token of "mother" or at a mental token of the corresponding concept. It does not follow at all that how things are related to one another in the external world is mind-dependent, or that the human mind imposes a relational scheme on the external world. Ockham is no precursor of Kant in this respect. If Mary is a mother, this is a fact of nature, and the corresponding sentence "Mary is a mother" is mind-independently true. In this sentence both the subject-term "Mary" and the relational predicate "mother" are in personal supposition, they both stand for a real person. In "*Mother* is a relation," by contrast, the subject-term "mother" must be in material or simple supposition for the sentence to be true. We have seen that a term can thus be taken only if the other extreme is a name of second imposition or second intention, and this is the case here since "relation" (in the required sense) is indeed a second-order term for Ockham. Thus understood, the sentence "*Mother* is a relation" means no more than that the term "mother" is a relational term. If "mother" was taken in personal supposition, on the other hand, the sentence would be false: real mothers are not relational terms, they are persons and hence substances. While "relation" itself is a second-order term, however, the terms it signifies are not. They are usually first-order terms, such as "mother," "friend," or "similar," which all designate things that are not signs themselves.

In this sense of "relation," saying that a relation holds between Socrates and Plato is saying that there is at least one relational term that can be truly predicated of Socrates with respect to Plato, or conversely. And saying that motherhood or similitude are relations is a somewhat misleading way of saying that "mother" and "similar" are relational terms. In none of these cases are the significates and the *supposita* of the term "relation" anything but spoken, written, or mental tokens, and all of those are singular qualities for Ockham. As to the significates and the *supposita* of the relational terms that "relation" refers to, they must also be singular substances and qualities. The relational term "mother," for example, primarily signifies certain women and connotes their children and it stands for the mothers (or some of them) when taken in personal supposition as in "Mary is a mother" or "A mother is a woman." When in material or simple supposition, on the other hand, as in "*Mother* is a relation" or "*Mother* is a relational term," it stands for singular linguistic or conceptual tokens, as must always be the case in the Ockhamist perspective when material or simple supposition are at play.

Relational statements

The truth-conditions of relational statements are of the same form as those of categorical sentences in general. Ockham analyzes a sentence such as "Mary is the mother of Peter" as a subject-predicate sentence with "Mary" as the subject and the complex term "mother of Peter" as the predicate. As in all other cases, the truth-conditions of such sentences depend on the suppositions of the subject and predicate terms on the one hand, and on the logical form of the sentence on the other hand. "Mary is the mother of Peter" is true if and only if the predicate "mother of Peter" supposits in this sentence for what the subject-term "Mary" supposits for. "Some philosophers are disciples of Aristotle," being a particular affirmative proposition, is true if and only if the complex predicate "disciples of Aristotle" supposits for some of the *supposita* of the subject-term "philosophers," and so on. One might wonder, then: how does the relational character of such statements contribute to their truth-conditions?

Although he does not elaborate on it, Ockham's answer can safely be reconstructed, at least in the general lines. The predicate-term in these sentences, according to his analysis, is a complex phrase composed of a relational term ("mother" or "disciples") and a nominal complement ("Peter" or "Aristotle"). Just like simple terms, such complex phrases can be said to primarily signify whatever it is that they are true of: "mother of Peter" primarily signifies the mother of Peter, and "disciples of Aristotle" primarily signifies the disciples of Aristotle. What they supposit for when taken in personal supposition, consequently, must be among these primary significates, as in the case of simple terms. Our question, then, comes down to this: how are the primary significates fixed for such complex phrases? What role, in other words, does the relational character of these phrases play in determining what individuals they are true of?

This is where connotation comes in. A relational term such as "disciple" primarily signifies the disciples and connotes their masters. A necessary condition for the complex phrase "disciple of Aristotle" to primarily signify anything, then, is that the individual designated by the complement "Aristotle" be among the *connotata* of "disciple" (Aristotle, in other words, must have disciples). If it is, then the primary significates of "disciple of Aristotle" will be those among the primary significates of "disciple" that are correctly associated with Aristotle. The rule is generalizable: the primary significates of a complex phrase composed of a relational term and a nominal complement, such as "mother of Peter" or "disciple of Aristotle," are the individuals among the primary significates of the relational term that are associated in the right way with those among its *connotata* that are designated by the complement.[57] The connotation of "mother" thus plays a decisive role in fixing the primary significate of "mother of Peter": the complex phrase "mother of Peter" primarily signifies any individual that is both primarily signified by "mother" and correctly associated with one of the individuals that "mother" connotes, the individual named "Peter" in this case. If there is such a person, "mother of Peter" will supposit for her in "Mary is the mother of Peter," and the sentence will be true if and only if the subject-term "Mary" also supposits for this person.[58]

This presupposes, obviously, that the *connotata* of a relational term are associated in a determinate way with its primary significates. Each single being that is connoted by "mother" must not only be related in some way or other with one of the primary significates of "mother." It must be related with it *in the right way*. Mary and Peter, after all, could be related in several different ways—Mary might be taller than Peter,

---

[57] Note that the complement does not need to be a singular term. Think of the sentences "Mary is the mother of twins" and "Some philosophers are disciples of Greek thinkers." My choice of singular terms in the examples is merely aimed at simplifying the exposition.

[58] If no such individual exists, the sentence "Mary is the mother of Peter" turns out false on Ockham's truth-conditions, since there is nothing in this case that the subject-term and the predicate-term both supposit for.

or Mary might love Peter, and so on—but for Mary to be a primary significate of the complex phrase "mother of Peter," she must be related with Peter in a very specific way. This is something that the nominal definition of "mother" is expected to express. "Mother," as we saw, can be defined as "a female animal that has a child." This makes it conspicuous that two conditions are required for a certain being to be a mother: she must be a female animal on the one hand, and she must have a child on the other hand.[59] In this particular definition, as it turns out, the properly relational content of "mother" ultimately rests on the verb "to have." "To have," however, is equivocal according to Ockham: something can be said to have a quality, or to have a quantity, or to have a part, or to have a possession, and so on, and the specifically relational content of the verb "to have" differs in each of these cases.[60] We can conclude that "to have" must correspond to several distinct relational concepts in mental language.

This suggests that there should be on the Ockhamist view a number of primitive relational concepts. These basic relational concepts would often be represented by the equivocal verb "to have" in spoken or written definitions, but certain other verbs or nouns might play a similar role. "Murderer" and "fertilizer," for example, must both have the concept of "cause" (or some equivalent) in their definitions; "adjacent" and "contact" might both have "to be contiguous to"; and so on. Ockham does not care to draw a list of these primitive relational concepts, but we will see in chapter 5 that his theory of human cognition does provide a plausible ground for reducing all relational concepts to a limited number of basic ones and for assuming that these primitive relational concepts can be acquired in pretty much the same way as the natural kind concepts.[61]

Whatever these basic relational terms are, however, their semantics must be the same as that of all other connotative terms: they primarily signify certain things and connote certain others, all of which

---

[59] Ockham insists that when two relational terms are correlative with each other, such as "mother" and "child" or "disciple" and "master," each should occur in the nominal definition of the other one: "child" in the definition of "mother," for example, and vice versa. Ockham has no qualms about circular definitions; see, e.g., SL III-3, 26, OPh I: 690.

[60] *Exp. in libr. Praedic.* 21, OPh II: 337–338.

[61] See below, pp. 153–156.

are but singular substances or qualities. "Cause," for example, which might very well be such a primitive, primarily signifies the causes and connotes their effects. Its correct application does require that the cause and the effect be associated with each other in a specific way: the effect must owe its existence to that of the cause.[62] This dependence, however, is no additional thing. As was shown in chapter 3, it is a fundamental tenet of Ockham's nominalism that things are mind-independently arranged in a few basic ways (causal dependence being one of them, along with spatial ordering, inherence, information, and essential similitude—among others maybe), but that these arrangements do not require the existence of special relational entities. The concept of "cause" thus connotes every singular thing that owes its existence to something else, and it primarily signifies any singular thing that is related in the right way with one of these *connotata*, any singular thing, in other words, that one of the *connotata* owes its existence to. Thanks to the connotation of relational terms, the statements in which these terms occur can thus describe how things are really arranged with respect to one another, without carrying with them extra ontological commitment.

Quantitative terms

"All names from the genus of quantity," Ockham writes, "are connotative."[63] They primarily signify certain things, then, and connote some others. When it comes to specific examples, however, it is not immediately clear what things exactly would thus be connoted. Take "body" (*corpus*). Ockham defines it as "a thing whose parts are separated from each other in length, breadth, and depth."[64] This definition indicates that "body" connotes the parts of the thing in question. And it incorporates the relational concept of "being spatially separated" (which might very well be basic), thus making it explicit that the

---

[62] See *Summ. phil. nat.* II, 3, *OPh* VI: 218, where Ockham proposes to define an "efficient cause" as "that to the existence of which something else owes it to exist" (my transl.). On this definition, see above, pp. 91–92.
[63] *SL* I, 10, *OPh* I: 37 (transl. Loux 1974: 71).
[64] Ibid.

application of the term "body" to a certain thing requires that the parts of this thing be spatially separated from each other. But how are we to understand the apparent reference to length, breadth, and depth in the definition, given that there are no special things in Ockham's ontology that correspond to the terms "length," "breadth," and "depth"? A practicable path in these cases might be to suppose that "length," "breadth," and "depth" are relational concepts naturally acquired by the human mind from perceptual experience.[65] A close look at the texts, however, reveals that Ockham actually uses certain additional semantic devices when dealing with particular quantitative terms. The present section will examine three of these that are of independent interest for any nominalist approach: the connotation of propositions, the linguistic formation of pseudo-names and collective designation. None of them is exclusively used for the analysis of quantitative terms by Ockham, but he takes them to be especially useful for it.

Propositions connoted

Certain terms, according to Ockham, connote *that* something is the case. "*Quantum*" (or its synonym "quantity"), for example, which is the most general term in the category of quantity, "connotes or signifies that one part of the thing is spatially separated from another part."[66] And "distance" (*distantia*) "conveys that there is some body in between the absolute things in question."[67] How is this to be understood? What is connoted in such cases cannot be a state of affairs, a fact, or an event, since Ockham does not countenance anything of the sort in his ontology. Things are related to one another in various ways, to be sure, but neither these ways nor corresponding connections are accepted as additional entities that could be signified, supposited for, or even connoted.

---

[65] Remember that Ockham has a relational conception of space; see above, pp. 82–83.
[66] *SL* I, 45, *OPh* I: 141 (transl. Loux 1974: 148; my italics).
[67] *Quodl.* VII, 8, *OTh* IX: 730 (transl. Freddoso 1991: 616).

The Ockhamist solution to the riddle is that the *connotata* in these cases are *propositions* (i.e., assertive sentences). When Ockham says that a certain term connotes that so and so, he normally uses an infinitive proposition as the grammatical complement of "to connote." The Latin for "connotes that one part of the thing is spatially separated from another part," for example, is "*connotat partem distare a parte*," where "*partem distare a parte*" (literally: "a part to be distant from a part") is an infinitive proposition. Ockham calls it a "*dictum*": "something is called the *dictum* of a proposition when the terms of the proposition are taken in the accusative case and the verb in the infinitive mood."[68] In English or French, the corresponding *dictum* would normally be a proposition in the indicative or the subjunctive mood introduced by a conjunction such as "that" or "*que*." This is the very same notion of *dictum* that Ockham employs when distinguishing modal propositions with a *dictum* from modal propositions without *dictum*.[69] A sentence such as "*Quantum* connotes that so and so" thus turns out to be a modal proposition with a *dictum* for Ockham. Remember that a modal proposition for him is characterized by the presence of a modal term, and that a modal term is any term that can be predicated of a proposition as a whole, including "true," "false," "known," "believed," "uttered," or "written."[70] We now see that "connoted" should also be counted among modal terms, since it is predicable of whole propositions: the logical form of "the term *quantum* connotes that so and so" really is "*that so and so* is connoted by the term *quantum*," where the *dictum* "that so and so" is the subject of which the complex modal term is predicated. When discussing the semantics of *propria* such as "capable of smiling," for example, Ockham is explicit that some of these terms connote mental propositions.[71]

In a sentence of the form "*That so and so is connoted by the term T*," the *dictum*, therefore, must be in simple supposition: it supposits for the corresponding mental proposition, a "proposition existing or

---

[68] *SL* II, 9, *OPh* I: 273 (transl. Freddoso and Schuurman 1980: 109).
[69] *SL* II, 9–10, *OPh* I: 273–279 (transl. Freddoso and Schuurman 1980: 108–115); see above, p. 112.
[70] *SL* II, 1, *OPh* I: 242–243 (transl. Freddoso and Schuurman 1980: 80–81).
[71] *SL* I, 24, *OPh* I: 81 (transl. Loux 1974: 102). The *proprium* is one of the five "predicables" that Porphyry discusses in his *Treatise on Predicables*.

capable of existing in the mind," as Ockham puts it.[72] The question arises, of course, as in all other cases of simple supposition, what precise mental tokens would be supposited for by a *dictum* such as "that a part is spatially separated from another part" when it occurs as the subject of "is connoted by the term *quantum*." There is a general difficulty here about simple and material supposition that Ockham never directly addresses, as I previously pointed out. One way of seeing it is to identify the *supposita* in such a case with the mental tokens that are semantically equivalent with the sentence "A part is spatially separated from another part." However that should go exactly, one thing that Ockham is explicit about is that these tokens need not actually exist in the mind of anybody: it suffices that they be "*capable* of existing in the mind" (my italics). Merely possible mental tokens are bona fide *supposita* in certain contexts for Ockham, as are merely possible things in general.[73] In sentences of the form "*That so and so* is connoted by the term *T*," the *dictum* "that so and so" thus supposits for actual or possible mental propositional tokens, just as it does in certain other modal propositions with a *dictum* taken in the sense of composition. And such propositional tokens are singular mental qualities in Ockham's ontology. The *connotata* in such cases, therefore, are mental qualities.

Taking mental propositions as the *connotata* of certain quantitative terms thus allows for much richness and flexibility in the semantic analysis of these terms, without overpopulating the ontology. The term "*quantum*" (or "quantity") has it in its semantic content that the parts of the things it designates are spatially separated from each other, but this content is not to be seen as a special abstract entity or a state of affairs. It merely consists in "*quantum*" connoting the (actual and possible) tokens of a certain mental proposition. This connoted proposition states the condition(s) that something must fulfil to be among the primary significates of "*quantum*." The proposition in question should not itself carry unacceptable ontological commitments, of course, but this constraint does not prevent it from having some primitive relational concept in it, such as "being spatially separated," since a concept

---

[72] Ibid.
[73] See above, pp. 96–100.

of this sort primarily or secondarily signifies nothing but substances or qualities.[74]

Pseudo-names

Apart from "quantity" itself (or "*quantum*"), the more salient terms that properly belong in the category of quantity, according to Ockham, are "line," "surface," "body," and "number."[75] The last of these has to do with discrete quantity; we will deal with it in the next section along with collective terms. The other three concern continuous quantity and the spatial dimensions of length, breadth, and depth. Ockham discusses them along with "point" in his treatise *On Quantity*, of which Question 1 (of three) mostly deals with "point," Question 2 with "line" and "surface," and Question 3 with "body" (*corpus*). The most striking aspect of his analysis comes out in Question 1, where he claims that the term "point" according to a certain use of it (and this holds for "line" and "surface" as well) "does not precisely have the force of a name" and cannot serve as the subject or predicate of a well-formed literal sentence.[76] One should not ask what a point is, therefore, since "point" is not a designative term at all and cannot serve as the subject of a literal sentence of the form "A point is so and so." Ockham's position with respect to sentences in which such quantitative terms occur as subjects or predicates turns out to be a variety of *fictionalism*: no such sentence is literally true, but we figuratively express ourselves *as if* the terms "point," "line," "surface," and "body" were designative names, while they are not.[77] A term like "point," according to Ockham, "is equivalent in signification to some complex expression composed of a name and a verb or a conjunction or an adverb, or a relative pronoun, or of a verb and an oblique case, that properly speaking cannot grammatically be used as the subject of a verb."[78]

---

[74] More on these primitive relational concepts below, pp. 153–156.
[75] *SL* I, 46, *OPh* I: 149 (transl. Loux 1974: 154).
[76] *Tract. de quant.* 1, *OTh* X: 24 (my transl.).
[77] On what fictionalism amounts to in contemporary philosophy, see Eklund 2019.
[78] *Tract. de quant.* 1, *OTh* X: 23 (my transl.).

Ockham does not actually provide a completely spelled-out analysis of "point," "line," "surface," and "body" that would make it clear what complex expressions exactly these terms are equivalent to, but what is interesting here is the general idea. The speakers of a conventional language, as he points out in the *Summa of Logic*, "can, if they wish, use one locution instead of several,"[79] but the abbreviated phrase in such cases might not always be fit to be the subject or predicate of a well-formed sentence. "Horseness," for example, might be used as an abbreviation for something like "[a] horse necessarily," as Ockham explains when discussing the semantics of abstract terms.[80] "Horseness" is not a quantitative term, admittedly, but the example nicely illustrates the abbreviative process we are now interested in. The salient feature here is that "[a] horse necessarily" is not a well-formed complex categorematic term, because the adverb "necessarily" in a sentence such as "A horse necessarily is an animal" does not belong on the subject side. It is part of the copula. The merging of this adverb with the subject "a horse" into the single word "horseness" is an artificial linguistic device that speakers might decide to use for the sake of elegance, brevity, or versification, but since "a horse necessarily" is not a well-formed nominal phrase, its abbreviation "horseness" does not genuinely designate anything. Any sentence in which "horseness" occurs in this sense as subject or predicate, consequently, must be taken figuratively: "Such propositions and similar ones," Ockham writes, "are not to be accepted as literally true, but should be explained by some grammatical figure of speech."[81]

Explications of this sort would usually require not only the replacement of the abbreviation by the abbreviated phrase, but some other transformations in the rest of the sentence as well. As Ockham puts it:

> Not only can one word be sometimes equivalent in signification to several words, but when it is added to another expression the resulting whole is equivalent to yet another complex expression, in which sometimes the part that is added will have a different case,

---

[79] *SL* I, 8, *OPh* I: 29–30 (transl. Loux 1974: 65).
[80] *SL* I, 8, *OPh* I: 29–34 (transl. Loux 1974: 65–68).
[81] *Tract. de quant.* 1, *OTh* X: 23–24 (my transl.).

mood, or tense, and sometimes it will simply be eliminated by being analyzed away and what it conveys being explicated.[82]

The sentence "Horseness is a sort of animality," to take an example of my own, might be rephrased as "A horse necessarily is an animal," where both the grammatical subject "horseness" and the predicate "a sort of animality" are replaced by concrete names ("horse" and "animal," respectively), while the apparently simple copula is replaced by the modal copula "necessarily is." There is no general rule, however, as to how these explanations should proceed. Each case is special. Ockham considers, for instance, the sentence "A point is indivisible." Since it is commonly accepted by mathematicians, it must be presumed to be true in some sense. If so, however, the term "point" cannot be taken in this sentence as being designative: there is nothing in the spatial world that is really indivisible, according to Ockham. In order to interpret the sentence, one must remember that "point" usually serves to indicate somehow that a certain line is not continued beyond a certain length. With this in mind, the sentence "A point is indivisible" can be taken as a figurative way of saying something like "A line is extended to a certain distance and not beyond."[83] This particular analysis, admittedly, sounds a bit far-fetched, but whether it is or not, the Ockhamist philosopher cannot stop there anyway in his attempt at reshaping the original sentence into one that is literally true. "Line," after all, is not a designative term, either. It is figuratively used in certain sentences when one considers spatially extended things from the sole point of view of their length.[84] "Line" should be analyzed away, therefore, in any literal reformulation of these sentences, and the same must be true with "surface" and "body." The resulting propositions might be rather intricate in the end when "point," "line," "surface," and "body" are all replaced, yet no reference whatsoever will be found in them but to substances and qualities.

---

[82] *SL* I, 8, *OPh* I: 33 (my transl.—Loux's translation does not follow the text closely enough in this case).
[83] *Quaest. in libr. Phys.* 63, *OPh* VI: 569; see also *Tract. de quant.* 1, *OTh* X: 24.
[84] See, e.g., *SL* III-3, 30, *OPh* I: 701.

The correct interpretation of a figurative sentence with a pseudo-name in it must depend in each case on the context of the utterance and the intention of the speaker. When these sentences occur in authoritative texts, whether in philosophy or in theology, it should be presumed moreover that what is meant is true. Ockham in such cases makes generous use of what we call today a "Principle of Charity" in favoring interpretations that make authoritative statements turn out true.[85] This means in practice that where authoritative texts are concerned, he usually proposes interpretations that "maximize the agreement" (to use Donald Davidson's phrase)[86] between the authority in question and what he takes himself to be true—nominalist reinterpretations, in other words: "It is not inappropriate," he insists, "to concede that philosophers and Saints thus spoke figuratively."[87] Aristotle, in particular, is understood by Ockham as defending a strict nominalist position with respect to quantitative terms, even though he sometimes figuratively speaks as if a point or a line were something real.[88]

The pseudo-name device is not restricted to the analysis of quantitative terms. It is also useful, Ockham thinks, in correctly understanding a whole group of abstract terms from other categories that are frequently used by philosophers and theologians.[89] "Horseness," for example, is interpreted by him as an abbreviation for "horse by definition" in Avicenna's famous statement that "horseness by itself is neither one nor many; nor does it exist in sensible things, nor in the soul."[90] Avicenna, Ockham charitably remarks, "clearly did not mean that horseness is some entity which is neither one thing nor many and neither outside the soul nor in the soul; for this is both impossible and absurd."[91] What he must have intended instead is the (true)

---

[85] On the Principle of Charity, see, e.g., Feldman 1998.
[86] See, e.g., Davidson 1984a: 101.
[87] *Tract. de quant.* 1, *OTh* X: 25 (my transl.).
[88] See *Quodl.* IV, 27, *OTh* IX: 433–440 (transl. Freddoso and Kelley 1991: 358–362), *SL* I, 44, *OPh* I: 132–139 (transl. Loux: 142–146). In the latter passage, Ockham even declines to endorse the nominalist position himself, presenting it only as Aristotle's view. It is clear from everything he wrote on the subject, though, that this is mere caution on his part to elude possible accusations of heresy.
[89] *SL* I, 8, *OPh* I: 29–34 (transl. Loux 1974: 65–68); see on this Panaccio 2022.
[90] *SL* I, 8, *OPh* I: 31 (transl. Loux 1974: 66); the original passage is from Avicenna's *Metaphysics* V, 1.
[91] Ibid.

metalinguistic statement that "none of these notions is part of the definition of 'horse'." Whether in the category of quantity or elsewhere, spotting such pseudo-names thus allows the philosopher to avoid misleading reifications by taking the sentences in which these terms occur as non-literal abbreviations.

Collective terms

The terms that are most closely associated with discrete quantity in Ockham are the numerals. Starting with "two," "three," etc., they are considered by him as "collective names," along with the term "number" itself and several others that do not belong in the category of quantity, such as "people," "crowd," and "army."[92] The distinctive semantic property of collective names is that they conjunctively (*coniunctim*) signify several things at once.[93] "Two" signifies couples and "three" signifies trios, just as "people," "crowd," and "army" signify certain groups. Couples and trios, however, are not distinct entities in addition to their members, any more than crowds and armies are. The significates in these cases as in all others are individual substances or qualities. It is just that several of them are jointly signified by such terms. What is special here is the mode of signification. Nothing is added to the ontology.

When they occur in personal supposition in the context of a sentence, collective names accordingly "supposit only for many things taken together."[94] In the sentence 'The Apostles were twelve,' for instance, the numerical term "twelve" stands for any dozen things that existed in the past.[95] And for each dozen, it conjunctively supposits for

---

[92] See, e.g., *SL* I, 9, *OPh* I: 34–35 (transl. Loux 1974: 69). The phrase "collective name" does not occur in this particular chapter of the *Summa*, but Ockham uses it elsewhere; see, e.g., *SL* II, 11, *OPh* I: 282 (transl. Freddoso and Schuurman 1980: 118), *Quodl.* VI, 25, *OTh* IX: 681 (transl. Freddoso 1991: 574), *Quaest. in libr. Phys.* 107, *OPh* VI: 681. On collective terms in Ockham, see Pelletier 2021.
[93] *Quaest. in libr. Phys.* 107, *OPh* VI: 681.
[94] *SL* I, 9, *OPh* I: 34 (transl. Loux 1974: 69).
[95] As we saw earlier, the supposition of the predicate is restricted by a past-tense verb to the individuals (or groups of individuals) that this very predicate applied to in the past (see above, pp. 117–118).

its twelve members taken together. It follows from this that a new variety of supposition is needed in such cases for the other extreme of the proposition. The subject-term "Apostles" in "The Apostles were twelve" cannot distributively supposit for the Apostles, as it normally does in sentences such as "The Apostles were men." While the latter entails that each single Apostle was a man, "The Apostles were twelve" should not entail, of course, that each Apostle was twelve.[96] "Apostle" in the latter sentence must conjunctively supposit, therefore, for the Apostles taken together, just as "twelve" conjunctively supposits for any dozen things taken together. The sentence will be true, then, if and only if the group that "Apostles" conjunctively supposits for in this particular sentence is one of the groups that "twelve" supposits for. Contrary to "twelve," however, the singular "Apostle" is not by itself a collective name. Separately taken, it distributively signifies the Apostles, just as "horse" distributively signifies horses. What comes out, then, is that a non-collective categorematic term can be endowed with a special collective supposition in certain propositional contexts.

Ockham does not develop the point in any detail, and he proposes no distinctive appellation for this special kind of supposition. He shows himself to be aware of its necessity, however, when discussing the syncategorematic term "all." "All," he says, can be taken either in "a collective or a distributive sense."[97] When it is taken distributively, the categorematic term that it determines distributively supposits for whatever it signifies as "Apostle" does in the sentence "The Apostles were men." When "all" is taken collectively, by contrast, "it is not asserted," Ockham says, "that the predicate agrees with each thing of which the subject is truly predicated," but "that the predicate belongs to all the things—taken at once—of which the subject is truly predicated."[98] This straightforwardly requires that the subject that is determined by the collective "all" should have a different mode of personal supposition in this context than it usually has. And the same holds in several propositional contexts in which "all" does not occur, such as in the sentences "The Apostles were twelve," "Peter and Mary are two,"

---

[96] *SL* II, 4, *OPh* I: 266 (transl. Freddoso and Schuurman 1980: 101–102).
[97] *SL* II, 4, *OPh* I: 266 (transl. Freddoso and Schuurman 1980: 102).
[98] Ibid.

and "Horses are many." The rule here must parallel the one Ockham introduces when dealing with second-order terms. Remember that a subject or a predicate term can be taken in material or simple supposition, according to him, only if the other extreme of the proposition is a second-order term.[99] The presence of the second-order term in a sentence, in other words, opens up the possibility for a first-order term to be taken in material or simple supposition in the same sentence. My point now is that although it is not expressed in so many words, a similar rule must apply when a collective name occurs: in such cases, the other extreme of the same sentence can be taken in collective personal supposition, even though it is not itself a collective name. "Peter and Mary are two" might mean that each one of them is two (which would be false in this case), but since the predicate "two" is a collective name, the complex subject-term "Peter and Mary" can alternatively be taken in what I just called "collective personal supposition." The sentence would then mean that Peter and Mary taken together are two—a true statement in this case. The difference, however, is only in the mode of supposition, not in the entities that are supposited for.

With respect to ontological commitment, in short, quantitative terms are on a par with natural kind terms and relational terms: they can occur in true sentences—or at least in acceptable figurative discourse—yet none of them ever requires anything but singular substances or qualities as primary significates, *connotata*, or *supposita*. Ockham's semantic theory is thus an essential component of his nominalism: it purports to show how languages with such terms in them can be adequate tools for describing a world exclusively made of non-relational individuals and for providing correct accounts of what is going on in this world. Several remarkable ideas are introduced by Ockham along the way. To conclude this chapter, let me recall a number of these that might still be useful for contemporary discussions over universals, relations, and quantities:

- the distinction between signification and supposition: taken in themselves, categorematic terms signify something and when

---

[99] *SL* I, 65, *OPh* I: 197–199 (transl. Loux 1974: 191–193); see above, pp. 106–107.

they are inserted in propositions as subjects or predicates, they acquire a new referential function—supposition, namely—that depends both on their pre-established signification and on certain elements of the context, such as the presence of *syncategoremata*, the semantic nature of the other extreme, and the intentions of the speakers;
- multiple denotation: general terms primarily signify several individuals at once and normally supposit for some or all of them distributively when taken in personal supposition (which is their most common use);
- connotation: many terms have a secondary signification (or connotation), they "obliquely" call to mind certain individuals that they might not be true of; this allows, among other things, for the existence of coextensive terms that are not synonymous with one another because their connotations differ;
- a theory of truth-conditions based on supposition: the truth-values of all atomic sentences, whether modal or non-modal, basically depend on the suppositions of their subject and predicate terms, given the syntactic structure of the sentences in question;
- an adverbial interpretation of modal terms: in *de re* modal propositions, the modal modifiers—for example, "possibly," "necessarily," etc.—are part of the copula and play a decisive role in determining what the predicate supposits for;
- a metalinguistic understanding of several propositions having to do with universals, relations, and quantities: certain especially important terms for these topics, such as "species," "genus," and "relation," are second-order terms; others are endowed with a metalinguistic connotation such as "*quantum*" or "quantity", and even non-metalinguistic terms are attributed special self-referential uses—simple or material supposition—in certain contexts, such as "horse" in "horse is a species" and "similitude" in "similitude is a relation";
- pseudo-naming: some apparently simple terms are conventional abbreviations for complex phrases that are not grammatically liable to be the subjects or predicates of well-formed sentences; in such cases, the sentences in which these terms occur are to be considered as figurative ways of speaking, and recovering the

underlying literal meaning usually requires that they be thoroughly reformulated;
- collective denotation: some terms—such as numerals—collectively (rather than distributively) signify several things at once.

The whole approach is essentially referentialist. The semantic properties of sentences are derived from those of their component terms (this is Ockham's semantic atomism), and the semantic properties of the terms relate them in turn to certain singular entities, whether actual or possible: what a term signifies, connotes, or supposits for are real or possible individuals. The connotative term "mother," for example, primarily signifies all singular mothers and supposits for them (or some of them) when taken in personal supposition, and it connotes their children. There are necessarily empty terms, admittedly, such as "square circle," which does not primarily signify anything and cannot, therefore, personally supposit for anything. The semantic content of such terms, however, still lies in their being semantically related with certain individuals. In Ockham's analysis, the phrase "square circle," for example, must be a complex connotative term, connoting the square things on the one hand and the circular things on the other hand. The term's being devoid of primary significates results from the fact that nothing can possibly satisfy the condition of being simultaneously associated in the right way with both sorts of *connotata*.

The theory is also a variety of mentalist semantics, in a sense. Conventional linguistic units receive their meaning by being subordinated to mental concepts. A striking feature of Ockham's view, however, is that these concepts must not necessarily be present to the mind of the speaker as she utters the words in question. The conventional subordination of a spoken sound to a concept is not something that every speaker does anew. It is accomplished by the agent Ockham calls the "impositor," the one who *originally* "imposes" a signification on a newly coined word by associating it with a given concept. The word "man," for example, signifies every man "for the impositor of the word 'man' intended that it would signify every thing the determinate mental concept is predicated of."[100] Once this is done, the word

---

[100] *Ord.*, dist. 2, q. 4, *OTh* II: 140 (transl. Spade 1994: 140).

retains this signification "for all those who are willing to use the word as it was imposed."[101] These later users might not themselves have an actual token of the relevant concept in mind when uttering the word. More than this: they might not even have the relevant concept at all in their conceptual baggage. Ockham explains, for example, that he does not himself possess the natural kind concept of "lion" because he has never seen a lion, but that he can nevertheless use the *word* "lion" as a natural kind term in spoken language—an "absolute" term—because the word was originally subordinated to the simple absolute concept of "lion" by someone who had this concept.[102] Even though Ockham's conception of the meaning of conventional words is mentalist, then, it is also a form of *linguistic externalism*: the precise meaning that a word has in the mouth of a particular speaker does not depend on what concept this speaker has in mind at the moment of utterance, but on an act of imposition that in most cases was accomplished by someone else, sometimes in a distant past.[103] How concepts acquire their representational content, on the other hand, will be discussed in the next chapter.

---

[101] *Ord.*, dist. 22, q. 1, *OTh* IV: 56 (my transl.)

[102] See *SL* III-2, 29, *OPh* I: 558–559 (transl. Longeway 2007: 195). In such a case, the concept Ockham himself would have in mind when uttering the word "lion" would be a complex connotative concept such as "a large feline with a mane" or something similar, but his spoken word "lion" would nevertheless be an "absolute" term because that is what it was instituted to be by the original impositor.

[103] For a defense of the externalist interpretation of Ockham's theory of linguistic meaning, see Panaccio 2015b: 167–173 and Panaccio 2017b: 226–229.

5
Epistemology

How is knowledge possible in Ockham's world? Realist philosophers often claim that nominalism inevitably leads to an extreme form of scepticism. Against the doctrine that everything is singular by itself, John Duns Scotus, for example, argued that an intellect that understands an utterly singular object under a general concept would therefore understand that object in a way that does not correspond to what it really is.[1] Similar worries arise with respect to relational and quantitative concepts if only substances and qualities exist, as Ockham holds. Insofar, then, as we think with general, relational, and quantitative concepts, how can we ever entertain true thoughts about reality, and how can we know these thoughts to be true? With these questions in the background, this chapter will successively outline Ockham's theory of cognitive acts, his theory of mental language, and his conception of knowledge.

Cognitive acts

Mental reality is made of substance and quality for Ockham, just as physical reality is. The sensory faculty and the intellectual faculty are substantial forms for him. These faculties are essential, intrinsic parts of human substances, along with matter and corporeal form.[2] The sensory substantial form is the subject of external sensory perception and physical affections, while the intellective substantial form is the subject of conceptual thought, volition, and reasoning. Two general kinds of mental qualities inhere in each of these substantial forms: acts

---

[1] John Duns Scotus, *Ordinatio* II, dist. 3, part 1, quest. 1, section 7 (transl. Tweedale 1999: 169–170).
[2] See above, pp. 72–73.

and *habitus*. The former are episodes of actually perceiving, feeling, thinking, and willing. They usually are of relatively short duration. *Habitus*, on the other hand, are acquired dispositional properties left in the mind by previous acts. Having learned, for example, that 12 times 12 is 144, I have internalized a disposition to assent to the proposition that 12 times 12 is 144 or to answer "144" when asked what 12 times 12 is. Such mental *habitus* are present in me even when I am thinking of something else. Yet mental *habitus* are not pure potentialities for Ockham. They are real qualities of the mind, just like the mental acts that they stem from and the mental acts that they are dispositions for. When describing the inner realm, Ockham's main focus is usually on acts, and so will ours be in this section, but let us keep in mind that mental life includes *habitus* as well for him. This will be especially relevant when we discuss knowledge in the last part of the chapter.

Although sensory perception is an indispensable component of human cognition for Ockham, as it is for Aristotle, he does not have much to say about it, and I too will mostly leave it aside. Our main interest will be on *intellectual* cognition. Cognition, admittedly, is not the sole function of the human intellect for Ockham. As a substantial form, the intellect is capable of various sorts of acts, he thinks, not all of which are cognitive acts. Acts of will—or "volitions" (*volitiones*)—are qualities of the intellectual part of the soul, too. It is one of Ockham's distinctive theses that there is no real distinction between intellect and will in a human person. The very same substantial form is called "intellect" when we want to stress its capacity for intellectual acts, and it is called "will" when its capacity for volitional acts is what matters.[3] Interesting as it is, however, Ockham's theory of volitions will not be discussed here.[4] We will restrict ourselves to intellectual cognitive acts.

These are of various kinds. First, Ockham distinguishes between apprehensive and judicative acts.[5] Intellectual apprehensive acts occur when something is actually grasped by the intellect, whether it is an external object, a concept, or a mental proposition. Judicative acts, on

---

[3] See *Rep.* II, q. 20, *OTh* V: 425–447: "Are memory, intellect, and will really distinct faculties?" (my transl.).
[4] More on Ockham's view on volitions in Panaccio 2012b.
[5] *Ord.*, Prol., q. 1, *OTh* I: 16 (transl. Boehner 1990: 18).

the other hand, have to do with propositions alone. They occur when the mind not merely apprehends a certain proposition, but also takes a stand with respect to its truth-value, either assenting to the proposition, doubting it, or dissenting from it.

Another important distinction that Ockham draws is between two kinds of simple apprehensive acts: intuitive and abstractive cognitions.[6] Intuitive acts are those non-propositional apprehensions on the basis of which the intellect can immediately and evidently assent to a true contingent proposition about the world, for example, that this thing here exists, that it is white, etc. Abstractive apprehensions, by contrast, are the intellectual acts that do not allow for such immediate assent: I can think of many things without thereby immediately knowing that such things presently exist, what color they are, where they are located, and so on.[7] Intuitive cognitions are the most basic kind of cognitive acts for Ockham, and I will first expound his views on the matter. I will then explain how natural kind concepts are abstracted for him; I will discuss the case of connotative concepts; and I will present his conception of judicative acts—or judgements.

Intuition

The cognitive contact with individual things is secured by intuitive acts in Ockham's theory. He acknowledges both sensory and intellectual intuitive cognitions. In normal situations, when an external thing is appropriately located with respect to us, we have a sensory grasp of it through sight, hearing, touch, smell or taste. This is the sensory intuitive act. This act is required for the intellect to grasp in turn the very same external object by a somewhat similar but different cognitive act: the intellectual intuitive cognition.[8] This postulation of two distinct intuitive cognitions, one sensory and one intellectual, has often been criticized as superfluous both by Ockham's contemporaries and

---

[6] *Ord.*, Prol., q. 1, *OTh* I: 30–47 (partial transl. Boehner 1990: 18–25), *Rep.* II, q. 13, *OTh* V: 256–261, *Quodl.* V, 5, *OTh* IX: 495–500 (transl. Freddoso 1991: 413–417).

[7] On the Ockhamist distinction between intuitive and abstractive cognitions, see Adams 1987: 501–550, Panaccio 2004: 5–20.

[8] See *Ord.*, Prol., q. 1, *OTh* I: 27.

by modern commentators,[9] but Ockham deems it necessary because of his view on the plurality of substantial forms in human beings. His point is that an act of the sensory part of the mind cannot suffice to cause an assent in the intellectual part,[10] let alone an *evident* assent. Experience shows, however, that we do evidently cognize certain contingent propositions such as that this thing here exists, that it is white, etc. Evident cognition for Ockham is a propositional assent that can be sufficiently caused by the more elementary cognitions that are parts of this proposition.[11] But a sensory act, he reasons, cannot be part of a proposition within the intellect, since it has a different substantial form as its substratum. The intellectual intuitive act, by contrast, can occur as an internal component of the mental proposition that it causes an assent to. When based on the direct apprehension of a thing, my propositional thought that this thing here is white has this very intellectual apprehensive act as its logical subject. The intuitive grasping of the thing by the intellect is the mental counterpart of the spoken demonstrative phrase "this thing here."[12]

When dealing with material objects, the normal process is thus the following for Ockham. As we come to be appropriately located with respect to some object, this object first causes a perceptual grasping in the sensory part of our mind: the sensory intuitive act. This act is immediately followed by an apprehension of the very same object by the intellect: the intellectual intuitive act. And this intellectual intuition in turn causes our assent to a number of true contingent mental propositions of which it is itself the logical subject, such as "this exists," "this is white," etc. All of these—the sensory intuition, the intellectual intuition, the mental proposition, and the act of assent—are mental qualities. And they are distinct from one another. It must be particularly stressed that neither the sensory nor the intellectual intuitive acts have any propositional content according to Ockham. We do not see or intuit *that* so and so. What we intuitively apprehend are singular substances or qualities. The mental proposition and the assent come

---

[9] See, e.g., Stump 1999: 194: "On Ockham's account, there is an odd doubling of cognition."
[10] See, e.g., *Quodl.* I, 15, *OTh* IX: 84 (transl. Freddoso and Kelley 1991: 73).
[11] *Ord.*, Prol., q. 1, *OTh* I: 5–6.
[12] See Panaccio 2014: especially 64–67.

afterwards and involve further mental qualities that are not themselves intuitive acts, such as the general concept "white," the predicative act of joining this predicate with the relevant intuitive apprehension, and the judicative act of assenting to the resulting proposition.

While there is no cognitive access to external material objects without the mediation of a sensory intuitive act in this world, no sensory perception is required, Ockham thinks, for reflectively apprehending our own intellectual and volitional acts.[13] Intellectual intuition suffices in such cases. If I have a thought or a volition, I can apprehend this thought or volition by means of a second-order reflective act of purely intellectual intuition. What happens then is that I reflectively grasp the first-order thought or volition, and this reflective intellectual grasping causes in me an evident assent to certain true contingent second-order propositions about myself, such as "I am presently thinking" or "I am presently willing." Long before René Descartes, this is how Ockham accounts for the evidence of the proposition "I am thinking" ("*ego intelligo*" in his case rather than "*cogito*"). No infinity of mental acts ensues, since we cannot as a matter of human limitation pile up more than two or three such reflective acts upon one another, Ockham thinks. A human being, he surmises, can intuitively grasp one of her own acts of thought, and then maybe intuitively grasp this second-order intuitive grasping by means of a third-order intuitive act, but the human mind being what it is, it cannot in practice go on much further along this line.[14]

Another remarkable thesis that Ockham holds about intuitive acts is that God can supernaturally cause in us the intuitive cognition of a *non-existent* object. God can produce in a prophet, for example, an intuitive apprehension of a temple or of a calamity that does not presently exist and maybe will never exist.[15] This is not naturally possible, though. In the natural world, the actual presence of the object is

---

[13] *Ord.*, Prol., q. 1, *OTh* I: 39–44.

[14] *Quodl.* I, 14, *OTh* IX: 78–82: "Does our intellect know its own acts intuitively in this life?" (transl. Freddoso and Kelley 1991: 68), and *Quodl.* II, 12, *OTh* IX: 166–167 (transl. Freddoso and Kelley 1991: 140–141), where Ockham confesses that he simply does not know how many reflective acts can pile up in the human mind in this way.

[15] *Ord.*, Prol., q. 1, *OTh* I: 38–39, *Rep.* II, q. 13, *OTh* V: 259–261, *Quodl.* V, 5, *OTh* IX: 496 (transl. Freddoso 1991: 414).

required for an intuitive act to occur. Naturally induced hallucinations, however strong they are, are not intuitive acts for Ockham, precisely because they are not brought about by the real presence of the object and are thus naturally delusive. "[T]he intuitive cognition of a thing," Ockham writes, "is this cognition in virtue of which it can be *known* whether the thing exists or not."[16] Yet since the intuitive act is a real thing—a quality, as we have seen—and it is really distinct from its object, God can supernaturally keep the intuitive act in existence when the object is destroyed. This is an instance of Ockham's separability principle: if two things are distinct from each other, there is a metaphysically possible world where one of them exists but not the other.[17] What is striking in Ockham's treatment of such cases is that the intellect, according to him, will thereby *correctly* judge that the object in question does *not* exist. Insofar as the prophet is endowed by God with an intuitive cognition of a non-existent temple, he is not deceived into thinking that this temple actually exists. Intuitive cognition is basically truthful for Ockham: "In no way does it lead the intellect in error," he says.[18] Once it exists in the mind, intuitive cognition, whether naturally or supernaturally caused, triggers a *reliable* cognitive process. This is not to say that God could not deceive us. He could directly produce in me false judgements, as well as completely misleading appearances or hallucinations. But this would not be by means of intuitive cognitions.[19] Although intuitive cognitions are usually quite recognizable in normal experience, their most distinctive characteristic lies not in how they subjectively feel (we might be deluded in this respect), but in their objective reliability, their capacity to bring about true contingent judgements. What matters to Ockham is that the most basic cognitive process that human beings are naturally capable of is an epistemically reliable one.[20]

[16] *Ord.*, Prol., q. 1, *OTh* I: 31 (my transl. with my italics). In the lines that follow this passage, Ockham admits that an intuitive cognition might occur in circumstances that do not allow it to bring about very precise true judgements about its object—if the latter is too far, for example, or if the in-between air is blurred. But insofar as a judgement is directly caused by an intuitive act, it will be true even if quite general sometimes (e.g., "something is moving there" or "there is an animal in the far distance").
[17] See above, pp. 33–35.
[18] *Rep.* II, q. 13, *OTh* V: 287 (my transl.).
[19] *Quodl.* V, 5, *OTh* IX: 498–500 (transl. Freddoso 1991: 415–417).
[20] See Panaccio and Piché 2010.

What makes this process epistemically reliable is that it is a *causal* process. Intuitive cognitions constitute a natural kind for Ockham, and they are governed by causal regularities. In the natural world, intuitive cognitions, whether sensory or intellectual, are caused by their objects and they in turn cause the intellect to assent to certain *true* contingent propositions about these objects (provided that these propositions are formed in the mind).[21] Indeed, the object of an intuitive act is the thing that naturally causes it for Ockham: "It is not because of a likeness that an intuitive cognition [. . .] is called a proper cognition of a singular thing [. . .]," he writes, "but only because of causality, nor can any other reason be given."[22] Suppose there are two very similar objects in my immediate environment, he explains. An angel who looks into my mind could not know which of the two objects I am presently intuiting unless he knew which one caused this particular intuitive act of mine.[23] Ockham's theory of intuitive cognition can thus be labeled as *externalist*. Externalism about mental content in recent philosophy is the view according to which "the contents of at least some mental states are not solely determined by occurrences falling within the biological boundaries of that individual that has them."[24] This is precisely what we find in Ockham's conception of intuitive cognition. The object of such a cognition is not fixed by the internal features of the intuitive act but by the relation of this particular act to the external object that naturally caused it. If the intuitive act is supernaturally caused by God alone, as Ockham admits that it can be, its object, he explains, is the one thing that *would* have caused it if it had been naturally caused. The intuitive apprehension of a non-existent temple by a prophet is a singular cognition of the particular temple that would have caused this very intuitive act if the latter had been naturally caused.[25] Even in such

---

[21] The formation of the contingent proposition in question is not automatically caused by the intuitive cognition, according to Ockham (*Quaest. var.* 5, *OTh* VIII: 170). His idea is that *if* it is formed, the intuitive act causes an immediate assent to it.

[22] *Quodl.* I, 13, *OTh* IX: 76 (transl. Freddoso and Kelley 1991: 66, with punctuation slightly amended).

[23] *Rep.* II, q. 16, *OTh* V: 378–379.

[24] Rowlands, Lau, and Deutsh 2020.

[25] See *Rep.* II, q. 13, *OTh* V: 287–291. This presupposes, as Ockham readily acknowledges, that each singular effect can only be naturally caused by a certain singular cause in the natural order that prevails in our world. A given heat trope cannot naturally be caused by just any fire; see *Quodl.* I, 13, *OTh* IX: 76: "[. . .] if [something] is caused

cases, then, the object of the intuitive act is fixed by an external relation of natural causality, albeit one that holds in nearby naturally possible worlds rather than in the actual one.[26]

Abstraction

The phrase "abstractive cognition," Ockham says, has two different senses according to whether we speak of abstraction with respect to singularity or abstraction with respect to existence and other contingent features.[27] The latter is the meaning he takes to be relevant when distinguishing abstractive from intuitive cognition. In this sense, an abstractive cognition of a certain object is one that does not suffice for us to evidently know any present-tense contingent proposition about this object. In natural circumstances, for example, my thinking of Mary in her absence does not allow me to evidently know whether she presently exists or not, or whether she is presently walking or not. Taken in this sense, abstractive cognition is a diversified category. It includes, for instance, the memories I have of a certain object. If I saw Mary an hour ago, I can vividly remember her, and this "recordative cognition" can suffice to make me give my assent to the true proposition that Mary was here just a short time ago or that she was walking and so on. Yet insofar as this simple act of apprehension does not allow me to evidently know that Mary presently exists or that she is presently walking or sitting, etc., it is not an intuitive cognition strictly speaking.

naturally, then it is caused by the one and not by the other, *and is not able to be caused by the other*" (transl. Freddoso and Kelley 1991: 66; my italics).

[26] See Panaccio 2015b. There is an ongoing discussion about the externalist interpretation of Ockham's theory of intuitive cognition. This interpretation is shared by several Ockham commentators (e.g., Normore 2003, King 2015), but it has been forcefully challenged by Susan Brower-Toland (2007, 2017). What is at stake is whether causation really is an external relation for Ockham. The question in the end boils down to this: are alternate natural causal orders metaphysically possible, according to Ockham? Could a given heat trope, for example, be naturally caused in some faraway possible world by a different fire than the only one that it can be caused by in *our* natural order? I think that Ockham is strongly committed to answer this question affirmatively and that causation, consequently, is an external relation for him; see, e.g., *Tract. de corp. Christi* 7, *OTh* X: 103: "God could change the total order of natural causes" (my transl.).

[27] *Ord.*, Prol., q. 1, *OTh* I: 30–31.

Since it nevertheless provides me with some contingent knowledge, albeit about the past, Ockham calls it an "imperfect intuitive cognition."[28] But imperfect intuitive cognitions, he adds, are in fact a kind of abstractive cognition, precisely because they do not suffice to cause evident knowledge about what is presently the case or not.

In Ockham's mature theory, general concepts constitute the most salient sort of abstractive cognitions. He had previously thought of concepts as purely ideal entities—or *ficta*—that would serve as objects for abstractive acts, but he came to realize that they could be identified with the abstractive acts themselves, seen as real qualities of the mind.[29] What happens when I form the general concept of "whale," say, is that a mental quality that represents whales occurs in my intellect. This conceptual act, however, does not suffice for me to evidently know that any whale presently exists. It is, therefore, an abstractive cognition in Ockham's sense. Knowledge usually involves at least one such general concept. Even the knowledge of atomic singular propositions such as "this exists" or "this is white," which can be brought about by intuitive cognitions in appropriate circumstances, involve general concepts such as the concept of "existing" or the concept of "white." The intuitive cognition in these cases is the subject of the known proposition, as we have seen, but a predicate is also needed, and this predicate will normally be a general concept or include one.[30] In order to understand how human knowledge is possible for Ockham, we must explain how we acquire general concepts in his view even though there are no universals outside of thought and language.

The natural process of concept acquisition, as Ockham describes it, always starts with intuitive cognitions of singular objects.[31] The idea is that intellectual intuitive cognitions immediately cause the formation

---

[28] *Rep.* II, q. 13, *OTh* V: 261–262.

[29] For references, see above, chapter 3, n. 5.

[30] The sole exception is a mental proposition in which both the subject and the predicate are intuitive cognitions, the negative thought, for example, that *this* here is not *that*. Ockham does accept the possibility of such thoughts (see, e.g., *Ord.*, Prol. q. 1, *OTh* I: 49), but they cannot constitute, obviously, the whole of human knowledge. Let me remark, by the way, that the mental copula is seen by Ockham as a syncategorematic unit rather than as a general concept; it should not be identified, then, with the general concept of "being" or "existing."

[31] See, e.g., Schierbaum 2014: 152–174.

of a number of simple abstractive acts in the mind. On Ockham's mature theory, the first abstractive cognitions that are thus formed are always *general* concepts. No abstractive representation is both simple and singular.[32] The reason for this is that an abstractive cognition, according to him, represents its object in virtue of some sort of resemblance that it has with it. If so, however, the abstractive cognition will equally resemble any object that maximally resembles the intuited one, and it will therefore represent all of these as well. Admittedly, the intentional resemblance that Ockham postulates between abstractive acts and their objects is rather peculiar—more will be said about it in the section on "Natural signs" later in the present chapter—but he obviously takes it to be important in his account of general cognition.

Strikingly enough, Ockham thinks that the concept of "being," which is the most general categorematic concept of all, is always one of the abstractive representations that are caused by an intuitive act.[33] All intuitive acts naturally bring along with them the general idea of existence. This explains why it is that they determine the intellect to assent to the singular proposition that this thing here *exists*. In most cases, more limited general concepts are also simultaneously produced, Ockham thinks. In particular, when the conditions of perceptual apprehension are optimal, the intuitive act induces in the intellect the most specific natural kind concept that the intuited object falls under. If I see a horse, for example, and the conditions of observation are favorable, the specific concept of "horse" is naturally produced in me. Indeed, Ockham holds that a single intuitive encounter suffices for the intellect to acquire such maximally specific concepts.[34] This must be for the same reason as before: if the abstractive cognition that is produced in me when I first see a horse in favorable conditions of observation resembles this horse in some way, it will equally resemble everything else that *maximally* resembles this particular horse. That

---

[32] See *Quodl.* I, 13, *OTh* IX: 77 (transl. Freddoso and Kelley 1991: 67) and *Quodl.* V, 7, *OTh* IX: 506 (transl. Freddoso 1991: 422–423). Ockham admits, however, that we can form a *complex* abstractive representation of a determinate singular thing by combining several general concepts.
[33] *Quodl.* I, 13, *OTh* IX: 78 (transl. Freddoso and Kelley 1991: 68).
[34] *Quodl.* IV, 17, *OTh* IX: 385: "[. . .] the concept of the species can be abstracted from a single individual" (transl. Freddoso and Kelley 1991: 317).

would be all horses for Ockham, and nothing else. The original acquisition of a genus concept, on the other hand, normally requires two or more intuitive encounters.[35] In order to acquire the generic concept of "animal," intuitive acquaintances with animals of various species are needed. The point here is that a generic concept resembles its objects to a lesser degree than more specific concepts do, and it will consequently represent more beings. Intentional resemblance comes in degrees for Ockham and can thus determine different degrees of representational generality.

We can now understand how it is that intuitive cognition inclines the mind to give its assent to certain true singular propositions with natural kind concepts as their predicates. On its very first intuitive encounter with an individual of a certain kind, the intellect is naturally caused to form a general concept that has in its extension all the individuals that are maximally similar to this one, that is, all those that belong to the same ultimate species. The intellect is thus naturally prompted to truly judge that this individual falls under that concept, that this thing here, for example, is a horse. As it successively encounters individuals of other species, the intellect acquires more and more general natural kind concepts and is similarly prompted on each particular occasion to truly judge that this thing that the intellect is presently intuiting falls under the newly acquired generic concept. Once a specific or a generic natural kind concept has thus been produced, a corresponding disposition (*habitus*) is left in the mind and the concept can be re-activated when the intellect next encounters an individual of the same natural kind as the original exemplar. The intellect, of course, could in principle be mistaken if the wrong natural kind concept is reactivated, but Ockham is confident that our inclinations to re-apply natural kind concepts are reliable under favorable conditions. Having internalized the concept of "horse" or the concept of "animal," for example, I can usually correctly judge whether something that I intuitively apprehend under optimal conditions is a horse or not, and whether it is an animal or not.

---

[35] *Quodl.* I, 13, *OTh* IX: 77: "[. . .] the concept of a genus is never abstracted from [just] one individual" (transl. Freddoso and Kelley 1991: 67).

Connotative concepts

Natural kind concepts in Ockham's view are the "absolute" terms of our mental language.[36] But how are *connotative* concepts acquired? The question is crucial for Ockham's nominalism, since all relational and all quantitative terms are connotative for him, as we have seen. How is it, then, that we can acquire concepts that correspond to such terms if there are no relations out there to be intuited, and no distinct quantitative entities, either?

An intriguing interpretation that was proposed a few decades ago by a number of prominent Ockham scholars is that all connotative terms should be reducible to complex combinations of absolute and syncategorematic terms in Ockham's mental language.[37] The spoken connotative term "white," for example, might be complexly represented in the mind as "a substance with a whiteness," where the concepts "substance" and "whiteness" are absolute mental terms linked to each other by a syncategorematic mental unit corresponding to "with." Only the acquisition of simple absolute concepts, then, would need to be accounted for along with the presence of certain basic syncategorematic connectors in the mind. No additional explanation would be needed for connotative concepts. A close examination of Ockham's texts shows, however, that he did accept simple connotative concepts in the human mind. It is certainly true that many connotative words in our conventional languages must correspond to complex combinations of simpler concepts for him—probably most of them, I would say. A word such as "foal," for example, might be represented in the mind as "young horse." "Young," however, is still a connotative term. It may be further reducible to some combination of simpler concepts, but Ockham does not hold that this reductive process should ultimately result in the elimination of all simple connotative concepts, nor is he committed to such a strong claim.[38]

Quite to the contrary, he thinks that if two things are spatially close to one another or otherwise related in some observable way, an intuitive

---

[36] On the idea of absolute term, see above, pp. 103–105.
[37] See, e.g., Spade 1975, Normore 1990.
[38] The case is argued for in detail in Panaccio 2004: 63–118.

grasp of these two things together suffices to make it evidently known that they are close to each other or that one of them is taller than the other, etc.[39] Certain simple relational concepts, then, such as "being spatially close to" or "being taller than," must be immediately acquired on the basis of intuitive cognition, just as natural kind concepts are. Otherwise, it would be impossible for us to even form the mental propositions that these things are close to one another or that this thing is taller than that other one. Yet, the intuitive cognitions that bring about the formation of these simple relational concepts do not have special relational entities as their objects. The point is that in normal situations a human person intuitively grasps several substances or qualities at once. She then acquires not only the natural kind concepts that each of these substances and qualities falls under, but some general relational concepts as well, that correspond to how they are perceivably related to one another in her immediate environment. And relational concepts are all connotative terms, as we have seen.

Exactly which connotative concepts would be acquired in this way is not something Ockham is explicit about, but some of his examples provide good clues for reconstructing his view. He writes, for instance, that "if Socrates really is white, this cognition of Socrates and of his whiteness in virtue of which it can evidently be known that Socrates is white is called an intuitive cognition."[40] This suggests that the simultaneous intuitive grasping of Socrates and his whiteness together suffices to cause the formation of the connotative concept "white." For Ockham, this concept primarily refers to the substances in which a whiteness inheres—such as Socrates in the chosen example—and secondarily refers to (or connotes) their whitenesses. The connotative concept "white" would thus be acquired on our very first intuitive encounter with a white thing, just as the specific concept "horse" is acquired on our first intuitive encounter with a horse. This account presupposes that the underlying substance and its whiteness are both simultaneously apprehended by the intellect. External material substances are never cognized without some accidents or other for Ockham, but this does not mean that material substances are not intuited at all. On the

---

[39] *Ord.*, Prol., q. 1, *OTh* I: 31–32.
[40] *Ord.*, Prol., q. 1, *OTh* I: 31 (my transl.).

contrary, Ockham's account of the acquisition of natural kind concepts such as "horse," as described in the previous section, requires that we do have intuitive apprehensions of horses, and horses are substances. The natural process that leads to the singular apprehension of a material substance is not an inferential one. We do not infer the presence of the substance from that of its qualities. The substance itself has a causal action on the cognizer's mind and what it thus naturally causes is an intuitive cognition. This intuitive cognition, then, has this very substance as its object. The intuitive apprehension of a material substance, however, is always accompanied by an intuitive grasping of some of its qualities, its whiteness for example, or its heat.[41] The typical situation, then, is that the intellect simultaneously intuits a substance and a quality together. While each of them causes the formation of some absolute concept, such as the absolute substantial concept of "horse" and the absolute qualitative concept of "whiteness," they also work in conjunction with one another to bring about the natural formation of certain connotative concepts, such as "white," "warm," etc.

Although they are connotative, neither "white" nor "warm" are relational concepts for Ockham, but his account of the natural acquisition of relational concepts must be very similar to what was just described: "Intuitive cognition," he writes, "is such that [. . .] when something is spatially distant from something else or otherwise related with something else, it is known right away in virtue of this simple cognition of these things [. . .] whether they are spatially distant from one another or not, etc."[42] This strongly suggests that the simple relational concept of "being spatially distant" is acquired on the basis of the joint intuitive apprehension of several things that are spatially distant from one another, just as the simple concept "white" is acquired on the basis of the joint intuitive apprehension of a substance and its whiteness. Intuitive encounters, therefore, must cause in the human intellect the formation of a number of primitive relational concepts, just as they cause the formation of certain primitive absolute (or natural kind) concepts such as "horse" or "whiteness" and the formation of

---

[41] Ockham says that intuited qualities are cognized *in se*, while the substances are cognized *in alio* (i.e., through the qualities); see on this Robert 2017.
[42] *Ord.*, Prol, q. 1, *OTh* I: 31 (my transl.).

certain primitive non-relational connotative concepts such as "white." In all cases, the intuited objects are singular substances and singular qualities, but when jointly intuited, several of them together cause the formation of simple connotative concepts, including certain basic relational ones such as the concept of being spatially distant.

The same account must hold for basic quantitative concepts. Relational spatial concepts such as "longer than," "wider than," "higher than," and "in between" might constitute the primitive basis for our intellectual representation of length, width, and height. And our most basic numerical concepts, such as "two," "three," and "four" might be directly caused by our intuitive grasping of two, three, or four things together. The rest of our geometric and arithmetic concepts would then be derivatively built as complex combinations of these and other basic concepts. The matter is not fully developed by Ockham, to be sure, but he clearly points in this direction. In a world where only substances and qualities exist, certain elementary relational and quantitative concepts can be naturally caused in the mind by the joint intuitive grasping of several individuals at once that collectively serve as exemplars for bringing similarly arranged groups under general conceptual representations.

Judgement

Once a general concept is thus acquired, the intellect can combine it with one or more intuitive cognitions to form a singular mental proposition corresponding, for example, to "This is a horse," "This is taller than that," or "These things are three." Or it can combine one general concept with another to form a general mental proposition, such as "some horses are white" or "all horses are animals." In Ockham's former theory, mental propositions, like concepts, were taken to be *ficta*, a sort of purely ideal entity that were the *objects* of apprehensive acts. In his mature theory, by contrast, mental propositions are identified with the cognitive acts by which they are formed. The formation of a mental proposition on this approach is just the proposition itself; there is no difference between the mental proposition and its apprehension.[43]

---

[43] *Quodl.* V, 6, *OTh* IX: 501 (transl. Freddoso 1991: 418). Ockham adds, however, that once it is formed, a mental propositional act can become the object of a second-order act

Propositional apprehensions, however, are not yet judgements. A judicative act is also needed.[44] It can be an act of assent, dissent, or doubt, but in all cases the judicative act is an additional mental quality that really differs from the proposition that is assented to, dissented from, or doubted. This distinction closely corresponds to one that is widely in use in today's philosophy of mind and language—and frequently associated with Frege—between the content of a thought and the judgemental force that accompanies it in a given cognizer.[45] The distinctive feature of Ockham's approach is that the judicative and the propositional act are taken to be distinct mental qualities of singular minds. Ockham indeed has no qualms about the possibility of several acts of different sorts being simultaneously present in the same individual intellect.[46]

The exact relation between the act of judgement and the corresponding proposition is somewhat complicated in Ockham's mature theory because of a distinction he draws between two sorts of assents.[47] The first one is the unreflective assent of the ordinary person (*laicus*) in daily life. In this case, the proposition that is assented to is formed in the mind—and therefore apprehended insofar as the formation of a mental proposition can be said to be an apprehension of this proposition, as we just saw—but it is not the object of a *reflective* apprehension. The example Ockham gives is that of an ordinary person who mentally assents to the proposition that a rock is not a donkey without even perceiving that she is thinking it. The judicative act of assent, then, is something like a mental nod of approval that accompanies the

---

of apprehension. The later apprehensive act, then, differs from the original one as a reflective act differs from its mental object. On Ockham's conception of reflective acts, see *Quodl.* II, 12, *OTh* IX: 165–167 (transl. Freddoso and Kelley 139–141).

[44] *Ord.*, Prol., q. 1, *OTh* I: 16–17.
[45] See, e.g., Frege 1918: "Consequently we distinguish: (1) the grasp of a thought—thinking; (2) the acknowledgement of the truth of a thought—the act of judgement [...]". Frege adds in a footnote: "It seems to me that thought and judgement have not been hitherto adequately distinguished" (transl. Geach and Stoothof 1984: 355).
[46] *Ord.*, Prol., q. 1, *OTh* I: 19. This was a matter of debate in the early fourteenth century; see Friedman 2009.
[47] *Quodl.* III, 8, *OTh* IX: 232–237 (transl. Freddoso and Kelley 1991: 196–199) and *Quodl.* IV, 16, *OTh* IX: 376–380 (transl. Freddoso and Kelley 1991: 310–313). Ockham speaks only of assents in these passages, but what he says there must hold as well for judicative acts of dissent and doubting; see on this Schierbaum 2014: 190–202.

unreflective formation of the proposition. The second sort of assent, by contrast, presupposes a reflective apprehension. A philosopher, most notably, will usually not be content with forming a certain proposition and unreflectively assenting to it. She will typically form a second-order act of reflection about this proposition, and her assent—if she gives it—will also be a reflective act, albeit a judicative one. It will not only accompany the formation of the proposition, but it will take this very proposition as its object. In the unreflective case, we can say, according to Ockham, that the ordinary person thinks that a rock is not a donkey, but the proposition that a rock is not a donkey should not be considered as the object of the ordinary person's judicative act. Her judgement is about rocks and donkeys, while the philosopher's reflective assent is about a proposition. The difference between the reflective and the unreflective assent, mind you, lies not in the proposition that is assented to. The philosopher who reflectively assents to "A human being is an animal" is not thereby assenting to a second-order proposition such as "'A human being is an animal' is true"; he is giving his assent "to the proposition 'A human being is an animal' by itself and absolutely", Ockham says.[48] While unreflective assent needs no second-order cognitive act at all, reflective assent is a second-order act of approval about a first-order proposition, and it always presupposes a second-order apprehension of that very same proposition.

Human cognition, in short, involves five different kinds of intellectual acts for Ockham:

- intuitive acts, the objects of which are singular substances or singular qualities;
- abstractive acts, especially concepts, whether absolute or connotative, that are acquired on the basis of intuitive acts by a natural process;
- syncategorematic acts, that serve to connect the other cognitions together into logically structured units;[49]

---

[48] *Quodl.* IV, 16, *OTh* IX: 377 (transl. Freddoso and Kelley 1991: 311). I must disagree on this with the interpretation proposed by Brower-Toland 2007b; for a detailed discussion, see Panaccio 2009.

[49] More about mental syncategoremata in the next section.

- propositional acts, that is, true or false combinations of items from the previous three categories;
- judicative acts, that is, acts of assent, dissent, or doubt that are associated either reflectively or unreflectively with one or more propositional acts.

Intuitive cognitions, of course, cannot be re-activated at will since, at least in the natural course, the presence of the object is needed for them to occur. But the cognitive acts of the other four categories all leave certain dispositions or *habitus* in the mind, according to Ockham, and these allow the cognizer to reproduce similar acts when she so wishes. Knowledge as Ockham conceives of it is made up of such cognitive dispositions. Before discussing which dispositions those would be, we need to say more about the structure and content of the mental propositions that can be known.

Mental language

The idea that there are propositions in the mind in addition to simple concepts was a common one in medieval Aristotelianism. Ockham's originality was to systematically conceive of these mental propositions on the model of spoken and written sentences.[50] For one thing, he thinks of mental propositions as being really composed of concepts, just as linguistic sentences are really composed of simple words.[51] His main innovation in the matter is to have systematically transposed the theoretical tools of medieval grammar and semantics to the fine-grained analysis of inner thought. This is not to say that he takes human

---

[50] On Ockham's idea of mental language (*oratio mentalis*), see in particular Panaccio 1999, 2017a: 179–197 and 247–258, Lenz 2003, Schierbaum 2014, Pelletier and Roques 2017.

[51] By contrast, some medieval authors, such as Gregory of Rimini, saw mental propositions as simple units (see, e.g., Ashworth 1981, Maierù 2004). Ockham did admit that mental propositions could sometimes be abbreviated as simple units in the mind (e.g., in *Quaest. in libr. Phys.* 6, *OPh* VI: 409–410), but his detailed analysis of mental language in the *Summa logicae* and the *Quodlibetal Questions* requires that they would normally be complex items (e.g., in *Quodl.* III, 12: "Is a mental proposition composed of things or of concepts?" [transl. Freddoso and Kelley 1991: 206]); see on this Panaccio 2017a: 250–252.

thought to be usually conducted in some conventional language like Latin, Greek, or English. On the contrary, in his view outwardly expressed linguistic sentences normally presuppose inner sequences of mental units that "belong to no language," as Augustine said.[52] Or at least to no conventional language. This approach is strikingly similar to modern "language of thought" theories such as Jerry Fodor's:[53] the basic medium of intellectual thought is a kind of mental language for Ockham. This language of thought has a *grammatical structure*, as we will now see in some detail; it is made up of signs, albeit *natural signs* rather than conventional ones, and it includes *syncategorematic terms* that play a decisive role in determining the truth-conditions of mental propositions.

Grammar

Ockham explicitly raises the question of which grammatical categories are suitable for the analysis of human mental language.[54] He starts this inquiry with a list of categories that were commonly used in medieval grammar—for the study of Latin in particular—and wonders which of them can be transposed to the realm of concepts.[55] This includes an enumeration of the "parts of speech" (names, verbs, pronouns, participles, adverbs, conjunctions, and prepositions) as well as an inventory of the "accidents" of names (such as genus, number, and case) and the accidents of verbs (such as mood, tense, and conjugation). The criterion Ockham invokes is semantic relevance. Mental language, he surmises, must have at least as much expressive power as any conventional language: anything that can be outwardly said can be thought by the intellect. Therefore, if a grammatical distinction sometimes makes a difference in signification or in truth-value, it must be present

---

[52] *SL* I, 1; *OPh* I: 7 (transl. Loux 1974: 49). Ockham's reference is to Augustine, *On the Trinity* XV, 10, 19.

[53] See Fodor 1975, 1987, 2008, Rescoria 2019.

[54] *SL* I, 3, *OPh* I: 11–14 (transl. Loux 1974: 52–54), *Quodl.* V, 8, *OTh* IX: 508–513 (transl. Freddoso 1991: 424–429).

[55] The list of categories that Ockham uses is borrowed from the *Ars Minor*, a short introductory grammatical treatise written in the 4th century A.D. by the Latin grammarian Donatus (a critical edition of this text is found in Holtz 1981: 585–602).

in mental language somehow. Grammatical distinctions that do not make any such difference need not be postulated in the language of thought.

Ockham's conclusions are: (1) that "mental concepts include names, verbs, adverbs, conjunctions, and prepositions," since all five of these categories are required for "signification or expressiveness (*expressio*)";[56] (2) that mental names can have number (singular or plural), case (nominative, genitive, etc.), and degree of comparison (for example, comparative or superlative); and (3) that mental verbs can have mood (indicative, subjunctive, etc.), voice (for example, active or passive), as well as number, tense, and person. The distinction between singular and plural, for example, is required among both mental names and mental verbs, since the mental propositions that correspond to "a horse is running" and "horses are running" can have different truth-values. A variety of verbal moods is also necessary, to take just one more example, since propositions such as "this horse runs" and "this horse would run" can have different truth-values. And so on.

That the distinction of grammatical cases such as nominative, genitive, or dative should be present in Ockham's mental language is especially noteworthy. Peter Geach for one saw this as an indication that Ockham "merely transfers features of Latin grammar to Mental, and then regards this as explaining why such features occur in Latin."[57] Geach points out that "'The farmer has one donkey, which is white' and 'The farmer's one donkey is white' plainly both express the same judgment, although the cases of 'farmer' and 'donkey' are different in the two sentences."[58] Ockham's idea, however, is not that the grammar of mental propositions should exactly parallel that of the spoken and written sentences by which we express them. It is that *some* distinction corresponding to that of grammatical cases is needed if mental language is to have at least as much expressive power as conventional languages. When applied to concepts, distinctions of case are not to be thought of, of course, as a matter of inflectional morphology as one

---

[56] *Quodl.* V, 8, *OTh* IX: 509 (transl. Freddoso 1991: 425). Note that adjectives are counted as names in medieval grammar.
[57] Geach 1971: 102.
[58] Ibid.: 103.

finds in Latin or Greek. Ockham's approach must be understood as quite similar to that of the twentieth-century linguist Charles Fillmore, according to whom the notion of grammatical case "deserves a place in the base component of the grammar of every language."[59] The plurality of cases in such a view corresponds to a plurality of semantic roles that a noun can play within sentences with respect to a given verb or to another noun. Fillmore conjectures, for example, that the base component of all human languages includes an "agentive" case (who did it?), an "instrumental" case (with what instrument?), a "locative" case (where did it happen?), etc.[60] As for Ockham, he never tries to provide a definite list of mental grammatical cases, nor he is explicit about how such grammatical cases are realized in the mind (for all he says, they might be reducible to combinations of prepositions and nouns). His point is that mental language should somehow allow for the various semantic roles that correspond to grammatical cases in external languages.

Other grammatical features, by contrast, do not correspond to distinctions at the conceptual level according to Ockham, but were introduced in conventional idioms "for the embellishment of speech or something of that nature."[61] A salient example is grammatical gender. The grammar of Ockham's mental language makes no distinction between masculine and feminine. The masculine Latin word "*lapis*" and the feminine word "*petra*," he remarks in support of this point, are strictly synonymous with each other, and the substitution of one of these for the other in a sentence changes neither the sense nor the truth-value of the sentence. It might affect grammaticality, to be sure, but that would only be at the surface level.[62]

Similarly, no distinction should be postulated in mental language between verbs and participles according to Ockham, "since a verb is always equivalent in signification to, and synonymous with, the participle of the verb taken together with the verb 'is.'"[63] "A horse runs" is strictly equivalent in meaning and truth-value to "a horse is running."

---

[59] Fillmore 1968 (Fillmore 2003: 23).
[60] Fillmore 2003: 46.
[61] *SL* I, 3, *OPh* I: 11 (transl. Loux 1974: 52).
[62] *Quodl.* V, 8, *OTh* IX: 510–511 (transl. Freddoso 1991: 426–427).
[63] *Quodl.* V, 8, *OTh* IX: 512–513 (transl. Freddoso 1991: 428).

Only one of these two forms, therefore, is needed in the language of thought. Ockham does not specify which it is, but he would probably favor the copula-plus-participle form, since it more obviously fits what Ockham takes to be the most basic structure of elementary propositions, namely, the subject-copula-predicate structure. All verbs but copulas, then, should be reduced to participles in mental language as he conceives of it.

Ockham laconically raises two more problems about the grammatical structure of mental language and leaves them open: Does mental language include pronouns in addition to names?[64] And is there a distinction between proper and common names in mental language?[65] The two questions are related to one another and it is interesting to dwell on them for a moment in the light of what we established about Ockham's theory of cognitive acts. What corresponds to demonstrative pronouns in Ockham's mental language, as we have seen, are intuitive acts.[66] The subject of the mental proposition that corresponds to "this is a horse" is the very intuitive act by which a certain individual thing—a horse, presumably—is immediately apprehended by the mind. There is a clear-cut distinction, then, between such mental demonstratives and the abstractive acts that can also occur in mental propositions, such as the concept "horse" or the concept "white." Since there is no properly singular simple abstractive cognition in the intellect according to Ockham,[67] it follows that the only simple singular terms in his mental language are the intuitive acts that correspond to spoken demonstrative pronouns. Is there a distinction, then, between mental pronouns and mental names? Ockham's answer should be "Yes," insofar as mental demonstrative pronouns are identified with intuitive acts and mental names with abstractive acts. Is there a distinction between simple proper names and simple common names

---

[64] *SL* I, 3, *OPh* I: 11 (transl. Loux 1974: 53).

[65] *Quodl.* V, 8, *OTh* IX: 510 (transl. Freddoso 1991: 426), *SL* I, 3, *OPh* I: 13 (transl. Loux 1974: 53). In both passages, Ockham simply asks whether the grammatical accident of "quality" is present in mental language and leaves it at that. To understand what the question amounts to, one should know that the "quality" of a name in Donatus's grammar is its being proper or common.

[66] See above, pp. 144–145. Pronouns other than demonstratives should be discussed too, of course, but I will leave them aside here.

[67] See above, pp. 150–151.

among concepts? The answer should be "No": there are no simple singular abstractive concepts in Ockham's mental language, and hence no proper names if the latter are supposed to be singular abstractive concepts. It is no wonder that Ockham left these questions open in his two short discussions of the grammatical structure of mental language, since they involve complex considerations about intuitive and abstractive cognitions, but even a brief discussion of them as I have just sketched neatly illustrates how strongly Ockham's theory of cognitive acts and his theory of mental language are dependent on one another.

Natural signs

As Ockham's grammatical analysis shows, the distinction between categorematic and syncategorematic terms carries over to mental language.[68] Mental conjunctions and prepositions corresponding to "if," "and," "except", "insofar," etc., as well as some mental adverbs corresponding to "not," "very," etc., are syncategorematic units.[69] They do not refer to anything by themselves, yet they decisively contribute to the logical structure and truth-conditions of the mental propositions in which they occur. Mental names and participles, on the other hand, are categorematic terms. They determinately signify (or connote) certain things in the world. I will discuss mental *syncategoremata* in the next section. As to categorematic concepts, their main characteristic is that they are natural signs. We have seen earlier how such concepts are acquired by human minds according to Ockham.[70] What remains to be accounted for is how it is that these mental items are *signs* rather than non-representational mental states, and how it is that they naturally represent *certain individuals* rather than others.

---

[68] The distinction between categorematic and syncategorematic terms is introduced by Ockham in *SL* I, 4, *OPh* I: 15–16 (transl. Loux 1974: 55). He includes it among the logical distinctions that pertain both to spoken and mental language.

[69] Not all adverbs, however, are pure *syncategoremata* for Ockham, as some of them "signify determinately the very things that categorematic terms signify, although they signify them in a different mode of signification" (*SL* I, 4, *OPh* I: 16; transl. Loux 1974: 55). Think of "generously," for example, that refers somehow to generous people and acts of generosity.

[70] See above, pp. 149–156.

In the narrow sense that is relevant for logic, a "sign," Ockham explains, "is anything which brings something to mind and can supposit for that thing."[71] It follows that all signs in the relevant sense are signs of something—the things that they "bring to mind"—and that they can occur as subjects or predicates in a proposition, since only then is supposition possible.[72] Semantic atomism is not to be renounced for all that. Every categorematic concept must have a signification by itself before it is inserted in mental propositions, according to Ockham, just like every spoken name has a signification before it occurs in sentences. But for a mental unit to have a signification, it must be *capable* of being a subject or a predicate in mental propositions. Now, the distinctive feature of propositions is that they are true or false. A mental sign, then, is a functional unit in a wider intellectual system in which certain complex arrangements have a truth-value. Where there is no such system, nothing is a sign in the relevant sense. Should an isolated conceptual quality be supernaturally transferred to a rock (as must be possible by God's absolute power in Ockham's metaphysics), it would no longer be a sign. Categorematic concepts are signs insofar as they inhere in a mind that can combine several of them in true or false complex arrangements and that can orient itself in the world by assenting to or dissenting from these propositional arrangements.

This functionalist perspective helps to understand how it is that intuitive cognitions naturally bring about the formation of general concepts, as Ockham thinks they do. Suppose you see a poison ivy plant for the first time and touch it. It is surely useful to you to form a general mental sign on the basis of this single encounter that will represent for you every other individual poison ivy plant. You will thus be able to subscribe to a mental proposition such as "poison ivy is to be avoided," the subject term of which is a categorematic concept that signifies every individual that is of the same species as your original exemplar. Ockham's conjecture is that human beings are thus endowed with an innate capacity for naturally forming general mental signs on

---

[71] *SL* I, 1, *OPh* I: 9 (transl. Loux 1974: 50).
[72] See *SL* I, 63, *OPh* I: 193–195 (transl. Loux 1874: 188–189). For a detailed analysis of Ockham's notion of sign, see Panaccio 2004: 47–53.

the basis of a very limited number of intuitive encounters (as few as one in certain cases). This sounds plausible if we see concepts as having the function of helping us navigate through the world. Ockham's approach to mental language can be seen as a "teleosemantic" theory in today's sense, that is, an approach according to which "the contents of mental representations depend, at least in part, on functions, such as the functions of the systems that use or produce them."[73]

Ockham does not explicitly speak of "functions," but his conception of the mental does presuppose a teleological perspective. Every natural agent, he says, has "an end fixed in advance by God."[74] The human mind, in particular, is supposed to be endowed by the Creator with innate inclinations and capacities, all of which have a purpose. This is a theological notion to be sure, but if a mundane conception of function is acceptable, as modern proponents of teleosemantics think it is, the Ockhamist approach to natural signs is of philosophical interest independent of its theological background. Whether a naturalistic notion of function is legitimate or not is still widely debated in contemporary philosophy.[75]

The picture, then, is the following. By naturally causing the formation of general mental signs, intuitive cognitions make it possible for us to form propositional thoughts about all the individuals that are relevantly similar to the ones that caused these intuitive cognitions in the first place. As we saw earlier, such a thought might be about all the individuals that are of the same ultimate species as the original exemplars; or all the individuals of the same genus if enough relevant intuitive acts have occurred; or all the couples, the threesomes, or the foursomes that are related in the same way as the original exemplars if several of them are jointly intuited. But whatever the details are, the acquisition of general signs through a natural causal process is a necessary condition for the human intellect to operate. Some of the resulting thoughts might turn out to be false, of course, since human beings are fallible, but the function of the whole system is essentially to

---

[73] Neander and Schulte 2021. The teleosemantic approach to mental content is advocated in particular by Ruth Millikan (1984, 2000, 2004).

[74] *Quodl.* IV, 1, *OTh* IX: 298 (transl. Freddoso and Kelley 1991: 248).

[75] See, e.g., Ariew et al. 2004, Garson 2016, Colin and Neal 2020.

make true judgements possible. This is how human intellects distinctively get around in the world. They are complex functional systems, the basic components of which are naturally acquired from immediate experience and can be combined into propositional arrangements that are true or false according to what is the case with certain determinate individuals.

There is a problem, though. It would seem on this interpretation of Ockham's view that the significates of a general natural sign are determined by the causal action of the intuited objects. An intuitive cognition that was caused by a chickadee, for example, brings about the formation of a mental sign representing all chickadees. But in several passages Ockham insists that some sort of resemblance must hold between concepts and their significates. Each simple concept, he says, "is equally a likeness of, and equally represents, all exactly similar individuals."[76] And this is the reason why "no such cognition is proper to the singular thing."[77] Isn't it intentional resemblance, therefore, rather than causality, that determines which individuals a given concept naturally signifies? Ockham, unfortunately, does not discuss the point in any detail and never makes it clear what intentional resemblance amounts to in his view. In my understanding, the key to the enigma is that concepts have a recognitional function for Ockham. Our concept of "man," he says, is that "in accordance with which we can judge about anything whether it is a man or not."[78] To fulfill this function, the concept must provide some sort of recognitional schema that would normally fit all the individuals of the same species or of the same genus. As I see it, this kind of fit is what Ockham calls the "similitude" (*similitudo*) of the concept to what it represents.

How this intentional resemblance works exactly is left unexplained. An attractive idea might be that our concepts—at least our concepts of material objects—are associated somehow with a perceptual profile that might include a sketch for outward shape, sound, smell, taste, typical environment, or typical behavior.[79] Errors, however, must be

---

[76] *Quodl.* V, 7, *OTh* IX: 506 (transl. Freddoso 1991: 422–423).
[77] *Quodl.* I, 13, *OTh* IX: 74 (transl. Freddoso and Kelley 1991: 65).
[78] *Ord.*, dist. 2, q. 8, *OTh* II: 278 (transl. Spade 1994: 222).
[79] See Panaccio 2015b: 175–177.

possible. To be sure, Ockham is confident that individuals of the same species or of the same genus usually resemble each other in recognizable ways and that our recognitional schemata are basically reliable. As Jerry Fodor puts it, the causal chain must be reliable from horses in the world to "horsy looks" and from horsy looks to the activation of our concept of "horse."[80] Yet it remains that the recognitional process cannot be infallible. Mistakes are possible even under optimal conditions of observation. Intentional resemblance, consequently, can be misleading. If so, intentional resemblance is not what fixes the significates of a given concept. The success or failure of conceptual recognition must be measured against some other way of fixing the extension of concepts. If the mental proposition corresponding to "this is a horse" can be false even when our recognitional schema fits the thing that is referred to, the significates of our concept of "horse" must be fixed otherwise. Ockham's best theory on this matter, I think, is that causality does the job for general natural signs as well as for intuitive cognitions. Intentional resemblance is required for concepts to fulfill their recognitional function and it is usually reliable, but the significates of a natural kind concept must be the individuals that are essentially similar (either specifically or generically according to the case) to the exemplars that originally caused the formation of that concept in the mind. And the same holds *mutatis mutandis* for our basic relational and quantitative concepts.

Syncategorematic terms

Mental conjunctions, prepositions, and basic adverbs cannot be acquired by abstraction, since they have no referents. Syncategorematic terms, Ockham says, do not have determinate significates.[81] How can they enter mental language, then? When he still subscribed to the so-called *fictum*-theory of concepts, according to which categorematic concepts are the correlates of abstractive acts, Ockham considered an account of mental *syncategoremata* that is quite surprising at

---

[80] Fodor 1988: 122.
[81] *SL* I, 4, *OPh* I: 15 (transl. Loux 1974: 55).

first sight.[82] They would be abstracted, on this view, from the corresponding spoken words and then used in mental propositions in the same ways in which spoken syncategorematic terms are used in spoken sentences. One might, for example, abstract a general representation from singular occurrences of the word "or" and then use this representation in mental propositions to fulfil the same role that "or" fulfils in spoken sentences. This is surprising, because it seems to make the language of thought dependent on conventional languages rather than the reverse, as is usually the case in Ockham. Reasoning, for him, must surely be an innate capacity of human beings. And reasoning involves operations such as predication, negation, quantification, disjunction, and so on that are expressed in conventional languages by syncategorematic terms. Human beings, therefore, should be capable of such operations before they learn any conventional language. Ockham's idea, as I understand it, must have been that spoken syncategorematic terms are introduced in conventional languages to make it conspicuous that the speaker is then performing such intellectual operations. When predicating "animal" of "horse," for instance, the intellect would produce the categorematic concepts of "horse" and "animal" (seen as ideal objects at this point in the development of Ockham's thought) and bind them together with a predicative act. This predicative act would be made conspicuous in communication by the use of a copula in external language, such as the verb "to be" in English. When such a conventional copula is available, the intellect can abstract from it a new mental representation—a representation of the verb "to be," for instance—and then include it in mental propositional wholes in addition to the subject and predicate terms. And the intellect could proceed similarly with the other basic syncategorematic terms of conventional languages, such as "and," "or," "all," etc., the advantage of this being that the intellect could now display complete mental propositions before itself and take them as its objects. Although it would not make the intellect capable of new logical operations, this mental objectification of the *syncategoremata* would presumably facilitate reasoning.[83]

---

[82] *Ord.*, dist. 2, q. 8, *OTh* II: 285.
[83] This interpretation of Ockham's former theory of mental syncategorematic terms is argued for in Panaccio 2004: 146–154.

When concepts are identified with intellectual acts in Ockham's later theory, however, there is no longer the need for this indirect process. Ontologically speaking, categorematic concepts and logical operations are now on a par: they are all mental acts, that is, real qualities of the intellect. Consequently, they can be directly combined with one another into complex propositional acts. Consider the copula again. It is a syncategorematic term for Ockham. The verb "is," he says, is not "a sign of things";[84] it is instead the very act of uniting the subject with the predicate:

> [...] the union of the extremes [i.e., of the subject and the predicate] in the mind is the concept of the copula, which is a quality of the mind, viz., an act of understanding, And this concept is really distinct from the subject and the predicate, which are also diverse acts of understanding. And when these three concepts are posited in the mind, then without any relation of reason one has a proposition [...].[85]

Similarly, when the mind associates a universal quantificational act (corresponding to "all") with the subject-term of a propositional complex, it *ipso facto* produces a universal proposition. When it adds a disjunctive act (corresponding to "or") to two propositional complexes, it produces a disjunctive proposition. When it adds a prepositional act (corresponding, for example, to "of," "to," etc.) to a categorematic concept within a proposition, it confers an oblique case (such as genitive, dative, etc.) onto this concept.[86] And so on for all the basic mental *syncategoremata*.

On this approach, the only plausible explanation of how such syncategorematic items enter the mind is that they are innate. Ockham is not explicit about this, admittedly, but how could it be otherwise? Human rationality for him is nothing but the intellectual soul itself.[87] And the intellectual soul is innate, of course, since it is a substantial

---

[84] *Exp. in libr. Perih.* I, 2, *OPh* II: 389.
[85] *Quodl.* VI, 29, *OTh* IX: 695 (transl. Freddoso 1991: 585).
[86] On prepositions in Ockham's mental language, see Panaccio 2004: 155–158.
[87] This identification is explicit in *Exp. in libr. Porph.* 1, 5, *OPh* II: 23 (transl. Kluge 1973–1974, ch. 2.5: 220).

form. Human beings acquire their categorematic concepts on the basis of experience, as we have seen, but they must be innately capable of combining concepts into predicative propositions and of combining the resulting propositions into copulative, disjunctive, or conditional wholes. And they must be innately capable of quantification and negation, as well as of some prepositional and adverbial operations. If it were not the case, then human beings could not be said to be rational. The logical capacities of the rational soul are not accidental properties. Having such capacities is nothing other than having a rational soul. It is not to be supposed, of course, that to each simple syncategorematic term of external languages there corresponds a distinct innate capacity of the human mind. Ockham's theory only requires that certain basic syncategorematic concepts be innate, the rest being combinations of these—with maybe some categorematic terms in some cases. Since Ockham does not develop the point, we do not know which syncategorematic concepts exactly he would have considered as basic, but he should certainly have included the copula, the negation, the conjunction, some quantifier, and presumably certain prepositions.

Mental propositions in Ockham's view are grammatically structured complex units that are really composed of simpler items, some of which are intuitive acts, common names, or participles, while others are syncategorematic functors corresponding to copulas, quantifiers, conjunctions, and prepositions. An act of will is normally required for mental propositions to be assembled,[88] but the basic constituents must have entered the mind in purely natural ways: categorematic terms are implanted on the basis of intuitive cognitions by a natural process of abstraction, and basic syncategorematic terms correspond to innate combinatorial capacities of the human mind. The semantics of mental language, then, parallels that of spoken and written languages, as described in chapter 4. Simple categorematic concepts signify (and sometimes connote) certain things. When they are combined into propositions with the help of mental *syncategoremata*, they acquire a referential function called "supposition," just as spoken words do. The truth-value of the resulting mental propositions then depends on their

---

[88] See *Ord.*, dist. 3, q. 4, *OTh* II: 438: "[...] the formation of a proposition cannot be done without the mediation of the will [...]" (my transl.).

logical structure and on the suppositions of their subject and predicate terms. This is how true thoughts are made possible in the human mind.

Knowledge

It is one thing, though, to be able to entertain true thoughts; it is another thing to know such thoughts to be true. Accounting for human knowledge requires more than a theory of mental language, and Ockham indeed has more to offer.[89] To introduce his ideas on the matter, I will use a distinction he draws between several senses of the term "knowledge" (*scientia*) as a guiding thread, but let me first mention a few features that he thinks knowledge has in every sense of the term.

Across the main definitions Ockham considers, knowledge always comes out as a mental *habitus*.[90] It is a disposition of the intellect to give its assent to a proposition. I can be said to know that 8 times 2 is 16 even when the corresponding mental proposition is not present to my mind, because I have internalized a disposition to assent to this proposition when I apprehend it. In Ockham's ontology, such *habitus* are singular qualities of individual cognizers just as cognitive acts are. My knowledge that 8 times 2 is 16 is something real in my mind, and it is ontologically distinct from your knowledge that 8 times 2 is 16. Contrary to the corresponding mental acts, it is not directly accessible to reflective introspection, but it is efficacious nonetheless insofar as it inclines the mind to certain judicative acts.

The proposition that the cognizer is thus disposed to give her assent to is the *object* of the knowledge *habitus*, Ockham says. The *subject* of knowledge, on the other hand, is the mental item that occurs as the subject-term in this proposition.[91] That only propositions and terms are objects and subjects of knowledge does not entail, however, as some commentators have concluded, that Ockham's account of knowledge "leaves us only in the realm of the mental."[92] The terms of known

---

[89] On Ockham's conception of knowledge, see, e.g., Goddu 1984: 21–80, Pelletier 2013: 11–70.
[90] *Exp. in libr. Phys.*, Prol., 2, *OPh* IV: 5 (transl. Boehner 1990: 3–4).
[91] *Exp. in libr. Phys.*, Prol., 3, *OPh* IV: 8–9 (transl. Boehner 1990: 8–9).
[92] King 1987: 118.

propositions are usually taken in *personal supposition*, according to him, and stand for extramental things. The knowledge that horses are mammals has the mental proposition "horses are mammals" as its object and the concept "horse" as its subject, but it reaches to real horses nonetheless, because the subject "horse" is in personal supposition in this proposition and stands for extramental horses. One reason why Ockham insists that knowledge primarily has to do with propositions and their subject-terms is that he wants to preserve Aristotle's principle that knowledge (in a strict sense) "is of universals"[93] without accepting external universals in the ontology. His strategy is to take advantage of a grammatical feature of the Latin verb *scire* (to know): it normally requires a propositional complement. The subjects of the known propositions, then, can be general terms accompanied by a universal quantifier such as "all horses," "all animals," etc., but these terms refer to nothing but individuals, as Ockham's semantics is intended to make clear.

Another condition for knowledge in all of its variants is that the known propositions should be *true*. It was a common dictum in medieval philosophy that "nothing is known but the truth" (*nihil scitur nisi verum*), and Ockham subscribes to it.[94] It does not follow that human beings cannot firmly believe certain falsehoods, but false beliefs are not to be *called* "knowledge."

More is needed for knowledge, of course, than a mere disposition to assent to a true proposition. One who believes a truth by sheer luck or for bad reasons cannot be said to have knowledge of it. I will now state the various additional conditions that Ockham considers as he introduces several senses of "knowledge." We will thus be led to successively discuss his conception of evident cognition, of demonstration, of induction, and of what scientific disciplines are.

---

[93] Aristotle, *Metaphysics* XIII, 10, 1086b33.
[94] The source is Aristotle, *Posterior Analytics* I, 2, 71b19–26.

Evident cognition

In the Prologue to his commentary on Aristotle's *Physics*, Ockham distinguishes four senses of the word "*scientia*," best translated in English as "knowledge" in most cases. The first definition is the only one that does not include "evident cognition." While general and non-technical, this first meaning is interesting nonetheless, since Ockham illustrates it with cases of testimonial knowledge, a topic that has attracted great attention in recent studies of epistemology.[95] Knowledge in this first sense is "certain cognition of something that is true."[96] We are thus said to know that Rome is a large city even if we have never seen it, or that a given person is our mother or our father. Our assent in these examples (given by Ockham himself) is induced by testimonies (*testimonia*) that we trust. Yet subjective confidence is not enough. The known proposition must be true, as in all other cases, and the source must be objectively reliable. The latter is what the mention of *certain* refers to in the definition. Not only is firmness of assent required, but the information-carrying process that brings it about must be veridical all the way through.

In a second sense, knowledge is identified with *evident cognition*.[97] This is a technical notion in Ockham: "evident cognition," he writes, "is the cognition of a true proposition that can be sufficiently caused immediately or mediately by the simple cognition of its terms."[98] A salient example is the assent we are inclined to give to an elementary true contingent proposition such as "this is a horse" in virtue of our intuitive cognition of a horse. Analytic propositions in today's sense are also evidently cognized in Ockham's sense: anyone who has the concept "bachelor" and the concept "married" is *ipso facto* disposed to give her assent to "no bachelor is married." The reason why Ockham mentions that evident cognition can be "immediately or mediately" brought about is that it can be directly induced by the cognition of the terms

---

[95] See, e.g., Shieber 2015, Adler 2017. On testimonial knowledge in Ockham, see Pelletier 2019.
[96] *Exp. in libr. Phys.*, Prol., 2, *OPh* IV: 5 (transl. Boehner 1990: 4).
[97] *Exp. in libr. Phys.*, Prol., 2, *OPh* IV: 6 (transl. Boehner 1990: 5).
[98] *Ord.*, Prol., q. 1, *OTh* I: 5 (my transl.). On Ockham's conception of evident cognition, see Perini-Santos 2006.

(or of their referents), as in the above examples, or it can be arrived at by way of a valid inference with evidently cognized premises. A deduction such as "this is a horse, all horses are animals, therefore this is an animal" would be an example of the latter; the two premises being evidently known, according to Ockham, by anybody who presently has an intuitive cognition of a horse and who possesses the concepts "horse" and "animal"; the conclusion is also evidently known, although in a mediate way.[99]

A crucial point about evident cognition in Ockham is that it is *causally* produced. The process that leads from the cognition of the terms to the disposition to assent is a natural one in such cases: "Whoever evidently knows a certain proposition," Ockham says, "cannot dissent from this proposition by the sole force of the will."[100] As always, an act of the will is required to form the proposition that is then assented to, but once the intellect actually considers the proposition, it cannot hold back its assent (unless it is moved by an even stronger force such as a supernatural intervention). Even when an evident cognition is mediately brought about and results from the joint action of prior evident cognitions, the chain is still causal for Ockham. If I form the true proposition that this intuited thing here is a horse and the proposition that all horses are animals, I cannot help being disposed to assent to the proposition that this thing here is an animal. The formation of the relevant proposition is not compelled, but the implementation of the corresponding judicative *habitus* is. And the *habitus* is implemented as a result of a purely causal process. Evidentness in Ockham is not a mere internal, experiential feature, as it requires a certain causal sequence: to be counted as evident, a propositional cognition must have been caused by the cognition of its simple components or of their referents.[101] Ockham's conception of evident cognition is thus an *externalist* one in today's sense. Externalism with respect to knowledge is the thesis that what makes a true belief a case of knowledge does not solely depend on the internal states of the cognizer, but on some external

---

[99] The claim that the general proposition "all horses are animals" is evidently known will be briefly discussed in the next section.
[100] *Ord.*, Prol., q. 1, *OTh* I: 192 (my transl.).
[101] *Ord.*, Prol., q. 1, *OTh* I: 5.

natural relation as well.[102] In Ockham's view, singular substances and qualities naturally cause intuitive cognitions and general concepts in the mind, as we have seen earlier. In appropriate circumstances, these in turn naturally cause certain adequate dispositions of assent, which can be called "knowledge" precisely because they are produced in this way.[103]

As it happens, this approach provides a solution to what is known as the Gettier problem in epistemology. Edmund Gettier famously called into question the definition of knowledge as "justified true belief" by pointing out that a belief can be both justified and true without qualifying as knowledge.[104] I could be justified, for example, in believing that my friend John owns a Ford because I have often seen his car, even very recently. Now suppose that unbeknownst to me John sold that car this morning and then, by mere chance, unexpectedly won another Ford in a lottery. My believing that John's car is a Ford is then both justified and true, but it hardly counts as knowledge, since the epistemic process that justifies it has nothing to do with what makes it true. Ockham's notion of knowledge as evident cognition avoids this difficulty by requiring that knowledge in this sense be naturally caused in a certain way in the cognizer. My cognition of John's present car plays no causal role in my belief that this car is a Ford; this belief, therefore, is not an evident cognition in Ockham's sense, because it has not been brought about in the right way. The same holds *mutatis mutandis* for the other three meanings of "knowledge" listed by Ockham. This is clear for senses 3 and 4, since they both incorporate the idea of evident cognition as we will presently see. But it also applies to the first definition: the condition that a true cognition be objectively certain in order to qualify as knowledge in this more general sense requires that it be acquired by an information-carrying process that is usually reliable *and* that is veridical in this particular case. My belief that John's car is a Ford is not certain in Ockham's sense, because the process that led me to it was triggered by the wrong car, and this belief, therefore, does not qualify as evident cognition.

---

[102] See, e.g., Kornblith 2001, Brown 2007, Engel 2020.
[103] On Ockham's epistemic externalism, see Panaccio 2015b: 180–184.
[104] Gettier 1963.

Demonstration

In Ockham's sense number 3, knowledge is the evident cognition of a necessary proposition. In sense number 4, it is the cognition of the necessary conclusion of a valid syllogistic inference from evidently known premises.[105] The latter is an obligatory tribute to Aristotle's technical vocabulary in the *Nicomachean Ethics*, where the acquired knowledge of demonstrable conclusions (*episteme* in Greek, usually translated as *scientia* in Latin) is contrasted with the cognition of first principles (*noûs* in Greek).[106] What matters to us at this point is that by introducing senses 3 and 4, Ockham shows his acceptance of the Aristotelian conception of scientific demonstration. Starting from necessary premises, a genuine demonstration on this view leads to a necessary conclusion by way of a valid syllogism. This raises a number of issues for Ockham's nominalism.[107]

For one thing, how can there be necessary propositions at all about the created world if nothing exists in it but contingent individuals? Even a proposition such as "all horses are animals" is contingent for Ockham, since "all horses are animals" would be false if no horse existed, and the existence of horses is a contingent matter.[108] But a proposition is necessary, Ockham says, only if it can never be false.[109] It follows, as Ockham is well aware, that no affirmative elementary proposition in the present tense can ever be necessary if it is about created things and that, consequently, "no such proposition can be a principle or conclusion of a demonstration."[110] What propositions, then, can ever occur in a genuine demonstration about the created world? Ockham's answer is twofold. On the one hand, he points out, conditional propositions can be necessary.[111] "All horses are animals" could

---

[105] *Exp. in libr. Phys.*, Prol., 2, *OPh* IV: 6 (transl. Boehner 1990: 5).

[106] Aristotle, *Nicomachean Ethics* VI, 3, 1139b18–35.

[107] On Ockham's theory of demonstration, see the Introduction to Longeway 2007: especially 101–140.

[108] On Ockham's semantics, any affirmative proposition with an empty subject is false; see, e.g., *SL* I, 72, *OPh* I: 218: "In affirmative propositions a term is always asserted to supposit for something. Thus, if it supposits for nothing the proposition is false" (transl. Loux 1974: 206).

[109] *SL* II, 9, *OPh* I: 275 (transl. Freddoso and Schuurman 1980: 111).

[110] *SL* III-2, 5, *OPh* I: 513 (transl. Longeway 2007: 160).

[111] Ibid.

thus be replaced by "if anything is a horse, it is an animal," which is true even if no horse exists. This opens up the way to a general replacement of syllogistic reasoning by chains of conditionals such as "if anything is a horse, it is an animal; if it is an animal, it can move by itself, therefore if anything is a horse, it can move by itself," every part of which is necessary. Even if Ockham does not mention it, however, this approach amounts to giving up the Aristotelian requirement that scientific demonstrations should follow strict syllogistic form, a requirement that Ockham explicitly endorses.[112] His second proposal is more promising in the Aristotelian context. It is to replace present-tense propositions by modal ones about the possible (*de possibili*) in scientific demonstrations.[113] "All horses are animals" will thus be replaced by something like "all possible horses are animals." As a rule, according to Ockham, the presence of the modal terms "possible" or "possibly" within a proposition extends the terms of this proposition to stand for all the possible things that these terms signify, and not only for the presently existing ones. "All possible horses are animals," then, turns out true even if no horse presently exists.[114] If true at all, propositions about the possible are necessarily true for Ockham and consequently they can occur in strict syllogistic demonstrations even in a world entirely made up of contingent individuals. This is one more reason why Ockham needs merely possible beings in his ontology.

This approach, however, raises yet another problem for Ockham's epistemology: how can such necessary propositions about possible beings ever be known if human beings are in cognitive contact with nothing but a limited number of actual contingent individuals? Ockham distinguishes between necessary propositions that are demonstrable and necessary propositions that are not.[115] His account of how they are known varies accordingly.

The former can be known by way of demonstration insofar as they logically follow from other necessary propositions. This is not merely a matter of logic, though. Knowledge of the premises, Ockham says,

---

[112] See *SL* III-2, 1–2, *OPh* I: 505–508 (transl. Longeway 2007: 154–156).
[113] *SL* III-2, 5, *OPh* I: 513 (transl. Longeway 2007: 160).
[114] See, e.g., *SL* III-3, 2, *OPh* I: 593: "[. . .] even if no man exists, 'A man can laugh' is true when the subject-term stands for that which can exist" (my transl.).
[115] *SL* III-2, 4, *OPh* I: 510–511 (transl. Longeway 2007: 158).

causes the knowledge of the conclusion. This is a natural process. If I give my assent to "all horses are animals" and to "all animals are able to move by themselves," I cannot help assenting to "all horses are able to move by themselves" whenever I mentally form this proposition. This is how the human mind naturally works. One might worry that on this view human beings would be caused to know everything that logically follows from whatever knowledge they have.[116] But this implausible consequence is avoided because Ockham would certainly require that the premises be *actually* assented to. Having a mere dispositional knowledge of the premises brings about no new knowledge. Judicative acts of assent are necessary in order for inferential knowledge to be caused. The premises, moreover, should not be too complicated and they should be simultaneously assented to in order to bring about the knowledge of the conclusion. A human being can presumably only entertain a very limited number of judicative acts at any particular moment. On Ockham's conception, then, necessary conclusions naturally come to be known because they obviously follow from a limited number of necessary premises that are actually and simultaneously assented to.

What about the premises? Some of them might have been reached by previous demonstrations, but that cannot be the case for all necessary premises on pain of infinite regress. Indemonstrable first principles are required for scientific demonstrations to get started. Some of them, Ockham says, are known by themselves (*per se nota*), while others are known by experience (*per experientiam*). Let us focus first on the former. In Ockham's vocabulary, principles known per se are those necessary universal propositions that are naturally assented to by anyone who possesses the concepts that are their parts.[117] Being known on the basis of their terms, they are evidently cognized in the sense defined earlier. Yet they are not all analytic in today's sense. They are not all true solely in virtue of the *nominal* definitions of their terms. Some of them are composed of terms that have no nominal definition at all. "All (possible) horses are animals," for example, is known

---

[116] The question is raised by Perini-Santos 2006: 183.
[117] *SL* III-2, 4, *OPh* I: 511 (transl. Longeway 2007: 158), *Ord.*, Prol., q. 2, *OTh* I: 83–84 (transl. Longeway 2007: 220).

per se, according to Ockham,[118] but its subject and predicate are absolute terms (or natural kind terms), and absolute terms do not have nominal definitions in his semantics.[119] Ockham, then, is committed to accepting what Immanuel Kant later called "synthetic *a priori* judgements": certain universal and necessary non-analytic propositions are naturally assented to when their terms are understood. Such are, for example, the physical principle that "every whole is larger than its parts"[120] or the moral principle that "the will ought to conform itself to right reason."[121] Unfortunately, Ockham provides no explicit account of how this is possible. In cases in which a genus concept is universally predicated of a species that falls under it, such as "all horses are animals," we can surmise that those who have the concept "horse" and the concept "animal" are naturally inclined to give their assent to "all horses are animals" because in these cognizers the species concept of "horse" has causally contributed to the original formation of the genus concept of "animal." It seems likely that someone who acquired the concept of "animal" as a result of having met with horses among other things would naturally be inclined to (rightly) believe that all horses are animals.[122] As to the other principles that are known by themselves, however, the only thing Ockham says is that we are naturally inclined to accept them: when the relevant necessary proposition occurs to us, we cannot resist assenting to it if we possess the concepts it is made of. Ockham simply follows Aristotle on this.[123]

Induction

Not all scientific demonstrations ultimately rest on premises that are known by themselves. Numerous indemonstrable principles come from experience, Ockham says.[124] An example he gives is the

---

[118] *SL* III-2, 29, *OPh* I: 558 (transl. Longeway 2007: 195).
[119] *SL* I, 10, *OPh* I: 35 (transl. Loux 1974: 70); see above, pp. 104–105.
[120] *Rep.* II, q. 13, *OTh* V: 257.
[121] *Quodl.* II, 14, *OTh* IX: 177–178 (transl. Freddoso and Kelley 1991: 149).
[122] I have developed this interpretation for such cases in Panaccio 2017c.
[123] See Aristotle, *Posterior Analytics* I, 10, 76a30–77a4.
[124] *Ord.*, Prol., q. 2, *OTh* I: 83–84 (transl. Longeway 2007: 220), *Exp. in libr. Phys.* I, 3, *OPh* IV: 45, *SL* III-2, 4, *OPh* I: 510 (transl. Longeway 2007: 158).

proposition "every heat is heat-producing." This proposition is not known in virtue of the mere cognition of its terms. Only experience teaches us that heat tropes normally cause other heat tropes in nearby substances. But experience deals only with singular things. It always involves intuitive cognitions of actual individuals. How can it lead to the knowledge of the necessary propositions that are needed for scientific demonstrations in Ockham's Aristotelian model?

In these cases, the mind must move from singular to universal propositions. This is what Ockham calls an "induction" (*inductio*), as we still do: "Induction," he says, quoting Aristotle, "is a passage from singulars to a universal."[125] Ockham usually prefers to reserve the term "induction" for inferences that are based on *all* the relevant singular instances, as he does in the chapters of the *Summa of Logic* where he deals with the logic of inductive inferences.[126] Yet his Aristotelian definition also fits the cases in which the enumeration of instances is incomplete. The latter is what happens when a cognizer moves from a finite number of singular propositions evidently known on the basis of intuitive cognitions to a necessary universal proposition suitable to serve as a premise in a scientific demonstration. A necessary premise must be about all possible individuals of a certain sort, as we have seen. But possible horses, possible heat tropes, and so on are infinite in number. No human being, however long she lives, can ever intuitively grasp all of them. In some situations, the cognizer might be justified to take it as *probable* that a universal proposition is true because she met with several singular instances of it and no counterexample. She might then be epistemically justified in using this proposition as a premise for syllogistic reasoning, but that would only yield a "topical syllogism," that is, a syllogism that "proceeds from probable propositions."[127] And topical syllogisms are not really demonstrative, Ockham says. They provide no *evident* cognition.

Yet Ockham is clear: there *are* cases in which the evident cognition of a limited number of instances naturally leads to the evident cognition of necessary universal propositions. This holds for causal

---

[125] *SL* III-3, 31, *OPh* I: 707; see Aristotle, *Topics* I, 12, 105a13–14.
[126] *SL* III-3, 31–36. *OPh* I: 707–721.
[127] *SL* III-1, 1, *OPh* I: 359 (transl. Boehner 1990: 83).

statements in particular. "This herb cures fever, therefore all herbs of the same species cure fever" is a good inference, Ockham claims.[128] And if the antecedent is evidently known, so is the consequent. The underlying principle here is that "all individuals of the same sort have effects of the same sort in equally disposed patients."[129] Ockham is explicit that where ultimate species are concerned, even a single experience may suffice. If it is well established in a single case that a certain plant has cured a given illness, it can safely be concluded that all plants of the same ultimate species will cure this illness in highly similar circumstances. Generalization to genera, on the other hand, is more demanding. The causal relation in such cases must have been established for a singular instance of each ultimate species of the genus in question. To conclude that all plants of a given genus have a certain curative effect, it is both necessary and sufficient that this has been shown for a singular instance of each ultimate species of this sort of plant.[130]

In these generalizations, the principle that all individuals of the same sort have effects of the same sort in sufficiently similar circumstances has the status of a rule of inference rather than that of a premise. With respect to the relevant inference, it is what Ockham calls an "extrinsic mean" (*medium extrinsecum*). All reasoning in his view makes use of such underlying "maxims" (*maximae*) that are not intrinsic parts of the argument itself, but that must be presupposed to move from the premises to the conclusion.[131] Although Ockham is not very clear about this, he does not seem to require that these maxims be evident to the cognizer. For a conclusion to be evidently known, it must be correctly inferred from evidently known premises, but it is not necessary that the rules of this inference and its underlying maxims also be evidently known. It suffices that they should hold in the relevant sort of case and that they be causally operational somehow in the mind of the cognizer.

What must be evidently known, on the other hand, in the kind of case we are now considering are the singular causal propositions on

---

[128] *Ord.*, Prol., q. 2, *OTh* I: 91–92 and 94–95 (transl. Longeway 2007: 224–225 and 226).
[129] Ibid.: 87 (my transl.).
[130] Ibid.: 92–93.
[131] See, e.g., *SL* III-2, 4, *OPh* I: 509–510 (transl. Longeway 2007: 157–158), where the point is developed about syllogistic inferences.

which the inductive inference rests. If they were not evidently known, the necessary universal propositions that are inferred from them would not be evidently known, either, and could not serve as premises in demonstrative syllogisms. Contrary to Hume, Ockham thinks that singular causal statements are sometimes evidently known on the basis of experience. Some preliminary work might be needed, to be sure: to evidently know that a given plant has cured fever in a particular case, one might have to rule out other possible causes, but once this is done, the cognizer "knows evidently that this herb was the cause of this health."[132] How is this possible? Ockham, of course, never discusses the now familiar Humean doubts about the empiricalness of causal beliefs, but the cognitive process that his nominalist theory suggests in such cases can be developed. Remember how basic relational concepts are acquired in his view.[133] It is not necessary that the relation itself be intuited. How could it be, since it is not a distinct entity? What is required is that certain singular substances or qualities be *jointly* intuited. In favorable circumstances, a relational concept that applies to all similarly related groups is thus produced in the mind. This is how the concept of efficient causality must be acquired on Ockham's theory: a singular cause and its effect are jointly intuited in such a way that the cognizer forms the general concept of a causal chain. This being done, the cognizer is naturally inclined to give his assent to the true contingent proposition that those things here are an instance of such a chain and she can thereafter detect certain other simple cases of causal connections. I can have a joint intuition of a person in front of me and of a certain vocal noise in such a way that I am naturally inclined to the true belief that this person causes this noise. Or I can have a joint intuition of a fire and of a pain in my hand in such a way that I am naturally inclined to the true belief that this fire causes this pain. Since these beliefs are true and they are immediately produced in me by the intuitive cognitions of the very things that are referred to by their terms, the corresponding propositions are evidently known according to Ockham's externalist conception of intuitive cognition. Not all singular causal connections can be cognized in this way, of course,

---

[132] *Ord.*, Prol., q. 2, *OTh* I: 87 (transl. Longeway 2007: 222).
[133] See above, pp. 153–156.

but when they are, inductive generalization is legitimate, and the necessary universal propositions that are reached are just as evidently known as the singular ones that they are grounded on.

Sciences

In the *Ordinatio*, Ockham introduces yet another sense of "*scientia*," best translated as "science" in this case. A science in this sense is an aggregate of several knowledge *habitus* thematically related to one another in various ways.[134] Thus taken, the term designates the mastery of scientific disciplines such as logic, physics, metaphysics, ethics, etc. Those are not abstract entities nor social institutions for Ockham. They exist in individual minds as clusters of singular qualities.[135] "Science" in this sense is a collective term like "army," "city," and "herd." It collectively refers to a plurality of cognitive dispositions. In a human person, a science typically involves the cognition of certain terms and the knowledge of principles and conclusions, as well as certain dispositions for drawing distinctions, refuting errors, and solving objections. The demonstration of necessary propositions lies at the core of such sciences, as the Aristotelian conception requires, but contingent statements, probable theses, uncertain conjectures, and arguments of various sorts must occupy in the end a large part of every science.

The unity of a given science in this perspective does not depend on its having a single object or a single subject. It is a matter of structure, of how, in particular, the conclusions are logically related to one another. And there are several possibilities for this. Given that each science is a cluster of *habitus*, that each *habitus* has a different proposition as its object, and that these propositions have different subjects and/or different predicates, all referring to individual things, there is quite a variety of ways in which a science can be organized. "The conclusions," Ockham says, "can be ordered in multiple ways, either according to

---

[134] *Ord.*, Prol., q. 1, *OTh* I: 9–11.
[135] See on this Pelletier 2018.

their predicate-terms or according to their subject-terms or according to both."[136]

Ockham's nominalist approach thus favors an open conception of how scientific disciplines are delimited. Certain truths can belong to different disciplines, and certain conclusions can be demonstrated in different ways in different sciences.[137] There is no a priori justification in his writings for how the array of scientific knowledge should be divided. He does make significant use of a general distinction between speculative and practical sciences according to whether the main conclusions are about what is the case or about what should be done;[138] he distinguishes between real and rational sciences according to whether the terms of the conclusions refer to extramental things or to mental items;[139] and he uncritically accepts traditional divisions such as the division of speculative sciences into metaphysics, mathematics, and natural philosophy.[140] In general, however, he is not strongly assertive about the fine-grained classification of disciplines and subdisciplines, and he seems to be sensitive to a certain amount of relativity in the accepted divisions. A scientific field, for him, basically corresponds at the outset to a given set of authoritative treatises.[141] Metaphysics is what Aristotle discusses in his eponymous treatise and logic is divided prima facie in accordance with Aristotle's and Porphyry's treatises, which were used for teaching logic in medieval universities. If necessary, however, any sector of the scientific realm can be supplemented and reorganized along the way, as Ockham does himself with logic in certain parts of his *Summa*.[142] Flexibility characterizes his attitude in such matters.

---

[136] *Ord.*, Prol., q. 8, *OTh* I: 219–220 (my transl.). Ockham's conception of the unity of a science is discussed in Perini-Santos 2006: 144–159 and Pelletier 2013: 26–38.

[137] *Ord.*, Prol., q, 1, *OTh* I: 10.

[138] *Ord.*, Prol., q. 11, *OTh* I: 310–323, *Summ. phil. nat.*, Preamble, *OPh* VI: 147–152.

[139] *Ord.*, dist. 2, q. 4, *OTh* II: 134–138.

[140] *Exp. in libr. Phys.*, Prol., 3, *OPh* IV: 6–7 (transl. Boehner 1990: 6); see Maurer 1990: 136–144.

[141] *Ord.*, Prol., q. 1, *OTh* I: 9.

[142] The chapters on supposition, for example, do not correspond to any particular part of Aristotle's *Organon* (*SL* I, 63–77, *OPh* I: 193–238; transl. Loux 1974: 188–221), and neither does the long development on truth-conditions (*SL* II, 2–20, *OPh* I: 249–317 [transl. Freddoso and Schuurman 1980: 86–154]).

The important point is that a rational individual who seriously engages in intellectual study can internalize a cluster of cognitive dispositions that allow him to truly master a body of organized knowledge, whatever its precise boundaries are, and to arrive at a series of inter-related necessary conclusions on the basis of valid demonstrations from evident premises, many of which are known by experience. Whether in logic, in metaphysics, in physics, or in ethics, several necessary truths are thus naturally accessible to human beings; these truths can be ascertained; and their logical relations can be spelled out.

The status of Christian theology, as may be expected, is of special interest for Ockham, and much of the long Prologue to his *Ordinatio* is devoted to whether theology can legitimately be counted as a science. His position is that it consists in an aggregate of cognitive *habitus* just as scientific disciplines do, yet insofar as it is naturally acquired, theology is not a science in the strict sense, since it does not lead to evident cognition.[143] For the most part, theology rests on faith, and faith in turn rests on preaching and testimonies that do not yield evident cognition of divine reality.[144] Christian theology, however, still qualifies as knowledge for Ockham, if only in the first sense, since he takes it to be both true and certain. Firmness of assent in religious matters does not evidently follow from previous evident cognitions, nor does it lead to evident cognition.[145] Yet it can be arrived at, Ockham thinks, by way of a veridical process, namely truthful preaching and testimonies from persons who have shown themselves to be reliable. The trust that the believer puts in these persons has no evident foundation, according to Ockham, and religious faith does require an intellectual leap, but this does not prevent it from reaching truth and objective certainty.

Whether in theological matters or in other fields, then, knowledge is possible for Ockham. Sometimes this is in the weak sense of the term, as in theology, but the strong senses do apply in several domains: evident knowledge of many propositions, whether singular or general,

---

[143] *Ord.*, Prol., q. 7, *OTh* I: 183–206.
[144] *Quodl.* IV, 6, *OTh* IX: 322–327 (transl. Freddoso and Kelley 1991: 267–271), *Quaest. var.* 5, *OTh* VIII: 184–185.
[145] *Quodl.* IV, 6, *OTh* IX: 326–327 (transl. Freddoso and Kelley 1991: 270–271).

contingent or necessary, is naturally accessible to human beings and it can be coherently organized in individual minds. Although Ockham did not devote much effort to refuting radical skepticism, which he took to be obviously false, it is effectively countered in his epistemology by an appealing combination of theoretical elements:

(1) an externalist approach to knowledge: that certain dispositions of assent qualify as knowledge does not depend mostly on their internal features but on the processes by which they were acquired;
(2) a view of the mind as a functional system innately endowed with a rich variety of natural capacities and liabilities, such as a capacity for conceptual abstraction, an ability to combine concepts into propositions, and a predisposition to be causally affected by simple inferential chains;
(3) a conception of thought as an inner discourse with a semantics that closely parallels that of spoken language; this makes it possible that mental propositions with general, relational, and quantitative terms in them are true even if the world is exclusively made up of singular substances and qualities, and it accounts for how conventional languages can be mastered;
(4) the foundation of the whole epistemic structure upon intuitive acts of direct acquaintance with individual things; intuitive contact, as we have seen, accounts for the acquisition of all simple categorematic concepts as well as for the evidentness of basic empirical cognition.

All knowledge is thus ultimately rooted in contingent cognitive encounters with singular substances and qualities.

Conclusion

Neither general terms nor relational terms nor mathematical terms involve anything in the world that is not referred to by singular non-relational and non-mathematical terms. This is the core of Ockham's nominalism and is what this introductory presentation has been centered on. When in doubt about the meaning or the truth of what is said, Ockham's general attitude is that the basic question to ask is: What are we talking about? What *things*, in other words, do we have to turn to in order to evaluate the proposed statements? This is why ontology and semantics are so important to him: we need to be clear about what kind of things exist in the world and about how exactly these things are referred to or evoked by what we say. When we use affirmative sentences, the presumption must be that we want to refer to something. It is a pernicious mistake, however, to presume that a special category of thing corresponds to every distinct category of terms. As Ockham puts it:

> Everyone who argues uses names for things; yet nevertheless, things are not arranged in the same way as names are, nor vice versa; therefore, he who believes that what holds for names holds for things, and vice versa, easily falls into sophisms, as happens frequently.[1]

For each category of terms, it must be clarified if and how they refer to external things. This is what Ockham does in great detail with general terms, relational terms, and quantitative—or mathematical—terms, and he builds a whole system around this project. To conclude this book, let me recall some of the most remarkable features of this Ockhamist system.

As we saw in chapter 2, Ockham's rejection of realism with respect to general, relational, and quantitative terms is based on a number of very

[1] *Exp. sup. libr. Elench.* I, 1, 3, *OPh* III: 8 (my transl.).

general principles. Two of them are especially salient in his works: the principle of separability and the Razor principle. The former is the idea that if two things are really distinct from each other, then either one of them can exist without the other. This principle has a theological foundation in Ockham, but it is also of independent philosophical interest. One thing that we must realize, however, is that this principle is not about natural but rather metaphysical possibility, which Ockham equates with everything that does not involve a logical contradiction. The Razor principle, on the other hand—it is vain to multiply entities without necessity—has been closely associated with Ockham's name since the nineteenth century, and he does indeed frequently use it, but it has a subordinate status in his view, since it yields only "probable" rather than definitive conclusions.

Once realism with respect to general, relational, and quantitative terms is discarded with the help of these principles and a number of others that were listed in chapter 2, Ockham's world is left with only singular substances and singular qualities in it, each one of which is primitively individuated by itself. As simple as it is, this ontological doctrine is characterized by a distinctive combination of theses. For one thing, it is a *pluralistic ontology*. It is often said that nominalism is a one-category ontology, but Ockham admits at least two basic kinds of individuals, namely substances and qualities (plus the essential parts of substances, that is, matter and substantial forms).

Essentialism is also considered alien to nominalism on occasion, but it is clearly part of Ockham's doctrine. There is a clear distinction to be drawn between essential and accidental properties in his view. While Bucephalus is white in virtue of being accidentally related with something *else*—a certain whiteness trope in this case—Bucephalus is a horse, an animal, and a substance in virtue of what it intrinsically is, and it cannot cease to be a horse, an animal, or a substance without ceasing to exist. Both substances and qualities intrinsically belong to natural kinds, and any one of them essentially resembles the other members of the same natural kind: a horse essentially resembles all other possible horses, and a given heat trope essentially resembles all other possible heat tropes. For Ockham, this means at the very least that all of the individuals of a same natural kind are intrinsically structured in the same way (if they are complex) and that they have similar causal powers.

Material substances, in particular, are composed of essential parts that they cannot lose without being destroyed, namely, a chunk of matter and one or more substantial forms. Each one of these parts, like everything else, is a singular thing. This is Ockham's version of Aristotle's *hylomorphism*, the doctrine that material substances are made of matter and form. I argued in chapter 3 that Ockham's view here can be illuminatingly reconstructed as a *nuclear trope theory*. In the vocabulary of today's metaphysics, tropes are singular properties, such as a particular patch of redness, that combine with other singular properties to form concrete singular objects. It is uncontroversial that Ockham's qualities are tropes in this sense, but I submit that the term also interestingly applies to substantial forms and chunks of matter as he conceives of them. On this view, the sensory substantial form of a horse, for example, is the singular sensitivity of this particular horse and its matter is the singular materiality of the horse. The point is that for Ockham, each basic component of reality—whether it is a chunk of matter, a substantial form, or a quality—is a singular entity that cannot exist by itself in the natural world and that combines with other such components into concrete qualified objects, just as today's trope theorists want it. Note, however, that Ockham's approach confers more structure to concrete things than contemporary trope theories usually do. While the latter often try to manage with compresence as the sole relation that tropes have among themselves in a given concrete object, Ockham wants matter and substantial forms to be the essential parts of a material substance, while qualities are accidentally attached to the resulting nucleus.

Another feature of Ockham's ontology that might seem surprising is that it is a variety of *possibilism*. It countenances merely possible beings by taking them as acceptable referents for the terms of some true affirmative sentences. As a consequence of this, the scope of Ockham's nominalism must be qualified in accordance with the distinction he draws between metaphysical and natural possibility. Nominalism with respect to general terms is radical: only singular beings are metaphysically possible. Nominalism with respect to relational and quantitative terms, on the other hand, is restricted to naturally possible worlds: no merely relational or merely quantitative entities can exist in the natural order, but nothing prevents God from creating such things if He so wishes.

Singular substances and qualities, however, are really related to one another in this world, and they are quantified. It is one of Ockham's central intuitions that things are *mind-independently ordered* with respect to one another, but that such orderings are not "small things" in between the substances and the qualities. Material things are spatially extended, they move from one place to another, and they are ordered according to before and after without space, movement, and time being extra entities. Qualities "inhere" in substances, and substantial forms "inform" chunks of matter without inherence and information having to be reified. Singular things naturally bring about the existence of other things without causation being something in addition to causes and effects. Each thing is one without its unity being something distinct from it. And several things are numerous without their number being an additional entity.

Ockham's nominalist project would be seriously jeopardized, of course, if this restrictive ontology turned out to be inconsistent with the truth of all sentences that have general, relational, or quantitative terms in them. If many of these sentences are to be accepted as true, as Ockham thinks, a detailed semantics is required to show how this is possible in a world that contains only singular non-relational things. This is something that Ockham devoted a great deal of work to. His semantics is *atomistic* and *referentialist*: the truth-conditions of elementary sentences are ultimately based on the relations of their component terms with singular objects. In developing this semantics, Ockham used or introduced, as we saw in chapter 4, a number of philosophically interesting ideas and suggestions, for example, about multiple denotation, supposition (in the medieval sense), connotation, collective reference, modal statements, etc.

Ockham's semantics is also *mentalist*. For him, words acquire their linguistic function by being "subordinated" to mental items. And human thought is a syntactically structured discourse composed of acquired natural signs and innate syncategorematic terms. This "language of thought," as contemporary cognitivists would call it, is what accounts for our capacity to create and master conventional languages.

Ockham's theory of mind can also be seen as a form of *representationalism* insofar as all categorematic units of thought are signs in his view. This holds not only for general concepts, but for intuitive acts as well: my intuitive apprehension of a singular object in front of me is a sign and a representation of that object insofar as it can stand for it in mental propositions, just as a general concept is a sign of those things that it can stand for in mental propositions. This, however, does not preclude direct cognitive access to external things. The objects of abstractive and intuitive acts are the external things themselves: my intuitive apprehension of Bucephalus has Bucephalus as its direct object, and my concept of "horse" has singular horses as its direct objects. What ultimately allows for this original blend of representationalism and direct realism is that Ockham's account of cognition is a *causal theory*: cognitive acts are real mental qualities, and their objects are fixed by what caused them. In the natural order, the object of an intuitive cognition is its singular cause; and the objects of a simple general concept are the individuals that are relevantly similar to the one(s) that caused this concept to be acquired.

All human cognition is thus ultimately rooted in singular encounters with individual things. Human beings are such that an object which is adequately located naturally causes an intuitive act in their minds, as well as a number of general concepts and certain dispositions for assenting to some true propositions. As we saw in chapter 5, this allows in the end for the evident cognition of both contingent and necessary propositions and for the development in individual minds of systematic bodies of scientific knowledge by way of our natural capacity for deductive and inductive inferences.

It is striking that along the way Ockham turns out to be committed to various forms of what is called today "externalism": linguistic externalism, mental content externalism, and epistemic externalism, all logically independent from one another. Although for him the meaning of a word ultimately depends on the meaning of a concept, this concept does not have to be present in the mind of the speaker who uses that word. The meaning of the word was conventionally given to it by the original "impositor," and from then on the word keeps that meaning for every speaker who—tacitly or explicitly—accepts the convention even if she does not re-activate—or even possess—the concept that the word has been subordinated to. This is a version of what is called today "linguistic externalism." Ockham also implicitly subscribes to *mental content externalism* insofar as he takes the content of a mental representation to depend not on how this representation internally appears, but on what originally caused it in the mind of the cognizer. In his best theory, as I have argued, this holds for general concepts as well as for intuitive cognitions. As for *epistemic externalism*, this is the view that a true belief has the status of knowledge in virtue of the process by which it was acquired rather than in virtue of how it appears to the mind. This is what we have in Ockham, both about testimonial knowledge and about evident cognition. Although Ockham does not explicitly discuss the ins and outs of these externalist positions, they do play a crucial role in his philosophy of mind and in his epistemology.

A final trait of Ockham's nominalism that must still be emphasized is that it is not at all a form of constructionalism or "irrealism" in Nelson Goodman's sense.[2] It is sometimes believed that nominalism is inevitably associated with such relativistic views, but this is not so with Ockham. However strongly he rejects realism with respect to general terms, relational terms, and quantitative terms, Ockham firmly subscribes to what is called today *metaphysical realism*, defined as the idea that "the world is as it is independent of how human or other inquiring agents take it to be."[3] There are only individual substances and qualities for Ockham, but what these are and how they are related to one another is in general utterly independent of how we look at them:

> We must understand that it does not depend on your consideration or mine whether a thing is mutable or immutable, contingent or necessary and incorruptible, any more than it does whether you are white or black, or whether you are inside or outside the house.[4]

Ockham's nominalism thus yields a unified and sophisticated theory that endorses metaphysical realism and essentialism as well as an atomistic semantics and a causal view of cognition and knowledge. This

---

[2] See Goodman 1978: x, 1–22, and 1984: 39–44.
[3] Khlentzos 2021.
[4] *Exp. in libr. Phys.*, Prol., 4, *OPh* IV: 13 (transl. Boehner 1990: 14).

approach, I believe, can still fruitfully contribute to the philosophical conversation. Each part of it, each thesis, each argument requires, of course, closer scrutiny and much more detailed discussion than what was appropriate in the context of this book. My intent here merely has been to take the reader through a guided tour of this beautiful theoretical construction.

Bibliography

Ockham's works

Editions (Latin text)
Guillelmi de Ockham Opera philosophica. Ed. Gedeon Gal *et al*. St. Bonaventure, N.Y.: The Franciscan Institute, 7 vols., 1974–1988.
Guillelmi de Ockham Opera theologica. Ed. Gedeon Gal *et al*. St. Bonaventure, N.Y.: The Franciscan Institute, 10 vols., 1967–1986.

English translations
ADAMS, Marilyn M. and KRETZMANN, Norman (1983). *William Ockham. Predestination, God's Foreknowledge and Future Contingents*. 2nd ed. New York: Appleton–Century–Crofts.
BIRCH, T. Bruce (1930). *The De Sacramento Altaris of William of Ockham*. Burlington, Iowa: The Lutheran Literary Board [to be used with caution].
BOEHNER, Philotheus (1990). *Ockham. Philosophical Writings*. Indianapolis, Ind.: Hackett.
BOSLEY, Richard N. and TWEEDALE, Martin W. (1997). *Basic Issues in Medieval Philosophy* (selected readings). Peterborough, Ont.: Broadview Press.
DAVIES, Julian (1989). *Ockham on Aristotle's Physics. A Translation of Ockham's Brevis Summa Libri Physicorum*. St. Bonaventure, N.Y.: The Franciscan Institute.
FREDDOSO, Alfred J. (1991). *William of Ockham. Quodlibetal Questions*, vol. II, Quodlibets 5–7. New Haven, Conn.: Yale University Press.
────── and KELLEY, Francis E. (1991). *William of Ockham. Quodlibetal Questions*, vol. I, Quodlibets 1–4. New Haven, Conn.: Yale University Press.
FREDDOSO, Alfred J. and SCHUURMAN, Henry (1980). *Ockham's Theory of Propositions. Part II of the* Summa logicae. Notre Dame, Ind: University of Notre Dame Press.
KLUGE, E.-H. W. (1973–1974). "William of Ockham's commentary on Porphyry." *Franciscan Studies* 33, 171–254 and 34, 306–382.
LONGEWAY, John Lee (2007). *Demonstration and Scientific Knowledge in William of Ockham. A Translation of Summa Logicae III-II: De syllogismo*

demonstrativo, *and Selections from the Prologue to the* Ordinatio. Notre Dame, Ind.: University of Notre Dame Press.
LOUX, Michael (1974). *Ockham's Theory of Terms. Part I of the* Summa logicae. Notre Dame, Ind: University of Notre Dame Press.
SPADE, Paul Vincent (1994). *Five Texts on the Medieval Problem of Universals.* Indianapolis, Ind.: Hackett Publishing Company, 114–231 (transl. of *Ord.*, dist. 2, q. 4–8).
TWEEDALE, Martin W. (1999). *Scotus vs. Ockham. A Medieval Dispute Over Universals.* Lewiston, N.Y.: The Edwin Mellen Press, 285–392 (selected transl. of *Ord.*, dist. 2, q. 4–6).
WOOD, Rega (1997). *Ockham on the Virtues.* West Lafayette, Ind.: Purdue University Press.

On Ockham and medieval philosophy

ADAMS, Marilyn M. (1979). "Was Ockham a Humean about efficient causality?" *Franciscan Studies* 39, 5–48.
—— (1987). *William Ockham.* Notre Dame, Ind.: University of Notre Dame Press, 2 vols.
ADEMOLLO, Francesco, AMERINI, Fabrizio, and DE RISI, Vincenzo, eds. (2022). *Thinking and Calculating. Essays on Logic, Its History and Its Applications.* Dordrecht: Springer.
AMERINI, Fabrizio, ed. (2010). *Later Medieval Perspectives on Intentionality.* Turnhout: Brepols [= *Quaestio* 10].
—— and CESALLI, Laurent, eds. (2017). *Universals in the Fourteenth Century.* Pisa: Edizioni della Normale.
ARLIG, Andrew (2019). "Medieval mereology." In E. N. Zalta (ed.), *The Stanford Encyclopedia of Philosophy* (Fall 2019 edition). URL = https://plato.stanford.edu/archives/fall2019/entries/mereology-medieval/.
ASHWORTH, E. J. (1981). "Mental language and the unity of propositions." *Franciscan Studies* 41, 61–96 (reprinted in Ashworth [1985]).
—— (1985). *Studies in Post-Medieval Semantics.* London: Variorum Reprints.
BIARD, Joël, ed. (2009). *Le langage mental du Moyen Âge à l'Âge classique.* Louvain: Peeters.
—— (2010). "Nominalism in the later Middle Ages." In Pasnau (2010b), 661–673.
—— (2017). "Le nominalisme au Moyen Âge tardif." In Amerini and Cesalli (2017), 5–36.
BOEHNER, Philotheus (1958). *Collected Articles on Ockham.* St. Bonaventure, N.Y.: The Franciscan Institute.
BOS, Egbert P., ed. (2013). *Medieval Supposition Theory Revisited.* Leiden: Brill.

BRAAKHUIS H. A. G., KNEEPKENS, C. H., and DE RIJK, Lambert M., eds. (1981). *English Logic and Semantics. From the End of the Twelfth Century to the Time of Ockham and Burleigh*. Nijmegen: Ingenium.

BROWER, Jeffrey E. (2016). "Aquinas on the problem of universals." *Philosophy and Phenomenological Research* 92: 715-735.

—— (2018). "Medieval Theory of Relations." In E. N. Zalta (ed.), *The Stanford Encyclopedia of Philosophy* (Winter 2018 edition). URL = https://plato.stanford.edu/archives/win2018/entries/relations-medieval/.

BROWER-TOLAND, Susan (2007a). "Intuition, externalism, and direct reference in Ockham." *History of Philosophy Quarterly* 24, 317-336.

—— (2007b). "Ockham on judgement, concepts, and the problem of intentionality." *Canadian Journal of Philosophy* 37, 67-110.

—— (2017). "Causation and mental content: Against the externalist reading of Ockham." In Pelletier and Roques (2017), 59-80.

CESALLI, Laurent (2016). "Propositions: Their meaning and truth." In Dutilh Novaes and Read (2016), 245-264.

——, EMAMZADAH, Parwana, and GOUBIER, Frédéric, eds. (2019). *Ontological Commitment in Medieval Logic, Medioevo* 44. Padova: Antenore.

CONTI, Alessandro (2010). "Realism." In Pasnau (2010b), 647-660.

——, ed. (2013). *A Companion to Walter Burley*. Leiden: Brill.

—— (2016). "Walter Burley." In E. N. Zalta (ed.), *The Stanford Encyclopedia of Philosophy* (Summer 2016 edition). URL = https://plato.stanford.edu/archives/sum2016/entries/burley/.

COURTENAY, William J. et al. (1992). *Vivarium*, 30/1 (issue on nominalism in the XIIth century).

DE LIBERA, Alain (1996). *La querelle des universaux. De Platon à la fin du Moyen Âge*. Paris: Éditions du Seuil.

DUTILH NOVAES, Catarina (2004). "A medieval reformulation of the de re / de dicto distinction." In L. Behounek (éd.), *Logica Yearbook 2003*. Prague: Filosofia, 111-124.

—— (2013). "The Ockham - Burley dispute." In Conti (2013), 49-84.

—— and READ, Stephen, eds. (2016). *The Cambridge Companion to Medieval Logic*. Cambridge: Cambridge University Press.

FAUCHER, Nicolas and ROQUES, Magali, eds. (2018). *The Ontology, Psychology and Axiology of Habits (Habitus) in Medieval Philosophy*. Dordrecht: Springer.

FRIEDMAN, Russell (2009). "Mental propositions before mental language." In Biard (2009), 95-115.

—— and EBBESEN, Sten, eds. (2004). *John Buridan and Beyond: Topics in the Language Sciences, 1300-1700*. Copenhagen: Royal Danish Academy of Sciences and Letters.

GALLUZZO, Gabriel (2004). "Aquinas on common natures and universals." *Recherches de théologie et philosophie médiévales* 71: 131-171.

GODDU, André (1984). *The Physics of William of Ockham*. Leiden: Brill.

GRELLARD, Christophe, ed. (2017). *Miroir de l'amitié. Mélanges offerts à Joël Biard.* Paris: Vrin.

HENNINGER, Mark G. (1989). *Relations. Medieval Theories 1250–1325.* Oxford: Clarendon Press.

HOLTZ, Louis (1981). *Donat et la tradition de l'enseignement grammatical.* Paris: CNRS.

JUN, Nathan J. (2003). "The letter of Fredegisus of Tours on Nothingness and Shadow: A new translation and commentary." *Comitatus: A Journal of Medieval and Renaissance Studies* (UCLA) 34, 150–169.

KALUZA, Zénon (1988). *Les querelles doctrinales à Paris. Nominalistes et réalistes aux confins du xive et du xve siècles.* Bergamo: Pierluigi Lubrina ed.

KARGER, Elizabeth (1981). "Would Ockham have shaved Wyman's beard?" In Braakhuis *et al.* (1981), 389–413.

KEELE, Rondo (2007). "Can God make a Picasso? William Ockham and Walter Chatton on divine power and real relations." *Journal of the History of Philosophy* 45, 395–411.

——— (2010). *Ockham Explained. From Razor to Rebellion.* Chicago: Open Court.

KING, Peter (1987). "John Buridan's philosophy of science." *Studies in History and Philosophy of Science* 18, 109–132.

——— (2015). "Thinking about things: Singular thought in the Middle Ages." In Klima (2015), 104–121.

KLIMA, Gyula, ed. (2015). *Intentionality, Cognition and Mental Representation in Medieval Philosophy.* New York: Fordham University Press.

———, ed. (2017). *Questions on the Soul by John Buridan and Others.* Dordrecht: Springer.

——— and Hall, Alexander W., eds. (2011). *Mental Representation.* Proceedings of the Society for Medieval Logic and Metaphysics 4. Cambridge: Cambridge Scholars Publishing.

KNUUTTILA, Simo (1993). *Modalities in Medieval Philosophy.* London: Routledge.

LAGERLUND, Henrik, ed. (2010). *Rethinking the History of Skepticism. The Missing Medieval Background.* Leiden: Brill.

———, ed. (2019). *Knowledge in Medieval Philosophy.* London: Bloomsbury Press.

LENZ, Martin (2003). *Mental Sätze: Wilhelm von Ockhams Thesen zur Sprachlichkeit des Denkens.* Wiesbaden: Steiner.

MAIERU, Alfonso (2004). "Mental language and Italian scholasticism in the fourteenth and fifteenth centuries." In Friedman and Ebbesen (2004), 33–67.

MAURER, Armand (1978). "Method in Ockham's nominalism." *The Monist* 61, 426–443; repr. in Maurer (1990), 403–421.

——— (1984). "Ockham's razor and Chatton's anti-razor." *Mediaeval Studies* 46, 463–475; repr. in Maurer (1990), 431–443.

—— (1990). *Being and Knowing. Studies in Thomas Aquinas and Later Medieval Philosophers*. Toronto: Pontifical Institute of Mediaeval Studies.

—— (1999). *The Philosophy of William of Ockham in the Light of Its Principles*. Toronto: Pontifical Institute of Mediaeval Studies.

McGRADE, Arthur S. (1974). *The Political Thought of William of Ockham*. Cambridge: Cambridge University Press.

NOONE, Timothy B. (2003). "Universals and individuation." In Williams (2003), 100–128.

NORMORE, Calvin (1990). "Ockham on mental language." In Smith (1990), 53–70.

—— (2003). "Burge, Descartes, and us." In Hahn and Ramberg (2003), 1–14.

NUCHELMANS, Gabriel (1973). *Theories of the Proposition. Ancient and Medieval Bearers of Truth and Falsity*. Amsterdam: North-Holland.

PANACCIO, Claude (1980). "Occam et les démonstratifs." *Historiographia Linguistica* 7, 189–200.

—— (1999). "Semantics and mental language." In Spade (1999), 53–75.

—— (2004). *Ockham on Concepts*. Aldershot: Ashgate.

—— (2009). "Le jugement comme acte mental selon Guillaume d'Ockham." In Biard (2009), 117–133.

—— (2010). "Intuition and causality: Ockham's externalism revisited." In Amerini (2010), 241–253.

—— (2012a). "Ockham and Buridan on epistemic sentences: Appellation of the form and appellation of reason." *Vivarium* 50, 139–160.

—— (2012b). "Intellections and volitions in Ockham's nominalism." In Pickavé and Shapiro (2012), 75–93.

—— (2013). "Ockham and Buridan on simple supposition." In Bos (2013), 371–384.

—— (2014). "Ockham: Intuition and knowledge." In Osbeck and Held (2014), 55–74.

—— (2015a). "Ockham's ontology." In Guigon and Rodriguez-Pereyra (2015), 63–78.

—— (2015b). "Ockham's externalism." In Klima (2015), 166–185.

—— (2017a). *Mental Language. From Plato to William of Ockham*. New York: Fordham University Press.

—— (2017b). "Linguistic externalism and mental language in Ockham and Buridan." In Klima (2017), 225–237.

—— (2017c). "Guillaume d'Ockham et l'épistémologie des genres." In Grellard (2017), 49–61.

—— (2019a). *Récit et reconstruction. Les fondements de la méthode en histoire de la philosophie*. Paris: Vrin.

—— (2019b). "Ockham's commitment to merely possible beings." In Cesalli, Emamzadah, and Goubier (2019), 81–98.

—— (2022). "Ockham on abstract pseudo-names." In Ademollo, Amerini, and De Risi (2022), 171–183.

—— and PICHÉ, David (2010). "Ockham's reliabilism and the intuition of non-existents." In Lagerlund (2010), 97–118.
PASNAU, Robert (2010a). "Form and matter." In Pasnau (2010b), 635–646.
——, ed. (2010b). *The Cambridge History of Medieval Philosophy*. Cambridge: Cambridge University Press.
—— (2011). *Metaphysical Themes 1274–1671*. Oxford: Oxford University Press.
PELLETIER, Jenny E. (2013). *William Ockham on Metaphysics*. Leiden: Brill.
—— (2018). "William Ockham on the mental ontology of scientific knowledge." In Faucher and Roques (2018), 285–299.
—— (2019). "William Ockham on testimonial knowledge." In Lagerlund (2019), 145–165.
—— (2021). "Kingdoms and crowds: William Ockham on the ontology of social groups." *British Journal for the History of Philosophy* 29, 24–44.
—— and ROQUES, Magali, eds. (2017). *The Language of Thought in Late Medieval Philosophy*. Dordrecht: Springer.
PERINI-SANTOS, Ernesto (2006). *La théorie ockhamiste de la connaissance évidente*. Paris: Vrin.
PICHÉ, David (2005). *Le problème des universaux à la Faculté des Arts de Paris entre 1230 et 1260*. Paris: Vrin.
PICKAVÉ, Martin and SHAPIRO, Lisa, eds. (2012). *Emotion and Cognitive Life in Medieval and Early Modern Philosophy*. Oxford: Oxford University Press.
PINI, Giorgio (2005). "Scotus's realist conception of the categories: His legacy to late medieval debates." *Vivarium* 43, 63–110.
ROBERT, Aurélien (2017). "A crucial distinction in Ockham's philosophy of mind: *Cognitio in se/cognitio in alio*." In Pelletier and Roques (2017), 39–57.
SCHIERBAUM, SONJA (2014). *Ockham's Assumption of Mental Speech. Thinking in a World of Particulars*. Leiden: Brill.
SPADE, Paul Vincent (1975). "Ockham's distinctions between absolute and connotative terms." *Vivarium* 13, 55–76 (reprinted in Spade 1988).
—— (1988). *Lies, Language and Logic in the Late Middle Ages*. London: Variorum Reprints.
——, ed. (1999). *The Cambridge Companion to Ockham*. Cambridge: Cambridge University Press.
—— and PANACCIO, Claude (2019). "William of Ockham." In E. N. Zalta (ed.), *The Stanford Encyclopedia of Philosophy* (Spring 2019 edition). URL = https://plato.stanford.edu/archives/spr2019/entries/Ockham/..
STUMP, Eleonore (1999). "The mechanisms of cognition: Ockham on mediating species." In Spade (1999), 168–203.
THORNDIKE, Lynn (1944). *University Records and Life in the Middle Ages*. New York: Columbia University Press.
TWEEDALE, Martin (1999). *Scotus vs. Ockham. A Medieval Dispute Over Universals*. Lewiston, N.Y.: The Edwin Mellen Press, 2 vols.

WEY, Joseph C. and ETZKORN, Girard J., eds. (2008). *Walter Chatton. Lectura super Sententias. Liber I. Distinctiones 3-7*. Toronto: Pontifical Institute of Mediaeval Studies.

WILLIAMS, Thomas, ed. (2003). *The Cambridge Companion to Duns Scotus*. Cambridge: Cambridge University Press.

WÖHLER, Hans Ulrich (2013). "Universals and individuals." In Conti (2013), 167-189.

Other works cited

ADLER, Jonathan (2017). "Epistemological problems of testimony." In E. N. Zalta (ed.), *The Stanford Encyclopedia of Philosophy* (Winter 2017 edition). URL = https://plato.stanford.edu/archives/win2017/entries/testimony-episprob/.

ARIEW, André, CUMMINS, Robert, and PERLMAN, Mark eds. (2004). *Functions. New Essays in the Philosophy of Psychology and Biology*. Oxford: Oxford University Press.

ARMSTRONG, D. M. (1978). *Universals and Scientific Realism*. Cambridge: Cambridge University Press, 2 vols.

—— (1989). *Universals. An Opinionated Introduction*. Boulder, Col.: Westview Press.

—— (1997). *A World of States of Affairs*. Cambridge: Cambridge University Press.

—— (2004). *Truth and Truthmakers*. Cambridge: Cambridge University Press.

—— (2010). *Sketch for a Systematic Metaphysics*. Oxford: Oxford University Press.

BACH, Emmon and HARMS, Robert T., eds. (1968). *Universals in Linguistic Theory*. New York: Rinehart and Winston.

BAKER, Alan (2016). "Simplicity." In E. N. Zalta (ed.), *The Stanford Encyclopedia of Philosophy* (Winter 2016 edition). URL = https://plato.stanford.edu/archives/win2016/entries/simplicity/.

BEEBEE, Helen and DODD, Julian, eds. (2005). *Truthmakers. The Contemporary Debate*. Oxford: Clarendon Press.

BERGMANN, Gustav (1967). *Realism. A Critique of Brentano and Meinong*. Madison.: University of Wisconsin Press.

BLACK, Max (1971). "The elusiveness of sets." *Review of Metaphysics* 24, 614-636.

BROWN, Jessica (2007). "Externalism in mind and epistemology." In Goldberg (2007), 13-34.

CAMERON, Ross (2018). "Infinite regress arguments." In E. N. Zalta (ed.), *The Stanford Encyclopedia of Philosophy* (Fall 2018 edition). URL = https://plato.stanford.edu/archives/fall2018/entries/infinite-regress/.

CAMPBELL, Keith (1990). *Abstract Particulars.* Oxford: Basil Blackwell.
CARNAP, Rudolf (1956). *Meaning and Necessity.* 2nd ed. Chicago: The University of Chicago Press.
CHURCH, Alonzo (1951). "The need for abstract entities in semantic analysis." *Proceedings of the American Academy of Arts and Sciences* 80, 100–112 (repr. in Fodor and Katz [1964], 437–445).
COLIN, Allen and NEAL, Jacob (2020). "Teleological notions in biology." In E. N. Zalta (ed.), *The Stanford Encyclopedia of Philosophy* (Spring 2020 edition). URL = https://plato.stanford.edu/archives/spr2020/entries/teleology-biology/.
DAVIDSON, Donald (1984a). *Inquiries into Truth and Interpretation.* Oxford: Clarendon Press.
——— (1984b). "Theories of meaning and learnable languages." In Davidson (1984a), 3–15.
EHRING, Douglas (2011). *Tropes.* Oxford: Oxford University Press.
EKLUND, Matti (2019). "Fictionalism." In E. N. Zalta (ed.), *The Stanford Encyclopedia of Philosophy* (Winter 2019 edition). URL = https://plato.stanford.edu/archives/win2019/entries/fictionalism/..
ENGEL, Mylan (2020). "Internalism and externalism in epistemology." In *Oxford Bibliographies.* Oxford: Oxford University Press. http://www.oxfordbibliographies.com.
FELDMAN, Richard (1998). "Charity, principle of." In *The Routledge Encyclopedia of Philosophy.* London: Routledge. https://www.rep.routledge.com/articles/thematic/charity-principle-of/v-1.
FILLMORE, Charles (1968). "The case for case." In Bach and Harms (1968), 1–88 (repr. in Fillmore 2003, 21–119).
——— (2003). *Form and Meaning in Language,* vol. I. Chicago: University of Chicago Press.
FINE, Kit (2002). "The varieties of necessity." In T. S. Gendler and J. Hawthorne (eds.), *Conceivability and Possibility.* Oxford: Clarendon Press, 253–281.
FODOR, Jerry (1975). *The Language of Thought.* New York: Thomas Y. Crowell.
——— (1987). *Psychosemantics.* Cambridge, Mass.: MIT Press.
——— (2008). *LOT 2: The Language of Thought Revisited.* Oxford: Oxford University Press.
——— and KATZ, Jerrold J., eds. (1964). *The Structure of Language.* New York: Prentice Hall.
——— and LEPORE, Ernest (1992). *Holism. A Shopper's Guide.* Oxford: Blackwell.
FREGE, Gottlob (1918). "Der Gedanke. Eine Logische Untersuchung," transl. as "Thoughts" by P. Geach and R. Stoothof in B. McGuinness (ed.), *G. Frege. Collected Papers on Mathematics, Logic, and Philosophy.* Oxford: Blackwell, 1984, 351–372.

GALLOIS, André (1998). "De re / de dicto." In *Routledge Encyclopedia of Philosophy*. London: Routledge. https://www.rep.routledge.com/articles/thematic/de-re-de-dicto/v-1.

GARSON, Justin (2016). *A Critical Overview of Biological Functions*. Dordrecht: Springer.

GEACH, Peter (1971). *Mental Acts*. London: Routledge and Kegan Paul.

GETTIER, Edmund (1963). "Is true justified belief knowledge?." *Analysis* 23: 121–123.

GOLDBERG, Sanford C., ed. (2007). *Internalism and Externalism in Semantics and Epistemology*. Oxford: Oxford University Press.

GOODMAN, Nelson (1956). "A world of individuals." In I. M. Bochenski, A. Church, and N. Goodman, *The Problem of Universals*. Notre Dame, Ind.: University of Notre Dame Press, 13–31; repr. in Goodman (1972), 155–172.

—— (1972). *Problems and Projects*. Indianapolis, Ind.: The Bobbs-Merrill Company.

—— (1978). *Ways of Worldmaking*. Indianapolis, Ind.: Hackett Publishing Company.

—— (1984). *Of Mind and Other Matters*. Cambridge, Mass.: Harvard University Press.

—— and QUINE, Willard Van Orman (1947). "Steps toward a constructive nominalism." *Journal of Symbolic Logic* 12, 105–122; repr. in Goodman (1972), 173–198.

GUIGON, Ghislain and RODRIGUEZ-PEREYRA, Gonzalo, eds. (2015). *Nominalism about Properties*. New York: Routledge.

HAHN, Martin and RAMBERG, Bjorn, eds. (2003). *Reflections and Replies. Essays on the Philosophy of Tyler Burge*. Cambridge, Mass.: MIT Press.

HINTIKKA, Jaakko (1971). "Semantics for propositional attitudes." In Linsky (1971), 145–167.

HORNSBY, Jennifer (2005). "Truth without truthmaking entities." In Beebee and Dodd (2005), 33–47.

JACKMAN, Henry (2017). "Meaning holism." In E. N. Zalta (ed.), *The Stanford Encyclopedia of Philosophy* (Spring 2017 edition). URL = https://plato.stanford.edu/archives/spr2017/entries/meaning-holism/.

KHLENTZOS, Drew (2021). "Challenges to metaphysical realism." In E. N. Zalta (ed.), *The Stanford Encyclopedia of Philosophy* (Spring 2021 edition). URL = https://plato.stanford.edu/archives/spr2021/entries/realism-sem-challenge/.

KMENT, Boris (2017). "Varieties of modality." In E. N. Zalta (ed.), *The Stanford Encyclopedia of Philosophy* (Spring 2017 edition). URL = https://plato.stanford.edu/archives/spr2017/entries/modality-varieties/.

KORNBLITH, Hilary, ed. (2001). *Epistemology: Internalism and Externalism*. Oxford: Blackwell.

LEWIS, David (1986). *On the Plurality of Worlds*. Oxford: Basil Blackwell.

―――― (2009). "Truth-making and difference-making." In Lowe and Rami (2009), 102–114.
LINSKY, Leonard, ed. (1971). *Reference and Modality*. Oxford: Oxford University Press.
LOWE, E. J. and RAMI, Adolf, eds. (2009). *Truth and Truth-Making*. Montreal/Kingston: McGill-Queen's University Press.
MACBRIDE, Fraser (2005). "Lewis's animadversions on the truthmaker principle." In Beebee and Dodd (2005), 117–140.
―――― (2020). "Truthmakers." In E. N. Zalta (ed.), *The Stanford Encyclopedia of Philosophy* (Spring 2019 edition). URL = https://plato.stanford.edu/archives/spr2020/entries/truthmakers/.
MARTIN, Richard (1958). *Truth and Denotation*. Chicago: The University of Chicago Press.
MAURIN, Anna-Sofia (2018). "Tropes." In E. N. Zalta (ed.), *The Stanford Encyclopedia of Philosophy* (Summer 2018 edition). URL = https://plato.stanford.edu/archives/sum2018/entries/tropes/.
MELAMED, Yitzhak Y. and LIN, Martin (2020). "Principle of sufficient reason." In E. N. Zalta (ed.), *The Stanford Encyclopedia of Philosophy* (Spring 2020 edition). URL = https://plato.stanford.edu/archives/spr2020/entries/sufficient-reason/.
MELIA, Joseph (2015). "Nominalism, naturalism and natural properties." In Guigon and Rodriguez-Pereyra (2015), 175–188.
MILLIKAN, Ruth (1984). *Language, Thought and Other Biological Categories*. Cambridge, Mass.: MIT Press.
―――― (2000). *On Clear and Confused Ideas. An Essay about Substance Concepts*. Cambridge: Cambridge University Press.
―――― (2004). *Varieties of Meaning*. Cambridge, Mass.: MIT Press.
MOORE, Michael (2009). "The nature of singularist theories of causation." *The Monist* 92/1, 3–22.
MORELAND, J. P. (2001). *Universals*. Montreal/Kingston: McGill-Queen's University Press.
NEANDER, Karen and SCHULTE, Peter (2021). "Teleological theories of mental content." In E. N. Zalta (ed.), *The Stanford Encyclopedia of Philosophy* (Spring 2021 edition). URL = https://plato.stanford.edu/archives/spr2021/entries/content-teleological/.
NELSON, Michael (2019). "The de re / de dicto distinction." Supplement to the entry "Propositional attitude reports." In E. N. Zalta (ed.), *The Stanford Encyclopedia of Philosophy* (Spring 2019 edition). URL = https://plato.stanford.edu/archives/spr2019/entries/prop-attitude-reports/.
OSBECK, Lisa M. and HELD, Barbara S., eds. (2014). *Rational Intuition. Philosophical Roots. Scientific Investigations*. Cambridge: Cambridge University Press.
PARSONS, David (2016). *Theories of Intensionality. A Critical Survey*. Dordrecht: Springer.

PEROVIC, Katarina (2017). "Bradley's regress." In E. N. Zalta (ed.), *The Stanford Encyclopedia of Philosophy* (Winter 2017 edition). URL = https://plato.stanford.edu/archives/win2017/entries/bradley-regress/.

PSILLOS, Stathis (2002). *Causation and Explanation*. Montreal/Kingston: McGill-Queen's University Press.

PUTNAM, Hilary (1975). "The meaning of 'meaning'." In Hilary Putnam, *Philosophical Papers*, vol. 2: *Mind, Language and Reality*. Cambridge: Cambridge University Press, 215–271.

—— (1981). *Reason, Truth and History*. Cambridge: Cambridge University Press.

QUINE, Willard Van Orman (1963). *From a Logical Point of View*. New York: Harper and Row.

RAMI, Adolf (2009). "Introduction: Truth and truth-making." In Lowe and Rami (2009), 1–36.

RESCORIA, Michael (2019). "The language of thought hypothesis." In E. N. Zalta (ed.), *The Stanford Encyclopedia of Philosophy* (Summer 2019 edition). URL = https://plato.stanford.edu/archives/sum2019/entries/language-thought/.

RODRIGUEZ-PEREYRA, Gonzalo (2016). "Nominalism in metaphysics." In E. N. Zalta (ed.), *The Stanford Encyclopedia of Philosophy* (Winter 2016 edition). URL = https://plato.stanford.edu/archives/win2016/entries/nominalism-metaphysics.

ROWLANDS, Mark, LAU, Joe, and DEUTSCH, Max (2020). "Externalism about the mind." In E. N. Zalta (ed.), *The Stanford Encyclopedia of Philosophy* (Winter 2020 edition), URL = https://plato.stanford.edu/archives/win2020/entries/content-externalism/.

SCHEFFLER, Israel (1979). *Beyond the Letter. A Philosophical Inquiry into Ambiguity, Vagueness and Metaphor in Language*. London: Routledge and Kegan Paul.

SHIEBER, Joseph (2015). *Testimony. A Philosophical Introduction*. London: Routledge.

SIMONS, Peter (1994). "Particulars in particular clothing: Three trope theories of substance." *Philosophy and Phenomenological Research* 54, 553–575.

SMITH, J.-C., ed. (1990). *Historical Foundations of Cognitive Science*. Dordrecht: Kluwer.

SOBER, Elliott (2015). *Ockham's Razors. A User's Manual*. Cambridge: Cambridge University Press.

WILLIAMS, D. C. (1953). "On the elements of being." *Review of Metaphysics* 7, 3–18 and 171–192.

Name Index

For the benefit of digital users, indexed terms that span two pages (e.g., 52–53) may, on occasion, appear on only one of those pages.

Abelard, Peter, 8, 15, 113n.34
Adams, Marilyn M., 4n.3, 19n.18, 22n.31, 41n.30, 51n.57, 65n.5, 70–71nn.15–16, 77n.40, 91n.82, 92n.87, 97–98, 144n.7
Adler, Jonathan, 174n.95
Albert the Great, 8n.2, 77–78
Aquinas, Thomas, 1, 4–5, 8n.2, 11, 31n.1, 71–72
Ariew, André, 166n.75
Aristotle, 5–6, 20–21, 22, 33, 34–37, 53, 57–58, 63–64, 66, 67, 70–71, 74, 76–77, 81–82, 86–87, 90–91, 109, 135, 143, 172–73, 173n.94, 177, 179–80, 181, 185, 190
Arlig, Andrew, 72n.20
Armstrong, David M., 9, 13, 15, 45n.43, 46n.45, 74–76, 94
Ashworth, Jennifer E., 159n.51
Augustine, 159–60
Avicenna, 135–36

Baker, Alan, 53n.61
Bergmann, Gustav, 75n.34
Biard, Joël, 8n.2
Black, Max, 104n.10
Boehner, Philotheus, 65n.5
Boethius, 19–20
Bradley, Francis, 42–43
Brower, Jeff, 20n.24, 31n.1, 41n.26, 44n.39
Brower-Toland, Susan, 97n.104, 148–49n.25, 158n.48
Brown, Jessica, 176n.102
Burley, Walter, 12–13, 32n.2, 77–78

Cameron, Ross, 43n.35

Campbell, Keith, 9, 73n.26, 89n.76
Carnap, Rudolf, 103–4
Cesalli, Laurent, 26n.40
Chatton, Walter, 94
Church, Alonzo, 112n.31
Colin, Allen, 166n.75
Conti, Alessandro, 13n.12, 32n.2

Davidson, Donald, 29, 135
Defense of Nominalism (anonymous), 12
De Libera, Alain, 31n.1
Descartes, René, 1, 146
Deutsch, Max, 148n.24
Donatus, 160n.55, 163n.65
Duns Scotus, John, 4–5, 8n.2, 11, 15, 37–38, 41–42, 43–44, 45, 47–48, 142
Dutilh Novaes, Catarina, 32n.2, 113n.34

Ehring, Douglas, 73n.26
Eklund, Matti, 132n.77
Engel, Mylan, 176n.102

Feldman, Richard, 135n.85
Fillmore, Charles, 161–62
Fine, Kit, 34n.10
Fodor, Jerry, 101n.1, 159–60, 167–68
Fredegisus of Tours, 27–28
Frege, Gottlob, 28–29, 108–9, 111–12, 156–57
Friedman, Russell, 157n.46

Gallois, André, 113n.34
Galluzzo, Gabriele, 31n.1
Garson, Justin, 166n.75
Geach, Peter, 161–62

NAME INDEX

Gettier, Edmund, 176
Goddu, André, 33n.5, 172n.89
Goodman, Nelson, 9, 15, 26n.37, 59–60, 104n.10, 193
Gregory of Rimini, 159n.51

Hamilton, William, 39n.23
Henninger, Mark, 20n.24, 31n.1, 41n.26, 44n.39, 48n.48
Hintikka, Jaakko, 104n.10
Hornsby, Jennifer, 50n.53
Hume, David, 15, 33–34, 91–92, 182–84

Jackman, Henry, 101n.1
John XXII (Pope), 6–7

Kaluza, Zénon, 8n.2
Kant, Emmanuel, 123–24, 179–80
Karger, Elizabeth, 99–100nn.113–14
Keele, Rondo, 7n.6, 39n.23, 94n.98
Khlentzos, Drew, 193
King, Peter, 148–49n.25, 172n.92
Kment, Boris, 34n.10
Knuuttila, Simo, 100n.114
Kornblith, Hilary, 176n.102

Lau, Joe, 148n.24
Leibniz, Gottfried Wilhelm, 1, 15, 61n.82, 96n.101
Lenz, Martin, 81n.50
Lepore, Ernest, 101n.1
Lewis, David, 33–35, 45n.43, 66
Lin, Martin, 61n.82
Locke, John, 15
Lombard, Peter, 5
Longeway, John L., 177n.107
Louis XI (King of France), 12
Louis of Bavaria, 7
Lowe, E. J., 15, 46n.45

MacBride, Fraser, 46n.45, 50n.53, 50n.54
Maieru, Alfonso, 159n.51
Martin, Richard, M., 103–4
Maurer, Armand, 4n.3, 39n.23, 61n.81, 70n.15, 94n.98, 185n.140
Maurin, Sofia, 42n.31, 73n.26, 79n.44
McGrade, Arthur, 7n.5
Melamed, Yitzhak, 61n.82

Melia, Joseph, 90n.78
Michael of Cesena, 6–7
Millikan, Ruth, 166n.73
Moore, George Edward, 15
Moore, Michael, 92n.86
Moreland, J. P., 75n.34

Neal, Jacob, 166n.75
Neander, Karen, 166n.73
Nelson, Michael, 113n.34
Noone, Timothy, 38n.19
Normore, Calvin, 148–49n.25, 153n.37
Nuchelmans, Gabriel, 26n.40

Panaccio, Claude, 3n.1, 7n.6, 16n.15, 18n.17, 65n.5, 74n.30, 96–97nn.103–5, 98n.107, 103n.8, 107n.22, 115n.37, 116n.41, 121n.49, 135n.89, 141n.103, 143n.4, 144n.7, 145n.12, 147n.20, 148–49n.25, 153n.38, 158n.48, 159nn.50–51, 165n.72, 169n.83, 170n.86, 176n.103, 180n.122
Parsons, David, 109n.24
Pasnau, Robert, 52n.60, 72n.23
Pelletier, Jenny, 20n.23, 136n.92, 159n.50, 172n.89, 174n.95, 184n.135, 185n.136
Perini-Santos, Ernesto, 174n.98, 180n.118, 185n.136
Perovic, Katarina, 43n.36
Peter of Spain, 109
Piché, David, 31n.1, 96n.103, 147n.20
Pini, Giorgio, 31n.1
Plato, 33, 34–35
Porphyry, 5–6, 19–20, 68–69, 130n.71, 185
Psillos, Stathis, 92n.86
Putnam, Hilary, 104–5

Quine, Willard Van Orman, 9, 10

Rami, Adolf, 46n.45, 50n.54
Rescoria, Michael, 160n.53
Robert, Aurélien, 155n.41
Rodriguez-Pereyra, Gonzalo, 11, 15
Roques, Magali, 159n.50
Rowlands, Mark, 148n.24
Russell, Bertrand, 15

Scheffler, Israel, 109n.24

Schierbaum, Sonja, 150n.31, 157n.47, 159n.50
Schulte, Peter, 166n.73
Shieber, Joseph, 174n.95
Simons, Peter, 15, 73–74, 75n.34, 78–79
Sober, Elliott, 53n.61
Spade, Paul Vincent, 7n.6, 153n.37
Stump, Eleonore, 145n.9

Tweedale, Martin, 38n.19

William of Sherwood, 109
Williams, D. C., 73–76
Wöhler, Hans Ulrich, 32n.2

Zeno of Elea, 81

Subject Index

For the benefit of digital users, indexed terms that span two pages (e.g., 52-53) may, on occasion, appear on only one of those pages.

abstraction. *See* cognition
appellation of form, 116–18
artifacts, 79–80
assent, 157–58, 175–76
  See also judgement
atomism, semantic, 26–27, 101, 165, 191

bare particulars, 74–76
Bradley's regress, 42–43

cases, grammatical, 120–21, 161–62
categories, theory of, 20–21, 63–64
causation, 90–94, 127–28, 181–82
  See also powers, causal
cognition
  abstractive, 144, 149–56
  evident, 144–45, 179–80, 181–84
  intuitive, 18–19, 144–49, 187
  of non-existent objects, 146–47
common natures, 11, 36–39
concepts
  abstractive (*see* cognition)
  acquisition of, 150–56
  of being, 151–52
  connotative, 153–56 (*see also* connotation)
  fictum vs *actus*-theory of, 64–65, 150, 168–70
  quantitative, 156
  relational, 127–28, 155–56, 181–82
  syncategorematic, 168–72
  See also terms
connotation, 103, 116–17, 120–22, 126–27, 128–32, 139
  See also concepts

definition
  nominal, 120–21
  real, 87–88
demonstration, 177–80
demonstrative pronouns, 18–19, 163–64
determinism, 60–61
dictum, 112–14, 130–31

essentialism, 94–95, 189–90
extension, 54–57
externalism, 140–41, 148–49, 175–76, 187, 192–93

faculties, sensory and intellective, 142–43
fictionalism, 132
finitism, 42, 49–50, 52
first principles, 179–80
formal distinction, 37–39, 44–45
forms, substantial, 70–73, 74–76, 142–43
  plurality of, 72–74, 144–45
functionalism, 165–67, 187

Gettier problem, 176
God's omnipotence, 33–34, 85–86, 94–95

habitus, 142–43, 159, 172, 175–76, 184
hylomorphism, 51–52, 70–71, 190

indiscernibility of identicals, 39, 40
individuation, 71–72, 78–79
induction, 180–84
inherence, 51, 67–68, 84–85
inscriptionalism, 108–9, 113–14

judgement, 143–44, 156–58, 178–79

judicative acts. *See* judgement

knowledge, 150, 172–87
   causal theory of, 175–76, 178–79
   testimonial, 174
   theological, 186

matter, 70–72, 74–76
mental language, 159–72, 187, 188–89
   grammar of, 160–64
mentalism, 140–41, 191–92
mereology, 36–37, 40
motion, 51, 81, 83–84

natural signs, 164–68
nominalism
   definition of, 9–17
   program, 27–30
numbers, 57–62
numerical unity, 32–33, 40

Ockham, biography of, 4–7
Ockham's razor, 39–40, 47–48, 52–53, 188–89
ontological commitment, criterion of, 97–98

place, 81–83
possibility, natural and absolute, 34–35, 70, 100
possible beings, 96–100, 117–18, 130–31, 177–78, 190–91
powers, causal, 93–94
propositions, 26–27, 109
   categorical and hypothetical, 109–10
   mental, 156–57, 171–72
   modal, 99–100, 112–19
   relational, 125–28
pseudo-names, 132–36, 139–40

quality, 66–70
   degrees of intensity, 69–70, 76–79
   and extension, 56–57
quantity. *See* concepts, terms
quantity, continuous and discrete, 22, 53, 132
quantum, 129, 131–32

recognition, conceptual, 167–68
referentialism, 140, 191

relational statements, 94, 125–28
relations. *See* concepts, terms
relations, internal and external, 45–46, 51–52
representationalism, 191–92
respectus, 65, 85–86, 94–95

sciences, 184–86
separability, 33–36, 40, 47, 58, 146–47, 188–89
signification, 102–5, 138–39
similarity, essential, 86–90, 94–95
space, 51–52, 82–83
state of affairs, 26–27
subordination, 102–3, 140–41
substance, 67–70
   composition of, 70–76 (*see also* hylomorphism)
sufficient reason, principle of, 55–56, 60–61
supposition, 97–100, 105–9, 110–16, 138–39
   collective, 137–38
   material and simple, 106–7, 108–9, 113–14, 124–25, 130–31
   personal, 106–8, 115–16, 117–19, 138–39

teleosemantics, 166
terms
   absolute, 103–5
   abstract, 23–26, 133–34
   collective, 59–60, 136–38, 140
   connotative (*see* concepts, connotation)
   modal, 112, 139, 177–78
   natural kind, 63–64, 101–19
   quantitative, 17, 22, 128–38
   relational, 17, 21, 41–42, 119–25
   singular, 18–19
   syncategorematic, 23, 102, 164–65
   See also concepts
theology. *See* knowledge
time, 51, 83–84
tropes, 67, 73–76, 88–90, 190
truthmaker principle, 46, 49–51, 94

universals, problem of, 9, 11, 19–20, 101–2

volitions, 143, 146

will, 143